The
Diary
of
Anaïs Nin

Works by Anaïs Nin

The
Diary
of
Anaïs Nin

1947-1955

Edited and with a Preface by Gunther Stuhlmann

A Harvest/HBJ Book
Harcourt Brace Jovanovich
New York and London

Printed in the United States of America

Library of Congress Cataloging in Publication Data (Revised)

Nin, Anaïs, date
The diary of Anaïs Nin.

(A Harvest book, HB 309)
CONTENTS: [1] 1931-1934.—[2] 1934-1939. [5]
1947-1955.
1. Nin, Anaïs, date   —Biography.
I. Stuhlmann, Gunther, ed. II. Title.
PS3527.I865Z5 1969   818'.5'203   77-2085
ISBN 0-15-626030-1

First Harvest edition 1975

C D E F G H I J

Preface

With the publication of this fifth volume drawn from the original diaries of Anaïs Nin we are gaining an ever larger view of this unique and massive literary undertaking. Each one of the published volumes—self-contained yet contiguous—exposed a fresh segment, a new chapter in this ongoing "novel" of a remarkable life. We saw Anaïs Nin emerge in Paris as a writer and catalyst to Henry Miller, Antonin Artaud, Dr. Otto Rank, and many others (1931–34); we followed her on a vibrant mission to the New World where her pursuit of psychoanalysis conflicted with her survival as a writer (1934–39); we watched the end of her "romantic life" in Europe and her reluctant return to the United States (1939–44); and we observed her efforts to come to terms with her second exile in America (1944–47). Each publication brought to light another portion of that grand store of varicolored, multishaped, multisized notebooks which, by 1947, amounted to some seventy-five hand-written volumes, a body of work that for years had defied all efforts at publication.

The present volume, drawn from the original diaries seventy-five to eighty-eight, and covering some eight years, to 1955, extends our total view of the *Diary* to a period of almost twenty-five years. From this vantage point we can discern the longer lines of growth and development. We can spot more easily the recurring themes—conflicts, conditioned responses, emotional patterns, the lifelong efforts to shake off the past, to create a "livable" present—that make up the essential warp and woof of Anaïs Nin's luminous tapestry. Beyond the individual event, the biographical fact, the nascent portrait, the captured high moment, the meditations and working notes, emerge deeper motivations, stronger connections. Indeed, the availability of all this material now may also explain the recent emergence of the first comprehensive critical studies of the published *Diary.**

The changes in tone and in the very function of the *Diary*, seen over a stretch of time, also seem more noticeable. What started out as

---

* See, for instance, *The Mirror and the Garden* by Evelyn J. Hinz, and *A Casebook on Anaïs Nin*, edited by Robert Zaller.

an enticing "letter," a Scheherazade, to bring back the lost father, had turned in the 1930s into Anaïs Nin's "kief, hashish, and opium pipe," and, by 1955, was evolving into an ever more consciously applied artistic instrument: "I have settled down to fill out, round out the diary. . . . I write about the developments and conclusions which took place twenty years later. It all falls into place."

But the essential need for the *Diary,* the tenacious, often joyous interplay between the *Diary* and its creator, which survived all moments of peril, remains. ("When I don't write I feel my world shrinking, I feel I am in a prison.") The urge to preserve is as strong as ever. ("The diary gave me a frightening mistrust of memory. Memory is a great betrayer. Whenever I read it, I find it different from the way I remembered the scenes and the talk.") The intensity of her struggle to resolve persistent problems, to shake off neurosis, to gain a firm hold on the "secret of personal freedom," which is a secret of creation, still reverberates through these pages.

Her enthusiastic response to new-found color and beauty in Mexico ("I felt a new woman would be born there") and her retreat from the arid frenzies of New York City to rustic serenity in California still do not resolve the conflict between *repose* (withdrawal?) and *activity* (succumbing to the outside world?). "This year," she writes, late in 1950, "the diary almost expired from too much traveling, too much moving about, too many changes. I felt pulled outward into activity, I did not want to meditate and examine. . . ." Using the two symbolic poles of New York and California, she feels "there must be a third way of life which I have to create myself."

The present, to her, is still unbearable at times. "I feel suffocated in my life," Anaïs Nin confides to her new psychiatrist in 1952, "overwhelmed by the demands put on me." The past still beckons as the paradise lost: "When I imagine the kind of life I like best, it was my bohemian life on the houseboat in Paris." But she also recognizes the past overshadowed by the father's critical eye, by the emotional camera lens that forever seemed to dog her steps. "That eye had to be exercised, or else, like that of a demanding god, pleased. I had to labor at presenting a pleasing image." The shedding of disguises is at the core of growing, and she knows that it takes courage "to be myself, rather than disguise myself." There is, after all, an Anaïs "who could love an ordinary tree which was neither symbolic, nor exotic, nor rare, nor historic, nor unique."

In a letter to Maxwell Geismar, in 1955, she measures her own progress ("I don't live here any more, I live in the future") toward that undisguised Anaïs:

This year I finally achieved objectivity, very difficult for a romantic. The divorce from America, as I call it, was painful, but has proved very creative and liberating. It was like breaking with a crabby, puritanical, restrictive and punitive parent. As soon as I overcame the hurt, I began to write better than ever. America, for me personally, has been oppressive and destructive. But today I am completely free of it. I don't need to go to France, or anywhere. I don't need to be published. I only need to continue my personal life, so beautiful and in full bloom, and to do my major work, which is the diary. I merely forgot for a few years what I had set out to do.

The *Diary,* we all know now, is indeed Anaïs Nin's major work. When she took up her pen on that first miserable journey into exile, at the age of eleven, she tried, by the sheer magic of her words, to bring back a golden past. She tried to lasso that universal dream of a father who will hold us safe from the realities of the world, from loss, separation, indifference, from the pain of growing up and dying and forgetting. She has never given up trying. Trusting forever in the magic of the word ("The role of the writer is not to say what we can all say but what we are unable to say"), she created, in the *Diary,* an instrument that shaped the very contours of her own life.

In answer to the question *"Why does one write?"* Anaïs Nin once replied: ". . . It is a world for others, an inheritance for others . . . in the end. When you make a world tolerable for yourself you make a world tolerable for others."

GUNTHER STUHLMANN

New York, N.Y.
November, 1973

The
Diary
of
Anaïs Nin

Acapulco, Mexico.

I am lying on a hammock, on the terrace of my room at the Hotel Mirador, the diary open on my knees, the sun shining on the diary, and I have no desire to write. The sun, the leaves, the shade, the warmth, are so alive that they lull the senses, calm the imagination. This is perfection. There is no need to portray, to preserve. It is eternal, it overwhelms you, it is complete.

The natives have not yet learned from the white man his inventions for traveling away from the present, his scientific capacity for analyzing warmth into a chemical substance, for abstracting human beings into symbols. The white man has invented glasses which make objects too near or too far, cameras, telescopes, spyglasses, objects which put glass between living and vision. It is the image he seeks to possess, not the texture, the living warmth, the human closeness.

Here in Mexico they see only the present. This communion of eyes and smiles is elating. In New York people seem intent on not seeing each other. Only children look with such unashamed curiosity. Poor white man, wandering and lost in his proud possession of a dimension in which bodies become invisible to the naked eye, as if staring were an immodest act. Here I feel incarnated and in full possession of my own body.

A new territory of pleasure. The green of the foliage is not like any other green; it is deeper, lacquered and moist. The leaves are heavier and fuller, the flowers bigger. They seem surcharged with sap, and more alive, as if they never have to close against the frost, or even a cold night. As if they have no need of sleep.

At the beach a child came forward from a group of children, carrying a small boat made of shells. She wanted me to buy it. She was small for her age, delicately molded like a miniature child, as Mexican children often are, more finely chiseled beings with small hands and feet and slender necks, tender and fragile and neat.

Everywhere guitars. As soon as one guitar moves away, the sound of another takes its place, to continue this net of music that maintains one in flight from sadness, suspended in a realm of festivities.

Festivities. Fiestas. Holidays. Bursts of color and joy. Collective celebrations. Rituals. Indian feasts and Catholic feasts. Any cause will do. Even the very poor know how to dress up a town with colored paper cutouts which dance in the wind. What was happened to joy in America? The Americans in the hotel spend all their time drinking by the pool. The men go hunting flamingos, which they shoot for the pleasure of it. Or they fish for inedible *mantarayas* and weigh their spoils to win prizes.

The eyes of the Mexicans are full of burning life. They squat like Orientals next to wide, flat baskets full of fruit and vegetables arranged with a fine sense of design, of decorative art and harmonies. Strings of chili hang from the rafters. The scent of saffron, and rhythms of Chagall-colored laundry hanging like banners from windows, and in gardens. Warmth falls from the sky like the fleeciest blanket. Even the night comes without a change of temperature or alteration in the softness of the air. You can trust the night.

There is a rhythm in the way the women lift the water jugs onto their heads and walk balancing them. There is a rhythm in the way they carry their babies wrapped in their shawls, and their baskets filled with fruit. There is a rhythm in the way the fishermen pull in their nets in the evening, and the way the shepherds walk after their lambs and cows.

The first night here I showered and bathed hastily, feeling that perhaps the beauty and the velvety softness of the night might not last, that if I delayed, it would all change to coldness and harshness.

When I opened the screen door, the night lay unchanged, filled with tropical whisperings, as if leaves, birds, insects, and sea breezes possessed musicalities unknown to northern countries, as if the richness of the smells kept them all intoxicated, with the same aphrodisiac which affected me. Perfume of carnation and honeysuckle.

Through labyrinthian paths bordered with bushes which caress you as you walk, on stone warmed by the sun, I walk from my room to the large terrace where everyone sits and waits for dinner or to meet with friends.

The expanse of sky is like an infinite canvas on which human beings cannot project images from their memories because they would seem out of scale with the limitless sea, the limitless sky and the stars, which appear nearer and larger. So memory is absent, dissolved. I lie on a chaise longue to watch the spectacle of sunset and the night's first act. Nature so powerful and drugging that it annihilates memory. People seem warmer and nearer, as the stars seem nearer and the moon warmer.

The sea's orchestration carries away half the words and makes talking and laughing seem more like an accompaniment, like the sound of birds. Words have no weight. They float in space. They have a purely decorative quality, like flowers.

Why are people so fearful of the tropics? "All adventurers come to grief." I heard this many times, it was a refrain. Was it because they could not surrender to the overpowering effect of nature? They resisted it. I abandon myself to it and I feel strengthened by it rather than weakened.

La Perla is the hotel's night club. It is built of driftwood, and overlooks the wild part of the gorge between two mountains of rocks, against which the sea hurls itself with fury, defeated by the narrowness, and spilling its fury in high waves and foam. Into this narrow gorge Mexican boys dive for the tourists. First they climb the rocks slowly and laboriously, then they stand at the peak, pause for a moment, and dive like birds into the foaming, lashing waves.

Red ship's lanterns illumine a jazz band playing for a few dancers. Because the hiss of the sea carries away some of the overtones, the main drumbeat seems more emphatic, like a giant heart pulsing.

Jazz is the music of the body. The breath comes through brass. It is the body's breath, and the strings' wails and moans are echoes of the body's music. It is the body's vibrations which ripple from the fingers. And the mystery of the withheld theme, known to jazz musicians alone, is like the mystery of our secret life. We give to others only peripheral improvisations.

I feel like a fugitive from the mysteries of the human labyrinth I was trying to pierce. I escaped my patterns. I escaped familiar and inexorable grooves. The outer world is so overwhelmingly beautiful that I am willing to stay outside, day and night, a wanderer and a pilgrim without abode.

I feel at home in Mexico, because I learned Spanish at the age of five, because the exuberance reminds me of my childhood in Spain, the singing reminds me of our Spanish maid Carmen, who sang all day while working. The gaiety in the streets, the children dancing, the flowerpots in the windows, the white-washed walls, the green shutters, the profusion of flowers, the liveliness of the people, all recall Barcelona and Havana. I realize that after years of life in America, I have finally learned to subdue my manners and my dress. I still remember that because my Cuban relatives sent me castoff clothes (and most dressing in Cuba was, as in Mexico, in a festive mood), I wore a red velvet dress to one of my jobs as model for a painter, and his expression when he saw me in a red velvet dress at nine in the morning was unforgettable. The walk with the weight on the heels, which Cubans and Spaniards do, the full-smile greeting, the gift for letting sorrow and worries slide off the shoulders, the predisposition for pleasure, all this is familiar and warm and comfortable.

Dr. Hernandez comes to the hotel several times a day for the tourists. He carries his black doctor's bag. He is my first friend here. After his visits he likes to sit on the terrace and talk a little and sip a drink.

He has written poetry, had a book published. He studied medicine in France. When he was first assigned to intern in Acapulco, he fought malaria, elephantiasis, and other tropical diseases. When his internship ended, he decided to stay on and practice.

He built a house on a protruding rock, extending out to the sea on the left of the Mirador, married, and had children. But his wife hates Acapulco and is always going to Mexico City because there are no schools for their children in Acapulco.

Since more than half of his life is given to the poor of Acapulco, to dramas and tragedies of all kinds, he does not like the tourists. "Because they live for pleasure only, because they pamper themselves, because half of their ills are imaginary. Most of the time they call me because they are frightened of foreign countries and foreign food."

He talks to me at length since he was told I am a writer. He wants to take me on his tour of the people of Acapulco. I plead that I have been deprived of all pleasure and rest for years and have a right to a period without sorrows and burdens.

I met Annette at the Hotel Mirador. I was sitting in the dining room. A stairway leads from the upper terrace to the dining room. It is lighted from above and gives the diners time to see those who are coming down the stairs. My eyes were caught by the brilliant colors and the textures of her dress. I watched her for several evenings. She used the full palette of Mexican colors. She wore barbaric jewelry, copies and fantasies inspired by Mayan and Aztec themes. She had a mass of short, curled hair aureoled around her head, unruly, in the style of Toulouse-Lautrec women, and under this a delicately chiseled face, a small straight nose, fawn-colored eyes, and a slender neck poised on a voluptuous body. Her movements have a flow and sweep and vivacity and seductiveness. She undulates her hips, her breasts heave like the sea, she is never still.

We were introduced. Her liveliness and joyousness incarnated the spices and colors of Acapulco. She sometimes thrust her breasts forward or else she tilted her head backward, or she laughed with a ripple which ran through her whole body. It was as if she lived a semidance which kept the jewelry tinkling and her earrings mobile. She swung into the dining room with a mambo rhythm.

We became friends.

We talked on the terrace at night, after dinner, while waiting to see what the evening would bring. In spite of her children, two boys of seven and nine, men treated her like a young woman. Her laughter was inviting, and as she lay on the chaise longue, her body seemed offered. All its exotic and brilliant covering was a plumage, and she was uncomfortable within it, her natural state was nudity, or a brief bathing suit at the beach.

She was without discrimination about men, so that I found it difficult to go out with her and her friends. I preferred solitude. Acapulco was a beautiful background for her. Her skin was naturally tan. She was like a native and in harmony with her surroundings.

She met Orozco, Diego Rivera, and Siqueiros in New York when taking a master's in fine arts at Teachers College, Columbia. They invited her to work on murals in Mexico. There she met her second husband, who was a powerful industrialist. Now she was married to a composer, Conlon Nancarrow.

She was natural, talkative, fluent, and always effervescent.

When I met her she had become so international, so well traveled, so multilingual, so at ease with all kinds of people, that no one could imagine her childhood, her origin.

Her dream was to build a house in Acapulco and stay there.

The past is dissolving in the intensity of Acapulco. The intense sunlight annihilates thought, and the animation of the crowd, the colors, the smiles, the dances at night, the gaiety of the beach close the eyes of memory. Freedom from the past comes from associating with unfamiliar objects; none of them possesses any evocative power. The hammock, the spectacles of sunrise and sunset, the exotic flowers, are all unfamiliar. From the moment I open my eyes I am in a new world. The colors are all hot and brilliant. Breakfast is a tray of fruit never tasted before, papaya and mangoes. All day long there is not a single familiar object to carry me back into the past.

The first human being I see in the morning is the gardener. I can see him at work through the half-shut bamboo blinds. He is raking the pebbles and the sand, not as if he were eager to terminate the task, but as if raking pebbles and sand were a most pleasurable occupation and he wants to prolong the enjoyment. Now and then he stops to talk to a lonely little girl who skips rope and asks him questions which he answers patiently.

Groups form in the evening on the terrace to plan whether to dance all night at the Americas Hotel, where there is a jazz band, or take an excursion to a little-known cove where one can swim nude and where the waves are phosphorescent. New groups form every night, new arrivals, new introductions.

The pool of the Mirador is another gathering place for those who love the night and a quiet swim before sleep.

Because someone had plunged into it from one of the rooms of the hotel late at night and drowned, the pool was now locked, but we all slipped over the gate. I heard one woman say to her young man: "Will you float me home?"

Tonight I met a young man who hitchhiked all the way from Chicago and was picked up by the patron of the hotel and given secretarial work. His candor, bewilderment, and wonder at everything rejuvenates the most indifferent visitors already accustomed to the beauty. I call him Christmas, because he said his first love-making was as wonderful as a Christmas tree. Annette's freedom fascinated him. She bubbles, her talk is like the foam of the sea, her laughter dispels all concerns.

The doctor and I sit in a hand-carved canoe. The pressure of the hand on the knife made uneven indentations in the scooped-out tree trunk which catch the light like the scallops of a sea shell. The sun on the rim of the carvings and the shadows within their valleys give the canoe a stippled surface like that of an Impressionist painting. As it moves forward in the water it seems like a multitude of changeable colors in motion.

The canoe was once painted in laundry blue. The blue has faded and has become like the smoky blue of old Mayan murals, a blue which man cannot create, only time.

The fisherman is paddling quietly through the varied colors of the lagoon water, colors which range from the dark sepia of the red-earth bottom to silver-gray when the colors of the vegetation triumph over the red earth, to gold when the sun conquers them both, to purple in the shadows. He paddles with one arm. His other arm was blown off when he was a young fisherman of seventeen first learning the use of dynamite sticks for fishing.

The mangrove trees in the lagoon show their naked roots, as though on stilts, an intricate maze of the silver roots as fluent below as they are interlaced above. The overhanging branches cast shadows before the bow of the canoe so dense that I can hardly believe they will open and divide to let us through. The roots look like a grasping giant hand, extending fingers into the water to hold on to a treacherous moving soil, fingers which in turn give birth to smaller fingers seeking a hold on the bank.

Emerald sprays and fronds project from a mass of wasps' nests, of pendant vines and lianas. Above my head the branches form metallic green parabolas and enameled pennants, while the canoe and my body accomplish the magical feat of cutting through the roots and dense tangles.

The canoe undulates the aquatic plants that bear long plumes and travels through reflections of the clouds.

The snowy herons and the shell-pink flamingos meditate upon one leg like yogis of the animal world. Iguanas slither away, and parrots become hysterically gay.

Now and then I see a single habitation by the water's edge, an ephemeral hut of palm leaves wading on frail stilts, and a canoe tied to a toy-sized jetty. Before each hut stands a smiling woman and several naked children.

I see the mud tracks of a crocodile. The scaly colors of the skin of the iguanas is so exactly like the ashen roots and tree trunks that you cannot spot them until they move. They lie as still as stones in the sun, as if petrified, and their tough, wrinkled skin looks thousands of years old.

———

A flowing journey.

I had a recurrent dream always of a boat, sometimes small, sometimes large, but invariably caught in a waterless place, in a street, in a city, in a jungle or a desert. When it was large it appeared in city streets, and the deck reached to the upper windows of houses. I was always in this boat and aware it could not sail unless I pushed it, so I would get off and seek to push it along so it might move and finally reach water. The effort of pushing the boat along the street was immense and I never accomplished my aim. Whether I pushed it along cobblestones or over asphalt, it moved very little, and no matter how much I strained I always felt I could never reach the sea.

Today on the lagoon, I felt that my dream of pushing the boat would never recur. I have attained a state of being which is effortless, a flowing journey. I am in harmony with nature, with the rhythm of the natives, and this is created not only by the presence of water (I experienced this feeling before in the houseboat on the Seine) but also by the fusion of my body with nature, the healing separation from our dissonant and harsh Western life.

I had read that certain Egyptian rulers believed that after death they would join a celestial caravan in an eternal journey toward the sun and the moon. Archaeologists had unearthed two wooden barques buried in a royal tomb which they recognized from ancient texts and mural paintings. There was a lunar barque for the night journey to the moon and a solar barque for the day journey to the sun.

In dreams I perpetuated such journeys in solar barques. There were always two. One buried in limestone and unable to float on the waterless routes of anxiety, the other flowing continuously with life. The static one made the repetitive journey of memories, and the flowing one proceeded into endless discoveries.

I am now in my flowing journey.

There is a quality in this place which does not come altogether from its beauty. Is it the softness of the air which relaxes body and soul? Is it the continuity of music which makes the blood rhythms pulsate?

I let my hand drop in the waters of the lagoon, to feel the gliding, to assure myself of the union with a living current, as if touching the flow of life within me, this life which blooms only in places where the life force is vital and expansive: Morocco, Mexico.

———

I took my laundry to a woman who lives down the road, recommended by the hotel. I came to a shack without a front wall, with a dirt floor. The woman was ironing with an iron which had to be heated over a coal stove. Her children were playing naked on the dirt. Behind her, on a steep hill, was the laundry drying over bushes. There was no running water. She washed the clothes at the river or at the village trough. But she was singing, full-throated, fluid, strong, like the song of the tropical birds in the trees above her. The song rose above the steam of the iron, above the dirty children, above the backyard, above the visitor standing at the front of the house with a bundle of summer dresses.

Sunday night the local people come to dance on the terrace next to the hotel. There is a native band. They only stop to watch the divers, or to take a walk down the steep descent to where the sea leaps and foams against the rocks.

I dance with the young men of the town. Some are future divers, dreaming of riches. Others dream of becoming guides, chauffeurs, bus drivers. One of the divers was "adopted" by a wealthy American woman. She paid to get him several new gold teeth, of which Mexican boys are very proud. This gave him an idea. Every new batch of tourists provided at least one godmother willing to pay for a gold tooth. The diver learned to take them out and reappear with missing teeth, and each godmother, compassionate for a young man with missing teeth, paid, and with each operation the boy made a little money from the sale of the gold.

An American was put in jail because he had no papers. The tourists were invited to visit him, to plead for him. They wrote to the American Consulate. But he stayed in jail, and he told whoever came to see him that a tip of fifty dollars to his jailer would get him out. The fifty dollars were paid, and he was out for a few days and then in jail again, awaiting new visitors. We saw the jailer and his victim celebrating at the Spanish restaurant on the square.

Once in a while I like to be alone. I walk down the hill to the square, which is full of interest. It is the heart of the town. The church opens its doors on one side, the movie house on the other, and in between, the square is lined with cafés and restaurants with their tables on the sidewalks. In the center is a small bandstand, surrounded by a park with old umbrella trees and plenty of benches.

On the benches sit enraptured young lovers, tired hobos, old men reading their newspapers. Because of the scraps of crackers and candies on the ground, the birds are concentrated here, and they fill the trees with merry chatter and songs. There is also a circle of vendors sitting on the sidewalks with their baskets full of candied fruit, colored fruit drinks, gold jewelry they learned to make from the Moors, delicate filigree work. Old ladies in black shawls walk quietly in and out of the church, children beg merrily, marimba players settle in front of each café and play for tips.

The flow of beggars is endless. A few change their handicaps. When they tire of portraying blindness they appear with wooden legs, concealing their good legs under them. The genuine ones are terrifying, like nightmare figures: A child shriveled and shrunken, lying on a board with wheels which he pushes with his withered hands; an old woman so twisted that she resembles the roots of very ancient trees; many of them sightless, with festering sores in place of eyes. They all refuse Dr. Hernandez's help. They do not want to be locked in hospitals. They want to remain a part of the religious processions, the fireworks, the funerals, the weddings, band concerts, and the display of foreigners with their eccentric costumes.

But custom will not allow me to sit alone in a restaurant. Not Mexican custom. A man came and threw some money on my table, and sat down. The patron of the restaurant had to explain that foreign women went about alone and it did not mean they were prostitutes.

Another time a comedy of errors. A young American student was stranded. He had been hitchhiking and no one was driving to Mexico City. He had no place to stay. He had spent the evening with two young women I knew, but they had no room for him. I offered him the hammock on my terrace. He accepted. In the morning, when I stepped out he was still asleep. While I was having breakfast he went into my room to shave and bathe. The maid found him there and reported to the "patron" who gave me a lecture on morality: "None of those American ways will be tolerated in my hotel."

One day we decided to visit the jungle *ranchita* of Hatcher, an American engineer who had married a local Mexican woman and was attempting to achieve the American dream of "going native." His place was near San Luis, north of Acapulco, on the road to Zihuatanejo. The road was dusty and difficult, but we had the feeling of penetrating into a wilder, less explored part of Mexico. Villages were few and far between; we met rancheros on horseback, in their white suits and ponchos and enormous hats, carrying their machetes rigidly. We saw women washing clothes by the river. Some huts were without walls, just a web of branches supported by four slender tree trunks. Babies lay in hammocks.

The river beyond San Luis was wide, and cars had to be ferried. We waited for the ferry, a flat raft made of logs tied together. The men pushed it along with long bamboo poles.

When we left the raft we started a journey into the jungle. A dust road with just enough room for the car. Cactus and banana leaves scraped our faces. When we were deep in the forest and seemingly far from any village, we saw a young man waiting for a ride. He carried a heavy, small doctor's bag.

"I'm Dr. Palas," he said. "Will you give me a ride?"

When he was settled he explained: "I have just delivered a child. I'm stationed at Zihuatanejo."

He was carrying a French novel like the ones Dr. Hernandez must have carried at his age, for they all studied medicine in France. Was he devoted to his patients? The Mexican medical plan rules that interns must work a year in a village where there is no doctor. This was the way Dr. Hernandez first came to Acapulco when it was a fishing village.

When we reached his village, where we were to spend the night, we had rooms across from his bungalow. A workman came in the middle of the night and called out to him, pleading and begging: "I have a splinter in my eye." But Dr. Palas did not come out. The poor workman stayed until dawn, and then the doctor deigned to come out and attend to him. I was shocked by his callousness. We went off without saying goodbye to him. I remembered his cynical words: "I have a year of this to endure."

Hatcher's place was deep in the jungle on a hill overlooking the sea. On a small open space he had built a roof on posts, with only one wall in the back. The cooking was done out of doors. A Mexican woman was bending over her washing. She only came to greet us when Hatcher called her. She was small and heavy, and sad-faced, but she gave Hatcher a caressing look and a brilliant smile. She showed only a conscious politeness to us.

"You must excuse us, the place is not finished yet. My husband works alone and he has a lot to do."

"Bring the coffee, Maria." She left us sitting around a table on the terrace, staring at an unbelievable stretch of white sand, dazzling white foam spraying a gigantic, sprawling vegetation which grew to the very edge of the sand. Birds sang deliriously, and monkeys clowned in the trees. The colors seemed purer and clearer, like those of a fresh place never inhabited before.

Maria came with coffee in a Thermos.

Hatcher said: "She is a most marvelous wife."

"And he is a wonderful husband," said Maria. "Mexican husbands never go around telling everyone they are married. He goes about buying presents for his wife, talking about his wife."

Turning to me she said in a low voice: "I don't know why he loves me. I am so short and squatty. He was once married to a tall, slim American woman like you. He never talks about her. I worked for him at first. I was his secretary. We are going to build a beautiful place here. This is only the beginning."

They had their bedroom in the back, protected by curtains. Visitors slept in hammocks on the terrace.

We took a walk to the beach. The flowers which opened their velvety faces toward us were so eloquent they seemed about to speak. The sand did not seem like sand, but like powdered glass which reflected the light.

The sea folded its layers around me, touching my legs, my hips, my breasts like a liquid sculptor with warm hands.

When I came out of the sea, I felt reborn. I longed for this simplified life. Cooking over a wood fire, sleeping out of doors in a hammock, with only a Mexican blanket. I longed for naked feet in sandals, the freedom of the body in summer clothes, hair washed by the sea.

When we returned Maria had set the table. The lights were weak bulbs hanging from wires. The generator made a loud throbbing. But the trees were full of fireflies, crickets, and pungent odors. There was a natural pool fed by mountain water where we could wash off the salt from the sea.

After a dinner of fish and black beans, Hatcher offered to show us the rest of his house. Behind the wall there was a storage room of which he was immensely proud. It was enormous, as large as the house itself, with shelves reaching to the ceiling. There was in it every brand of canned food, medicines, tools, hunting guns, fishing equipment, garden tools, vitamins, seeds. He reveled in the completeness of it. "What would you like? Cling peaches? Asparagus? Quinine? Magazines? Newspapers? I even have a pair of crutches in case of need. I have ether, and instruments for surgery."

I felt immensely tired and depressed. I lay in my hammock pondering why I was so disappointed. I had imagined Hatcher free. I admired him as a man who had won independence from our culture and could live like a native, a simplified existence with few needs. And here he demonstrated complete dependence on complex and artificial products. America the mother and father had been transported into a supply shed, bottled and canned. He was not able to live here without possessions, with fresh fish and fruit and vegetables in abundance, with cow's milk and the products of hunting.

His fears made me question: was there no open road, simple, clear, unique? Could I live a new life here in Mexico, free of all that had wounded me in the past, and free of dependency? Hatcher was not free of his bitterness about his first marriage, nor free of America. He was not free of the past.

My lacquered nails reminded him of his first wife. He was hostile to me because of his first wife.

I wanted to stay in Mexico, I wanted to have a little house in Acapulco, overlooking the sea, where I could watch the dawns like Oriental spectacles, watch the whales at play, without need of books, concerts, plays, provisions of any kind.

When I awakened I first saw a coral tree with orange flowers that seemed like tongues of flames. Between its branches rose thin wisps of smoke from Maria's *brasero*. Maria was patting tortillas between her hands in an even rhythm.

I did not want to stay and Hatcher was offended. He thought our battery was too low and that we should get a new one. He tinkered with the car. I felt that now he represented slavery to an inescapable past and not the freedom of a natural, native life. He loved all this only because he had been hurt by the other. He loved Maria because she was not the American woman with painted nails who had hurt him. It would take days to get a new battery and I refused to stay.

When the car was repaired we left. Driving back in the violent sun we did not talk. The light filled the eyes, the mind, the nerves, the bones, and it was only when we drove through the shade that we came out of this anaesthesia of sunlight.

A truck full of Mexican workmen with guns was driving a short distance behind us. Our car stalled. They caught up with us. They offered to tow us to the nearest town for a new battery.

But they did not know I understood Spanish, and among themselves they discussed how easy it would be to get both our money and the car. I had to think quickly.

We explained that Mr. Hatcher was following close behind us and would soon be here with a new battery.

It was, as I knew, a lie. But I thought it would drive them away. They all knew Mr. Hatcher, and he had guns. They hesitated. And then Hatcher arrived! He had been uneasy about us and had decided to follow. The men filed quietly into the truck. Hatcher said they would have taken our money and the car and left us there. He towed us to San Luis and left us in the hands of a very dubious Mexican garage to wait for a new battery.

It was New Year's Eve. We had reached San Luis in time for fireworks and dancing in the street. At seven o'clock, when we arrived, the streets were silent and it began to grow dark. The owner of the café was a pale-faced Spaniard with the manners of a courtier. He fixed us a dinner. Then he told us we could not go out that night.

"San Luis looks quiet now, but it is only because they are dressing for New Year's Eve. Pretty soon they will all be out in the streets. There will be dancing. But the men will drink heavily. The women know when it is time to leave. I advise you not to mix with them. The women go home with the children. The men continue to drink. Soon they begin to shoot at mirrors, glasses, bottles, at anything. Sometimes they shoot at each other. I entreat you, I beg you to stay right here. I have clean rooms I can let you have for the night. Stay in your rooms, I advise you strongly."

At ten o'clock music, fireworks, shouts and shooting began.

I lay on my plain white cot, in a whitewashed room, bare and simple, shivering with cold, imprisoned by mosquito netting, listening to the noise, and feeling lonely and lost.

In the morning the streets were littered with confetti. The street vendors' baskets were empty and they were asleep beside them rolled in their ponchos. The scent of malabar was in the air and that of burnt firecrackers. There were three men dead and a little boy injured by the fireworks.

In Acapulco I looked for a house I could afford. Even if I had to return to the United States, this would remain the place of joy and health.

I found the smallest house in Acapulco at the very tip of the rock I loved, the highest one above Caleta Beach, looking out to sea and to the island where the beacon light stood.

It was built of stucco, all open on the sea side, and the walls on the side of the street were latticed to let the breeze through. I was euphoric. The people who sold it lived below me. I startled everyone who had heard me say I never wanted to be tied down anywhere by announcing that I had chosen a place to live.

I bought simple native things at the market, pottery, serapes, straw mats, baskets. There was a bed there already. I was deliriously happy. A walk down the hill and I was at Caleta, the Mexican beach. The tourists swam at other beaches.

The beach is lined with thatched roof shanties where one can eat fresh clams and shrimp. The guitar players clustered around the shanties. They were treated to beer and sang all day.

The glass-bottomed boat was tied there, and the trips on it were full of marvels: coral, sea plants, and colorful fishes. The American who ran it was also collecting animals for his zoo. They could be seen at his house—monkeys, kinkajous, birds of all kinds, parrots, iguanas, snakes. He paid the native boys to hunt for him.

But several things happened in the little house. The tank on the roof which supplied water for the bath and for cooking would either run dry or overflow during the night. The insects I pursued with Flytox turned out to be scorpions, who liked to nest behind the straw mats. Rats came at night, ate the food, ran over my body and frightened me to death.

When I asked advice from the Mexicans, they counseled resignation. I bought rat poison and began to fight them, but a new batch came every night through the terrace.

The young men of the town found out I was living alone and came to call me, or serenade me behind the latticed walls. I would put out the lights and lie in the dark.

I had to walk up the steep hill with food and ice.

I invited Alice Rahon to stay with me. She brought her long

beautiful black hair, her radiant smile, her superb swimming. Her talk was full of fascination. She was a painter and also known for her surrealist poems. We talked endlessly and formed a deep friendship.

I had finally frightened away the scorpions and the rats. But now I had a new enemy. It was the neighbor's rooster. He was not only the most arrogant rooster I ever met but he crowed ahead of time. He did not wait for the dawn, he wanted to show that he could bring it on, cause it to happen by his sonorous announcements and prophecies.

So at four in the morning I was awakened by the rooster, who did not surrender until the dawn gave in and appeared.

When the rooster crowed that was a signal for the old man next door to start his asthmatic cough, a long, continuous, raucous cough which seemed to strangle him.

I was told about the early Acapulco. There were no hotels, only Mexican boardinghouses. You arrived on a donkey because the train did not go that far. You ate purée of black beans and fish for breakfast, lunch, and dinner, for a dollar a day.

Painters had discovered it. It must have seemed like Tahiti. The women did not wear bathing suits, just a piece of cloth resembling the Tahitian *pareu*. The children went about naked. There was an abundance of fish. The people were poor but lived with a certain kind of beauty. Always a palm-leaf hut with a garden filled with flowers.

Their boats were painted in soft colors. The fishermen repaired their nets on the beach. The pottery people used, the baskets, the water jugs were all beautiful and handmade. It was only later that they built tin shacks, without gardens, like the ones behind the bullring, shacks crowded together with no room at all so that they hung their laundry in the narrow alleys. Animals and children slept together.

The beauty of Acapulco was unspoiled.

I took delight in the market. The mere arrangement of ribbons women wore in their hair, the decorative way fruit was laid out in huge round baskets, the birdcages, the smell of melons and oranges, the playfulness of the children. I took delight in the animated and crowded square, in the jetty where the fishing boats returned with their colored pennants flying. I loved to watch the fishermen pulling in their nets at sundown.

Every scene in Mexico is so natural that it alters the color of violence itself, of death. A stabbed Mexican staggered across the night club, his shirt all bloody, but the fatalism of the Mexicans subdued the horror, the shock. It was all made to seem a part of nature, natural, inevitable. Violence and innocence, the two natural aspects of man.

Everything was natural, the dirt floors in the huts, the babies in hammocks, the minimum of possessions: one shawl, one fan, one necklace, one trunk of clothes, no sheets.

I made friends with Pablo at the post office because he was interested in my stamps from foreign countries. He collected post cards from America.

It was he who took me dancing to the places where the people of the town went, the poor. I had to leap over an open sewer. These cafés were antechambers to the whorehouses. A young man with absolutely no hair was singing. ("Complete baldness results from a tropical disease," Dr. Hernandez solemnly informed me.) The prostitutes were modest, not arrogant or overdressed as in America, gentle and courteous.

The music was marvelous, native dance music far better than at the hotel night clubs. People danced in bare feet. My friends were shocked when I threw off my sandals. I loved the texture of the earth, and the touch of other feet.

Everyone knew each other. The town policeman was there, enjoying himself. He had discarded his belt and gun to dance with the prostitutes.

A widower asked me: "If I rent a motorboat for tomorrow will you come and see the sunrise with me at La Roqueta?"

His offer was known to the whole town. He was always looking for women who would be willing to see the sunrise with him on a desert island.

Paul Mathiesen arrived. I was in a frivolous mood. His appearance of a Nordic mystic, far from the earth, seemed to interfere with my pursuit of joy. He was the pale dreamer, I felt; he was ill at ease dancing and swimming and I was hungry for it. His muteness, his withdrawn, mysterious self seemed like a reproach from nonsensual worlds. He seemed detached from our pleasures, lying on surfboards sunning, dancing in native shacks. Paul seemed to call me back into art, the myth, the dream.

Once, I remember, we were all coming out of a bad film which we attended only for the sake of the crowd, the men, women, and children who went there, their gaiety and expressiveness. As we came out I found Paul eating at one of the communal tables in the market where they served fish soup to the workmen and fishermen. He sat there, silent, seemingly remote, and also reproachful. I sought forgetfulness and no personal, intimate friendships.

The dreamer was here again, to take me away from the vivid physical world I loved.

There was a guitar-playing Mexican doctor, quite young, who had abandoned his career to live in Acapulco. He worked at the hotel desk. The two American girls I went to the beach with fell in love with him. He fell in love with the dark-haired one. The other I found weeping on the steps of the bungalow one day. He loved the wrong one. She made him spend all his money, she wrecked his car while she was drunk, and was frightened by the intensity of his love-making. She asked me: "Why does he keep calling me 'mi vida, mi vida'? It frightens me, all that emotion."

You are my life, my life. How could I explain to her that even one night of love-making can make one say: "You are my life, mi vida, mi vida."

If you give toys to the children, they grab for them so desperately they scratch your hand. The mature grin of the seven-year-old boy who sat on the hood of the car to direct us through the shallowest part of the river. He straddled it as if it were a bull, and with his small hand indicated left or right in the dark; his face was illumined with pride and a feeling of superiority over the blind voyagers.

The children barefoot, in rags, but joyous, alive. Playing with discarded tires on the beach. Small rations, little food, an orange is a luxury, but their smile and their gaiety are overwhelming. They filled the streets of Acapulco with their vivacity, their games, their mischievous begging.

The bullfights, which I hate, make me ill. But after staying away for four Sundays, feeling I was not sharing in a community experience and everyone looked upon me as abnormal, I went. It was torture.

The disillusion of finding a charming Mexican reading *How to Win Friends and Influence People.*

Then came time to leave.

The taxi driver who had sworn to come for me never came, and I had to drag my valise down the hill to take the bus. The day before at the beach I had witnessed cruelty toward a dog, who had fallen off a surfboard and was tottering on the beach, inflated with water, suffering, while the Mexicans laughed. I screamed at them and forced them to help the dog expel the water.

But when I left, the beauty was uppermost in my eyes, I could only remember the softness, the gold patina over everything, the long, unthinking, memoryless days, days filled with the scent of flowers, sunrises and sunsets to eclipse all the paintings of the world.

The return to New York was brutal. Grit, harshness, anger above all, the anger of the bus driver, the anger of the subway ticketman, the sullenness of the taxi drivers, the angry tone of newspapers, the anger on the radio, in the street, from the policeman, the doorman, the delivery boy, the shopkeepers. The mechanical service at cafeterias, unsmiling, not looking. No one looks at anyone. People are like numbers.

It was pouring rain, to make the contrast sharper.

But having the little house in Acapulco made me feel I would be able to return.

I asked Dutton for an advance on *Under a Glass Bell.*

My dear Anaïs:

Nick tells me that like the rest of us you are in need of some extra pennies. One of these days when we are really scratching the bottom of the barrel I think I will write to five hundred of our authors and suggest that they send us $100 each. That will come to $50,000 and help no end. Keeping up with present-day costs is as tough for a publisher as for an author, and there does not seem to be an end towards the increase.

At any rate, I enclose a check for $250 which is the amount of the initial advance due on November 1 1947 on *Under a Glass Bell and Other Stories.*

I hope that you are well and happy. With kind regards,

Sincerely,
E. P. Dutton & Co., Inc.
Elliott [Macrae]
President

New York.

I had many duties in New York, many unfinished tasks and responsibilities. The months in Mexico had been like one long reverie, but what a deep effect they had on me. They loosened chains, they dissolved poisons, fears, doubts, healed all the wounds. To look into the dark, bottomless eyes of the Mexicans and see warmth, humanity, emotion, to be assured of their existence, to hear the sweetness and tenderness of their voices and be reassured of their existence, to see the lovers, as in France, dissolved in ecstasy, to be reassured of love's existence, to see people who could dance, sing, swim, laugh in spite of poverty, and be reassured of the existence of life and joy. To see and hear joy.

There was a book by Georges Bernanos I once carried around with me, not so much for its content as for its title: *La Joie*. Joy. There was in it the description of joy, a joy which became ecstasy. The young woman experienced it as religious ecstasy. I translated it into physical ecstasy. The cynical man who did not believe in it spied upon her and could only attribute it to madness.

I found this joy in Mexico. And it was pagan and human. It was in the sun, in the light, in the colors, in the voices, in their smiles and in their fiestas. Poverty could not destroy it, invasions, revolutions, tyranny could not destroy it. It is a gift of dark people, those for whom the real life begins at night deep within themselves and where everything flowers.

Joy, for many years, was the unattainable state (except intermittently). It was the unknown land.

When I left New York in a small Model A Ford last spring I did not know it was to be a voyage not only across the United States, but ultimately to this land, this unfamiliar country of *La Joie*.

I forgot to write about my visit to Black Mountain College. It was in October, 1947, and I was invited by Mary Caroline Richards.

The place was in a wild and beautiful setting, the country of Thomas Wolfe. I knew it was the fruit of a rebellion by several teachers, and a brave experiment in education. There were only about one hundred students, and the spirit of it attracted special, unique teachers.

The students had built their own studios; they shared all the work from cooking to taking care of children, from raising funds to gardening. It was ideal communal living.

My visit began with an individual talk, one hour with each student in his own studio. It was good to see them alone, in their own atmosphere. I only had time to talk to those interested in writing.

Among them was a young student named James Leo Herlihy. He had laughing Irish eyes, a swift tongue, and seemed outwardly in full motion in life until he showed me a chart he kept in his journal. It was designed like a fever chart, only instead of fever it recorded the ups and downs of his moods, the outline at times rising, at times plunging into the depths. Jim said, pointing to the lowest ebb of the chart: "The day it goes below that point I will commit suicide."

He said this without the expression which would ordinarily accompany such words. He said it smiling, defiantly. It was as if he wore the mask of youth, alertness, gaiety even, and that this dark current was so far below the surface it had not yet marked his face or his voice, or invaded his eyes. Yet I believed him, and I began to talk about how I dissolved my depressions.

"I begin to look at what happens to me as a storyteller might look at it. What a good story it makes! I take my distance. I look at the dramatic possibilities. Try that. The depression falls away, you are changed into an adventurer faced with every obstacle, every defeat, every danger, but as they increase the sense of adventure increases too."

After my talks with the students I was exhausted. When I returned to my room I found a note of thanks from Mary Caroline Richards:

Here is my poem. I hope to see you at breakfast. You are good and wonderful. I hope the kids have not exhausted you, but of course they have. Goodnight. M.C.

I slipped it under my pillow like a sweet reward.

I had talked about my printing press, and the students dug out an old press which was lying inactive in the garage, and began printing poetry.

A few days later I received my first letter from Jim Herlihy and a story.

————

New York on my birthday, February 21.

I had told my friends about the way Mexicans celebrate birthdays. How they rise at dawn and come to serenade one, so you will be born to music and the dawn. My poor New York friends got up before dawn on a bitter cold morning and rang my bell to serenade me.

In New York there were work and duties, but I was detached from them. I accepted a lecture at Houston, Texas. Signing books in a bookstore, being feted with a dinner, seeing a person I would like to know better, like someone you see out of a train window, and wistful that it should all be so swift and superficial. What do you leave of yourself? What do I remember? It passes too swiftly.

I return to Los Angeles for another book-signing party.

Los Angeles is not as deeply natural or joyous as Mexico, but the white houses, the palm trees and the sun give a feeling of lightness; people are tanned, they seem carefree, they prefer the beach to an exhibition, the beach to a concert, the beach to a theater. The cars shine and carry surfboards on their roofs. Or the drivers ride in bathing suits, with the top down, hair flying. There are parts of the beach which are deserted, rocks to sunbathe on. I am awakened by the singing of the mocking birds. They sing at night like Keats' nightingale. It is a forest of billboards, each bigger and louder than the next. It is Nathanael West's Hollywood, a fair, grotesque, vaudeville, a grade B film. The people on Hollywood Boulevard dress as though they bought their clothes in a thrift shop, a fur coat and sandals, slacks and gold shoes, satin waists and sport skirts. Dyed hair tired of being dyed. They live in boardinghouses, awaiting roles, jobs, stardom.

[Spring, 1948]

I met Kenneth Anger in San Francisco. He is a very handsome young man with Latin eyes and dark hair (he has Cuban blood). He wanted to meet me because of *Under a Glass Bell* and spent his whole week's salary on taking me to an expensive Russian restaurant, where we ate flaming shish kebab. It was the ritual he thought appropriate for the author of *Under a Glass Bell*, and when I found out how poor he was I made vain efforts to make him see the real Anaïs who does not like deluxe restaurants.

At someone's house I was shown his film *Fireworks*. The sadism and violence revolted me, but the film has power and is artistically perfect. It has a nightmare quality. Everyone had mixed feelings, horror and recognition of Kenneth Anger's talent.

The films of Curtis Harrington are different. They are entirely surrealistic, suggesting the dream, mysteries, and metamorphosis, with a touch of magic in the camera work. What he does with natural settings, his friends as actors, is imaginative.

In different ways, both promise to become unusual film makers.

I write every day.

I gave a reading at a small theater.

I go to the beach with Curtis Harrington, Paul Mathiesen, Kenneth Anger.

We talk about films. They are educating me in the history of films, passing on to me the knowledge they gained in UCLA film-making classes. Leonard W. is on his way back from Korea and scolds me because my letters have become impersonal. I answer that is an art I learned from him. Two years of training and I passed with honors.

Clippings and reviews of *Under a Glass Bell*. Not one line of understanding.

Visit to San Francisco. Ruth Witt Diamant invited me to read at San Francisco State College. Her home is the guesthouse of the poets she invites to her Poetry Center: Dylan Thomas, W. H. Auden, Kenneth Patchen, Harold Norse, Kenneth Rexroth, et cetera. She is warm and witty and hospitable, and devoted to poetry. She owns some of Janko Varda's collages.

The deep life runs securely like a river and the rest is adornment. I no longer fear the shallowness of my father when I give time to take care of my body, lie in the sun, swim, learn to drive a car.

In Denver, during my trip out West, I met Reginald Pole. He is an actor, dramatist, a stage director, a composer. He is famous as a Shakespearean actor. At the time he was directing his own play, *Malice Toward None,* a dramatization of Abraham Lincoln's last years in which he also played the title role.

He was born in Japan, where his father was continuing the work of his grandfather, William Pole, who was awarded the third order of the Rising Sun for his work in establishing Japan's railroad system.

He did not talk about Japan, but he talked a great deal about his life at King's College, Cambridge University, from which he graduated. He was trained in theater by his uncle, William Poel, [the original spelling of the name was forbidden for professional use], the most famous producer of Shakespeare since James Burbage of the old Globe Theatre. He talked about his friendship with Rupert Brooke, and their founding of the Marlowe Dramatic Society to produce plays at Cambridge. He knew the group which was later to become the famous Bloomsbury circle. He would have fitted in with Virginia Woolf, Thomas Hardy, John Cowper Powys. But he was plagued with asthma, which drove him out of England.

He had intended to join Rupert Brooke in Tahiti. He stayed in Tahiti long enough to engage in a romance with a princess of the reigning family. He read me her letters in French. He was deeply immersed in the beauty of Tahiti, as he described it in his autobiographical novel, and he was, according to his English upbringing, discreet about the romance. But it was as easy to imagine the princess in love with a romantic-looking young Englishman, as handsome as Aldous Huxley and Rupert Brooke, who courted her with poetry, as it was to imagine him being in love with a Tahitian princess. Reginald must have seen Tahiti as Rupert Brooke did, though he may not have been as playful and exuberant.

Her parents became alarmed that the romance would become serious and interfere with the marriage planned for her for the benefit of royal succession. Reginald never told me how they informed him of their wishes that he should continue on his journey.

Whether it was done with the courtly tact of the Tahitians, or more directly, I never knew. Nor did Reginald's natural reticence permit him to inform us of details. But a note from the widow of Robert Louis Stevenson asking him to come and visit her in a most wonderful place called Palm Springs, California, determined his leaving. He came away with a conch shell, which he had learned to blow as the Tahitians do, to call everyone to the feasts.

Once in Los Angeles he had to find out where Palm Springs was. The train went as far as Whitewater, and then, as he was told by an old Indian, he must wait for the buckboard. "How long?" he asked. "Oh, it might be hours, it might be days. But wait there. It will come." The buckboard did come at last, and he found himself in the desert.

There were only two houses in Palm Springs, one now the Desert Inn, where Mrs. Kaufman had set up tents for tubercular patients, and the other occupied by Dr. White, a woman who collected collie dogs.

Reginald met Mrs. Stevenson, who was ill. He was entranced by the desert.

In Los Angeles he produced Shakespeare, Greek dramas, Ibsen, with the collaboration of Lloyd Wright and Lawrence Tibbett.

In New York in the early twenties, he directed and acted in his own version of Dostoevsky's *The Brothers Karamazov* and *The Idiot* with Estelle Winwood and Boris Karloff. Later he acted the ghost in John Barrymore's *Hamlet*. His American-Indian ballet was performed by Ernst von Dohnányi with the New York State Symphony, and at the Metropolitan Opera House, and in Boston in 1925.

He married an actress, Helen Taggart (later Mrs. Lloyd Wright). They built the third house in Palm Springs.

He shared with his friend and mentor, John Cowper Powys, the gift for lecturing with an actor's sense of drama. Powys wrote that they both had the dramatic quality of born actors.

He played Christ in the yearly performances of the *Pilgrimage Play* in the Hollywood Hills. He gave lectures on:

The Emergence of Woman in the Modern World
The Spiritual Foundation of Art
The Meaning of Beauty
Greek Drama
The Value of Repose

His erudition was vast. He was an unusually handsome man, tall, very thin, with the long lean face of the Anglo-Saxon, pale-blue eyes under bushy eyebrows, refined features. My first impression of him was: this is the father I would have liked to have.

He was only in his late fifties, but he lay down on the couch after a performance as if he were about to die. His eyes were closed, his voice was a whisper. When the conversation touched upon a subject which interested him, he suddenly recovered his energy, his voice became the resonant actor's voice, his gestures vehement and emphatic. A few minutes later he would lie back again as if the effort had drained him.

It seemed appropriate that Reginald should have acted the ghost in *Hamlet*. By the time I met him, I was seeing a ghost of himself. The underlying self-destruction which was corroding his marvelous gifts was already at work.

He preferred to sit and talk. He would have fitted in the café life of Europe, to discuss art and philosophy, the theater and literature.

His passion for the theater and literature did not rule his life. What ruled his life was an abnormal preoccupation with his body, his ambulant anxiety which made him move from one dismal hotel to another, sleep all day in darkened rooms, prowl at night when his friends were asleep and could not see him.

He comes to visit me in Los Angeles, late in the evening, and wants to talk most of the night, which means I cannot work the next day because I do my best work in the morning.

I grew to dread his inactivity and need of talk. It was as if he sought constantly to fulfill an unfulfillable hunger, which was a return to the passivity of the child and a mother's care. He sought the mother throughout his life. There was always a woman of his age willing to play the role until he wearied them with his demands and they were replaced by another.

But if the mother made the slightest demand on him, such as wanting him to accompany her to a concert or an exhibit, he pleaded illness.

Strange destiny which makes one encounter the same figures many times. I purposely described in full the fascination of Reginald and the danger he presented. He was Helba again. They are always about to die, always using their dramatic power to make their slightest illness a major tragedy, always dramatizing their need, to engage others into serving them, waiting on them, helping them. They had the same way of skillfully working on the compassion of others.

But karma is evolution. I am not the same woman who was helpless and victimized by Helba's demands. I admire Reginald, but I know exactly what his demands would do to a human being. Unknowingly he has the most destructive effect on those around him.

J. C. Flugel [in *Man, Morals and Society: A Psychoanalytical Study*] has something interesting to say about the artist, and distance from reality:

> The artist can neither be too distant because the myth distorts reality, nor too close to it for then its uninteresting and irrelevant details also distort the essential outline which gives us the quintessence of reality. We have to face the fact that for many adults, and for still more children, the frustrations and conflicts aroused by reality are often more than can be born, and that at least an occasional retreat from reality into some form of artistic thinking [in spite of all the dangers of such wishful thinking, to which Flugel gives a whole chapter] is almost inevitable, even if only for the purpose of backtracking to better leap forward.

Reginald Pole took me to meet Charlie Chaplin at his home. Chaplin is an enchanting storyteller, acting out each story. He had just come back from Bali, and he was miming everything he saw. His face is pink and healthy, and he stands in the middle of the room performing while Oona sits quietly and unobtrusively in a corner. He was bitter about America's treatment of him, but only spoke briefly about that.

When I read *Steppenwolf* by Hermann Hesse, I felt it was a description of Reginald. The self-created loneliness which nothing can assuage, the self-enclosed walls separating him from human beings. One can only feel compassion for that incurable illness of the soul.

I wanted to say: "Reginald, come out of your darkened rooms. Come out in the light and the sun of day. Live with the friends who love you."

But his message seemed to be: "Come and die with me. Keep me company in my death. Hold my hand while I lie in a state of non-existence."

Reginald takes me to meet Cornelia Runyon. She looks as the Queen of England should look. She is suntanned from living at the beach and her sculpture studio is on the terrace, out of doors. Her house is beautiful, sits high on the rocks above the sea at Zuma Beach, north of Malibu. In the living room her sculptures of semi-precious stones are standing against the window, and so the sun makes them incandescent.

She gives the impression that she is one of her own sculptures. Her beautiful deeply tanned face is molded with finesse and strength to express wit and liveliness and something undefinably enduring, eternal as stone. Hers is a beauty sculptured by intelligence and quality. There is a harmony between her appearance, her house high above the beach, and her work, which looks like a part of the sea, the rocks, and the sky. It was here that she started late in life to work with stones which she found on the beach. She began with stone because she felt it more alive than clay. Later she discovered semiprecious stones in the desert and began to work with blue calcite, howlite, rose quartz, aventurine, jade, jasper, basalt, ob-sidian, malachite, and granite.

From the first she had an essentially feminine attitude toward her material. She began with a respect for what the sea or the earth had already begun to form in the stones. She contemplated and meditated over them, permitting them to reveal the inherent pat-terns they suggested. She never imposed her own will over the image tentatively begun by nature. She discovered and completed the image so that it became visible and clear. She assisted the birth of chaotic masses into recognizable forms. She watched, mused, observed, to allow the potential in the stone to reveal its hidden qualities, color, texture, bulk, half-born animal or man. She carved with care for what was already there, so that every head or animal remained simultaneously at one with nature, not torn away while yet acquiring a personality, an individual character our eyes can identify.

In this way, her way, what came through was not some abstrac-tion torn away from its basic roots, its textures, its organic growth; but something her tender, maternal, intuitive hands allowed to grow organically, without losing its connection with the earth or sea. It is necessary to stress this, because at this time critics favored pure abstraction and advised her to impose her will on difficult materials. Her work, I believe, is the opposite of an act of will. It is an act of creativity which remains rooted in nature, more like an act of giving birth. It reminds one of the ancient myth about the image asleep in the block of marble until it is carefully disengaged by the sculptor. The sculptor must himself feel that he is not so much inventing or shaping the curve of a breast or shoulder as delivering the image from its prison.

I believe this myth fits the attitude of Cornelia Runyon toward her work. The ego is absent. She writes humbly: "I am so grateful for those twenty years with stone," as if the stone had given itself to her, as if there had been a collaboration between them. And again: "Many artists came to see and said to me: 'You must impose your will.' I listened but went on my own way, the way I found most happy, to feel the content of the stones and listen closely to their richly mysterious messages."

Because she revealed the forms, moods, messages of nature without tampering with them, they retained their intense, vivid life and their mystery. Her lack of egocentricity is like that of cathedral builders who refused to sign their designs. Everything lies asleep until she touches it like some intuitive mother, and then it discloses its inner life which she has liberated. *The Eagle* reveals his hesitations before his first flight, her *Seal* is graceful and playful in spite of his shining wet density.

She tells of the days when she loved swimming under water and how she saw fish moving around her. She found this shining fish in calcite and he seems to be glistening with water. She utilizes the dimensions of the stone's own colors, transparencies, and inner fire. She integrates its veins, stratas, contours, and textures. Her *Head of a Woman* in rose quartz has the incandescence of real flesh illumined with poetic radiance. Her *Cathedral* is a quintessence of light and lyrical aspirations. Her *Sleeping Bird* is not only asleep, he shivers with dreams. Another *Head* has as many facets as the Goddess Shiva has arms and legs in Hindu mythology. Her *Snake* flips its tail with arrogance, and her *Buffalo* butts its head with delight. Her *Turtle* clings to his carapace but scans the horizons. Her *Walrus* is a gracious comedian and the *Creeping Creature* may be born of a vision into the future.

Cornelia Runyon captures the vital emotional existence of man and animal in the living mobility and fluidity of the forms not entirely separated from the elements in which they were born. Here is no cold abstraction or mathematical equation but the eloquence of moods, the human messages from mute flesh: I fly, I crawl, I weep, I laugh, I swim, I grow, I fall, I need, I want, I follow, I break, I sink, I love, I exist.

She was born in 1887 in New York, and had little formal training, a few short months at the Art Students League. But she is a descendant of the men who built and sailed the great clipper ships out of Boston. Perhaps for this reason she chose the challenge of the hardest stones, the least tractable. She accepted the difficulty of giving subtle life to such unyielding masses.

A child of seven returning from a visit to Cornelia, falling asleep on the way home, murmured: "It was so alive-ing."

A king snake sleeps in the eaves of her porch. She feeds the birds and the sea gulls. During the war she offered her services to patrol the beach.

She reminds me in her queenly ways of the *grandes dames* who people our world as the image of the grandmothers we would have liked to have, Isak Dinesen, Virginia Woolf, the Madwoman of Chaillot, but she carries her strong personality on the light wings of humor.

She tells the story of being taken as a girl of ten to the christening of a ship. The ceremony was lengthy, the speeches interminable, it was bitterly cold, and when she was handed the ribbon to pull, the gesture suggested pulling the chain of a toilet, a signal for something which she could not control.

She is a descendant of the patriot Nathan Hale.

She does most of her work on the terrace, out of doors, overlooking the sea. A path leads down a rugged sand, rock, and heather hill to a rather somber sea dotted with rocks.

Her sculptures are placed either against the open sky, or profiled against the sea. They rest on the sand in her terrace. One of them is on a stand, indoors, but in profile against the sea and often struck by the sun and shining like a diamond.

In another epoch she would have had a salon, and all the famous artists would have sat at her feet. But our age is not an age of worship or admiration. She had that gift toward other artists.

[Summer, 1948]

I am working at the fiction of Gonzalo become Rango [*The Four-Chambered Heart*]. The present Gonzalo is dead for me. He has destroyed every vestige of friendship. I work at the fiction with mixed feelings of love and pity for the dream he destroyed. I know how human beings destroy themselves, every step of the way, and one can only feel pity. Do I begin the fiction to re-create him? To keep what was beautiful? The illusion of Gonzalo, his tales of Peru, his guitar playing, his singing and his Heathcliff wildness? The fiction breaks away from the actual facts. It is another life. It is another character. It conveys other messages. It takes its place in a continuum. Fiction teaches us that the sorrows of living are meaningful. Fiction restores the meaning. The experience which is being lived day by day may seem futile, destructive because the vision of its totality is lacking. In the novel it acquires a pattern. It is fiction. It reaches beyond pain to the pattern of meaningfulness which consoles us for all the agonies, and uncovers elevations.

There remains as residue an unbroken love of the dream itself, the myth, in spite of its human death. Thus must Henry have buried June over and over again, with misgivings, because the corpse of our human love is illumined and kept alive by our first illusion, and one is uneasy at burying it, doubting its death. Will it rise again and remain a part of our life forever?

I feel depressed, invaded by the past because my writing forces me to remember, because that is the source of my stories. If only I could create fiction out of the present, but the present is sacred to me, to be lived, to be passionately absorbed but not transfigured into fiction, to be preserved faithfully in the diary.

The alchemy of fiction is, for me, an act of embalming.

Dream: Marijuana has been planted in my room with directions to melt it in a bottle to disguise it. I have not finished when I hear a noise. I throw everything into a drawer and go out. My room is searched and I know I will be imprisoned.

Inexplicable dream because I have had so little to do with marijuana. Once I tried it in Acapulco, out of doors, and it produced no results. Another time George Leite gave me some in Berkeley and all I felt is my usual love of dancing. Do I feel guilt at my frequent elated moments which come out of passionate moments and not from any herb? Do I think my enjoyments should be punished by imprisonment?

I am suffering again from the mysterious malady of anxiety and marvel at whatever alchemy transmutes this and gives it to others as a life source, wondering if it is not the alchemy itself which is slowly killing me, as if I kept the poisons of doubt and fears in my being and gave out only the gold. Everywhere I go life and creation burst open, yet I remain anchorless, uprooted.

Anxiety is love's greatest killer, because it is like the stranglehold of the drowning. It took me years of sorrow to learn these airy bird's spirals around the loved ones so that the love should never crystallize into a prison. Flights, swoops, circles. For our anxiety is the one thing we cannot place on the shoulders of others, it suffocates them. It is the one contagious illness of the spirit one must preserve others from, if one loves. For it has nothing to do with love, it is its antithesis, and no love can thrive within the walls of fears.

This fear of loss, which haunted my childhood, my adolescence, my young woman's life, the fear of love being doomed to vanish as my father did, is a secret not to burden others with, for then the love will seem heavy and not survive the airless anxiety.

Life in Los Angeles is not as toxic as in New York. The proximity to the Orient and to Mexico has made people less obsessionally ambitious and more in love with life. Everyone has a garden, and people are not enslaved by the clock. The Japanese have designed the gardens, the Mexicans influence the rhythm. You feel the presence of the desert when people speak of the Santa Ana winds, which recall the simoom in Mallorca. You feel the fruitfulness of the canyons, and the presence of the sea. The sun pulls you out of the house. The artificial presence of film makers does not seem part of the land. The surrealists would be pleased with the sudden appearance of a subway station on a truck being taken to a studio, by the movie villages Nathanael West wrote about, the reproductions of Western towns, of Swiss villages, of Southern mansions. As you are walking along a street suddenly you see a whole house approaching on wheels; it fills the streets. It is being moved. I thought it would be marvelous to film a party going on as the house moves;

it reminded me of the Haitian stories about the trees which moved from place to place in the night. One never thinks of a house moving.

I am awakened by the singing of birds. I cannot introduce them. I ask their names and then forget them like a careless hostess. But they sing well and gaily. The sun always shines through the Venetian blinds. I have a choice of two new dresses to wear. I walk down the hill to breakfast at Musso's, where they make the most fragile pancakes. The banality and vulgarity of Hollywood Boulevard do not bother me. Nathanael West understood it. I see another Hollywood, young artists of all kinds, making films without money, doing pottery and weaving, painting, engraving, sculpture.

I am learning to drive. A new freedom. A quest for health and beauty, to efface some of the harm from my years in hell. At times I feel like a convalescent from hell. The sun shines on the chromium of my car, on my new dress, on my new dash and my new confidence. The quest for sun and suntanning and swimming is of major importance here and it suits me.

The white houses, the perpetual sun, and the major theme "we are going to the beach," "will you come to the beach?" "today is a good beach day," et cetera, is Grecian. When I return to my desk there is an envelope filled with newspaper clippings on *Under a Glass Bell*. There are telephone messages from Kenneth Anger and Paul Mathiesen, Curtis Harrington. Now I can write. I can extract the essence of the past for fiction without pain. The present is beautiful. As in Acapulco there is a more subdued but perpetual air of fiesta. The birds sing at night.

After hearing music I was elated, keyed up, and with friends we decided to go to the sea, to the Amusement Park in Venice. And there I found my fear again, all the fears I thought I had conquered: fear and terror of speed, heights, the scenic railway, of violence, of the labyrinth, enclosures, of chutes, of darkness, traps. Why?

Am I not made for happiness, I asked inside of the dark house of terrors, facing sudden skeletons, traps, sudden plunges into total darkness? Will I hear the birds sing again? Will I feel pleasure tomorrow when I see the jacaranda tree in bloom?

———

The ugliest, most prejudiced review was written by Elizabeth Hardwick in *Partisan Review*. How can anyone go into a tantrum of insults over *Under a Glass Bell?* What is there to hate so fiercely? For example:

. . . In Anaïs Nin the attraction to the inexpressible is fatal and no writer I can think of has more passionately embraced thin air. Still, she has nerve and goes on her way with a fierce foolishness that is not without beauty as an act, though it is too bad her performance is never equal to her intentions. I suppose it is true that nothing is so boring as intransigence that does not lead to art superior or even equal to that which is dramatically snubbed. The dreary, sour side of programmatic purity—egotism, piety, boastfulness—annihilates what was meant to be joyful and releasing and leaves only the vanity, like that outrageous pride one sees on the faces of the more interesting American derelicts, those who know they can, if they pull themselves together, still go into the family business.

No doubt this middle-class bum is vanishing; martyrdom and the illusion of righteous protest are just as "dated" on the Bowery as elsewhere. In the same way Anaïs Nin, one of our most self-consciously uncompromising writers, seems old-fashioned. She is vague, dreamy, mercilessly pretentious; the sickly child of distinguished parents—the avant garde of the twenties—and unfortunately a great bore. . . .

[Fall, 1948]

In San Francisco, walking around Ruth Witt Diamant's neighborhood, I looked into a vast garden and saw a tiny Japanese teahouse which looked unlived in. I visited the old couple who owned the estate and they agreed to rent it to me. But it was left to me to empty it of trash kept there for many years, old newspapers, old magazines, broken furniture, discarded valises. It took many weeks to clean, to paint, and to install a shower. I loved the teahouse. I felt I was living in Japan. But winter came. The teahouse had no heat and was terribly cold and damp in the middle of so many trees, vines, and moss. My health forced me to give up my beautiful teahouse I had worked so hard on and move into an apartment which had a huge central fireplace and received sun all day through big windows overlooking the bay.

This reminded me very much of looking for a gypsy wagon with Gonzalo, then a houseboat, as if I always wanted to live outside and beyond the reality of the place where I was.

Ruth comes every day to tell me it is my duty to the community to go to gatherings, parties, et cetera. But my feeling is that my duty is to write. If I go out every night, I cannot work well the next day.

Gangster Dream: I am walking with an older couple. Suddenly we notice there are three or four gangsters, dressed as they are in the movies. Dark clothes, dark glasses, and a brutal, fixed, hypnotic immobility. I seek to escape. Then I realize it is not me they want but the couple. The woman, as she is led away, turns an agonized face toward me. I am distressed but also glad not to be involved. I was only a passing friend. However, later in the dream, the same couple is free, in their own house, but the gangsters are coming. The couple asks me to answer the bell and give them time to escape. I know I am risking revenge from the gangsters but this time I feel I should risk my life in contrast to my first impulse to escape the situation completely.

It is not imagination which stirs in the blood obscurely at certain spectacles, certain cities, certain faces; it is memory. Some memories lie dormant, like hibernating animals, atrophied memories, but others survive in the genes and easily reappear in the present. Idea of memory very persistent. I think of it all day. I believe the body carries cells of memories down through the ages, in the same way it transmits physical traits. These memories lie dormant until aroused by a face, a city, a situation. A simple explanation of "we have lived this before." Of recognition and familiarity. Racial and collective memories have continuity, forming unconscious layers.

In California the white buildings, the sun and the palms re-create Cuba for me, childhood memories of sea, of gaiety, and of a kind, caressing climate.

Have I walked away from my demons?

In San Francisco I can work better. I am not dissolved in nature.

Exhausted with writing, and with the conflict of making a river-bed for the flow of the diary so that it may not seem like a diary but an inner monologue, a series of free associations accompanying the life of several characters. Not yet solved. The diary cannot be published in its entirety. How can I convert it into a Joycean flow of inner consciousness?

Last night I wanted to give up writing. It seemed wrong to make a story of Gonzalo. I felt the inhumanity of art. I thought of my fictionalizing of Paul in *Children of the Albatross*. It destroyed nothing. It touched his heart. The story of Gonzalo may be the only undestroyed image of him, because he set about to destroy himself. It may be an inspiration to other Gonzalos not to destroy themselves.

Last night I was a woman, hurt by memories and acknowledging the ever recurrent continuity of love. This morning I am a writer and have come to terms with the woman by saying: "It must be sincere, it is fiction but it must be sincere, it must be truthful to the feelings if not to actual facts." And I worked gravely, sincerely.

In my fiction there is no death, as there is occasionally in the diary. Do I extract the death-dealing parts? Shall I go to the end this time and describe dissolution and death?

One handles truths like dynamite. Literature is one vast hypocrisy, a giant deception, treachery. All the writers have concealed more than they have revealed.

But paradoxically, we create fiction out of human concern for the victims of the revelations. This concern is at the root of literature.

I remember D. H. Lawrence complaining that nature was too powerful in Mexico, that it swallowed one. If I lived there, would the need to write disappear? When the external world matches our need, our hunger, our inner world, might not the need to create cease? Morocco did that. It made me contemplative, content with a spectacle of life so vivid that it stilled all needs. Would a mere change of culture put an end to our restlessness, our dissatisfaction, our need to create what is not there?

In Acapulco I felt for the first time the slackening of this tension I suffer from in my dealings with the world. The contact was established without difficulty. I felt at one with the people and nature.

I do not feel this tension when I am writing, I am at ease in the diary. When will creation and life fuse for me, and when will I be equally at ease in both?

[Winter, 1948]

We receive a fatal imprint in childhood, at the time of our greatest plasticity, of our passive impressionism, of our helplessness before suggestion. In no period has the role of the parents loomed as immense, because we have recognized the determinism, but at the same time an exaggeration in the size of the Enormous Parent does not need to be permanent and irretrievable. The time has come when, having completed the scientific study of the importance of parents, we now must re-establish our power to revoke their imprint, to reverse our patterns, to kill our fatal downward tendencies. We do not remain smaller in stature than our parents. Nature had intended them to shrink progressively in our eyes to human proportions while we reach for our own maturity. Their fallibilities, their errors, their weaknesses were intended to develop our own capacity for parenthood. We were to discover their human weakness not to overwhelm or humiliate them, but to realize the difficulty of their task and awaken our own human protectiveness toward their failures or a respect for their partial achievement. But to place all responsibilities upon them is wrong too. If they gave us handicaps, they also gave us their courage, their obstinacy, their sacrifices, their moments of strength. We cannot forever await from them the sanction to mature, to impose on them our own truths, to resist or perhaps defeat them in our necessity to gain strength.

We cannot always place responsibility outside of ourselves, on parents, nations, the world, society, race, religion. Long ago it was the gods. If we accepted a part of this responsibility we would simultaneously discover our strength. A handicap is not permanent. We are permitted all the fluctuations, metamorphoses which we all so well understand in our scientific studies of psychology.

Character has ceased to be a mystery and we can no longer refuse our responsibility with the excuse that this is an unformed, chaotic, eyeless, unpredictable force which drives, tosses, breaks us at will.

Claude Fredericks I never had time to describe. He was an enthusiastic and loving friend, spontaneous and generous. He worked with us at the Gemor Press, to learn printing, and then set up his own press, the Banyon Press, and published a few books before going to

Italy. He was a friend with whom one could exchange confidences. He writes a diary. I read some pages of it. His descriptions of sexuality are very specific and he may not be able to publish it.

We argued about *Nightwood*. He prefers *Anna Karenina*. "It has more scope." But I answered that scope was not as important as depth.

Everyone speaks of scope, but what they mean is a bigger screen, more people, and they do not realize that in this there is no hope of knowing human beings. Masses make human beings anonymous and one-dimensional.

Claude presents to the world an Oriental-cast face, but if you seek to know him, he also presents the Oriental smile, a reflection of yours, a sympathy which is ever present, like a supreme act of politeness, an opinion which at the slightest opposition vanishes. He is difficult to know because he offers you only his charm and thoughtfulness.

He was the born confidant, the shadowy friend, the evasive supporter. What you assert he does not deny. In a sense he acts out feminine attributes in relationships, he yields, he consoles, he sustains. He is the felt in the bedroom slipper, the storm strips on the wintry windows, the wool lining back of piano keys, the interlining in conversations, the shock absorber on the springs of cars, the lightning conductor. He is the invisible man. When he worked at the press with us, and Gonzalo's anarchism, erratic hours, caused us so much anguish and extra work, he was the receptive ear, the devoted helper. In his diary he asserted his physical hungers and fulfillments. But I have yet to know this enigmatic friend.

Of the fragments I did in San Francisco only a few survived. Nothing of what I wrote in Acapulco. Out of one hundred pages only twenty are good. I am only beginning now to work seriously.

To write is to descend, to excavate, to go underground.

Humanity and art were always opposites for me. When will they integrate? I see that when I want to be human, I have to slacken the tension which I always feel in my dealings with the world, in my work, and not in my diary or in my love.

I can feel it now, how I have to loosen the overcharged tensions which created a kind of precious stone, and petrified the blood. It was the Petrified Forest of Fear, always. Now when I strike in writing, I say: too high, too high, and I try to lower my tone. Even if

I am inventive, creative, innovative, I still feel I have to rid myself of the influence of the beliefs of the men I knew. I was influenced by Henry's anarchy and amoralities. I was influenced by Gonzalo's dogmatism and prejudices, his blind acceptance of Communism. I was influenced by others' admiration of classical literature and music and their suspicion of modern contemporary writing.

The feminine desire to espouse the faith of those you love as I espoused my father's and then my mother's. I only swerved from each as my love changed. I swerved from admiration of my father's values to that of my mother's. But I am slowly finding my own. In my life today there is a freedom of emotion, a keenness of sensation, an explorative, adventurous attitude which is mine.

Jerry Kaiser, a warm and clever friend, who works now for the Telephone Company in Chicago, invited me to lecture. As the workmen are there all day, and it is a large city in itself, at their lunch hour they have programs: concerts, films, lectures. Jerry asked me to come and read from my books, and to bring the copper plates by Ian Hugo from which we had pulled the engravings that illustrate the books. He thought it would be interesting for the workmen who handled copper to see how an artist uses it.

First I was invited to watch the making of copper wires, from an ingot the size of a tree, being fed by the men into the furnace. When this large piece becomes red-hot, the men in hip-high boots carrying giant tongs have to catch the red-hot snake and slip it into a smaller furnace. It is dangerous work requiring great skill. At each furnace the snake becomes thinner, until it comes out as wire and is rolled into a bobbinlike thread. The scene in the cellar, with furnaces spewing fire, tall men like strong Wagnerian giants in the flaming caves of the earth, was like a Dantesque scene in hell. One whip blow from the red-hot snake of copper spells death.

In another part of this hell huge vats filled with acid were used to dissolve the scraps. The copper in the acid acquires a beautiful moss green through which the copper color still shows.

It was strange and fascinating to see the workmen arrive at the recreation hall to look at the exhibit of copper plates, at the needle-thin designs. They listened attentively to the reading. The women responded particularly to my passage on sewing from *Ladders to Fire*.

Later I went to a bookshop party to sign books at the Red Door Bookshop run by Ward and Lolajean Sherbak.

In New York I wear a wool dress of winter white.

I see Lila Rosenblum again.

Talking with her I am reminded of things I did not write about because they were too painful. Lila was crippled by an unusual illness. Half of the time she was bedridden. But in contrast to Helba her spirit is undefeated. She helped me even before we met.

When *House of Incest* was out of print and we were collecting money to reprint it, Lawrence Maxwell borrowed money from her. He owned a bookshop and was a mutual friend. When we finally met we talked like sisters, though Lila was much younger. She worked, how I do not know. Her place was filled with books. We talked analysis and life. When she was in Los Angeles she was going through a dark period. She was on dangerous drugs like Nembutal. She would be half unconscious and then call Jim Herlihy. She had a slight tremor, which gave her talk and even her laughter a tremulous quality.

October 28 I gave a lecture at Dartmouth College.

Sunami, the famous Japanese photographer, took photographs of me.

I had a book-signing party at Lawrence Maxwell's Village shop.

November 5 I lectured at Bennington College.

November 9 I lectured at Washington Art School.

November 12 I lectured at Chicago University, presented by Wallace Fowlie as one of the surrealist writers.

At the art school, a student kept repeating stubbornly and obsessively: "Literature does not help us to live." He prevented all discussion and had not even read my work.

I cannot find in American literature the metaphysical and poetic qualities of a Bernanos, a Pierre Jean Jouve, a Léon-Paul Fargue, a Giraudoux of the novels.

A Frenchman who knew him well describes Jean Giraudoux:

He was outstanding in every way, even physically, six feet tall, thin, distinguished in bearing; a thoroughbred face, rather ascetic, head held high. Everything about him spoke of an exceptional human being. Wit, finesse, a total lack of vulgarity emanated from him. Few people pleased him, but he was so gentle and kind he did not show his antipathies. He had to keep above platitudes, mediocrities of life not to be shocked constantly. He avoided them. For this reason he preferred the company of women. With men he had to feel that they respected his talent before he came out of his shell. He was a dazzling storyteller, his imagination was constantly surprising you. He liked to improvise a story, embroidering as he went along, knowing only vaguely what the climax would be. He loved tennis, billiards, and Ping-Pong. He could have been an excellent chess player due to his power of analysis, but he did not have the concentration.

Simenon. The pattern is the same in every book. It is the fall of man. Simenon is aware that this fall is caused by the fatality of an impulse of self-destruction more often than by external fatality. He is aware of the germ which may or may not develop, may grow and kill the other or the self.

He is a past master at tracing the early formation of this germ, the conditions which led to its growth, the slow germination, development, and climax of its destructiveness. He is perhaps our best psychologist in the novel.

[Spring, 1949]

San Francisco.

At six o'clock the electric clock buzzes and makes me jump. In the long, wide bed I turn from my left side to see through the slit of the Venetian blind a little garden stretching up, filled with flowers, the reflection of a ceiling of fog. On these cold mornings duty tears me out of the warmth, cuts the sleep, sending me out of bed to wash my face and comb my hair and button on my dress and sweater. I start the coffee and light the oven for the rolls. I turn on the button which gives heat. I open the Venetian blinds. The fog has lifted and I see the bay, the bridges, the ships, the other white houses, children starting off for school, garages opening like the jaws of monsters to let out the cars of people going to work. I see women waiting for the bus. The clouds of San Francisco are not airy like those of France; even when cotton-colored, they seem charged with future rain and storms. When the sun's rays pierce through them it is like the aura of God in ancient paintings, a shaft of illumination transcending darkness. It will hit a group of houses which look as white as Mediterranean houses, but leave the rest gray and rather ominous. The sun gives no assurance.

Then I go to work.

At eleven o'clock the postman comes. I await news from Dutton. I sent them a few weeks ago my new book, *The Four-Chambered Heart,* the story of Gonzalo, fictionalized, without the sordid ending, for Gonzalo, like June, had the power to descend to the greatest vulgarities when he poisoned and degraded in one instant of destructiveness all the romance and idealism he built up over the years. In one moment of anger he could corrode nine years of poetry and romanticism.

The belongings I left stored in France when the war broke out finally arrived. I was happy to see my books. But when I saw the furniture, I realized it did not belong in my new life. It harmonized with Louveciennes, with the houseboat, it was catalogued in the diary, described in *Under a Glass Bell* stories, but it did not belong in a modern, white, San Francisco apartment. Objects die when they are no longer illumined by certain experiences and heightened mo-

45

ments of one's life. My attachment to them died, and they lost their glow as soon as I stopped loving them. When they arrived from France, after years of storage, I saw that they were dead. Wreckage from a great emotional journey. I had moved away from them. I sold them.

I telephoned the antique dealers: "Will you come and see some antiques I have? A Spanish Moorish headboard, an Indian lamp, an Arabian mirror, a Turkish coffee set of silver, a Kali goddess, a Venetian vase."

(If you had seen how beautiful these objects looked in the houseboat, the shadows and patterns designed by the carved copper lamp, the encrustations of ivory and mother of pearl and copper arabesques on the headboard gleaming in the light of passing boats. If you could have seen what was reflected in the tall Arabian mirror.)

But the antique shops were not interested and I ended by disposing of them among my friends. The Arabian fairy-tale bed was bought by the painter Zev and taken to his Monterey house.

The front room is flooded in sunlight. I wash dishes, I clean the apartment, I market. I never minded the monotony of housework as long as my life has its lyrical climaxes, its high moments, the certitude of full living.

A night of fog. Music on the radio. Leave the past alone except to fictionalize and transform, and turn sorrows into tales.

My collection of Japanese dolls on the shelves, princesses of a lavish glitter of gestures and clothes, like a Christmas tree of light, tinsel, satin, jewels. Elaborate and iridescent. I love their porcelain faces, delicate hands, the sway and grace, the stylized gestures. One carries a birdcage, another a musical instrument, the third a fan.

They are not the dolls of a child, which I never liked, but dolls of a highly sophisticated beauty.

I am not refusing to grow and mature in the so-called mature world, but I cannot grow in arrogance, in a hard finish, in a gold-plated irony, in the impertinence and cynicism of the wealthy.

Brahms' Double Concerto on the phonograph.

When I need drugs, when the present is unacceptable, I reread all my French books, saturate myself with the delectable Giraudoux, with the poetic analysis of Jouve. Above all, with the certitudes of people who never refused or eluded experience, for whom experience of life was the primary motivation, who were unafraid of love, sex, even madness or evil.

46

The backyard is wistful with the persistence of the drizzle. The flowers hang their heads. Some of them adopt the raindrops like dazzling bastard children and make them look like flowers. I saw an unusual flower, bent over it, it melted in my fingers. It was raindrops pretending, expanding in bridal costume reflected from the clouds, spreading false, illusory tentacles of white lace on the heart of the leaves.

The ballet of Japanese dolls dancing on the shelves looks down at me.

When I was ten years old I started out writing adventure stories. In reading Simenon I remembered this. He is my favorite storyteller. He has a good story to tell, and he works subtly at characterization. His characters are beautifully wrought, his details significant. He is primarily a psychologist, for whom action has to be analyzed and understood. Each detail counts because it is related to the drama, and the drama happens because of the character and childhood, et cetera. He keeps the design of the adventure story (suspense) and embroiders upon this a psychological drama with care and skill. People do not appreciate his novels as they should because he made his reputation writing detective stories. His latest book, *Le Passage Clandestin,* is wonderful. I forgot my bronchitis, my foggy head. I am in Tahiti, I am inside of others' lives. I feel as if I had been there. His knowledge of the workmen, trades, professions, of humble crafts and occupations is far deeper than Zola or Balzac. He truly knows the life of the poor, the workmen, the most ignored of little men.

With all their emphasis on plot and narrative, no American writers have ever told as good a tale because Simenon tells it in depth. Everything is indicated, outer and inner equally. The psychological drama is there too. The little people with their miseries are the ones he likes to bring out of the shadows, but the origin of his compassion is the knowledge of what makes them cruel, desperate, alcoholics or murderers, so that even his most repulsive character, Felix in *Le Cheval Blanc,* became so because he was accused of a crime he did not commit. In his adventure stories, such as *Le Passage Clandestin,* the suspense and drama is tremendous but based on a subtle study of self-destruction. In *Le Touriste de Banane* he studies the adventurer better than any writer I know, delves into his desire for isolation and the fear of solitude.

———

No rest for me anywhere. No rest from writing, awareness, in-sights, memories, fantasies, analogies, free associations. Writing becomes imperative for a surcharged head.

Occasionally I think of death. I can easily believe in the disin-tegration of the body, but cannot believe that all I have learned, experienced, accumulated, can disappear and be wasted. Like a river, it must flow somewhere. Proust's life flowed into me, became a part of my life. His thoughts, his discoveries, his visions, each year visit me, each year bring me deeper messages. There must be continuity.

The mocking birds of California sing intermittently but sumptu-ously.

Once in Paris I had a record I loved, music by Erik Satie, poem by Paul Éluard. I searched for it in New York. I could not remember the title. I never found it again. It was the ever recurrent song of remoteness, the same one which appears in Debussy's Sonata for Piano and Violin, in the *Chansons d'Auvergne,* in Carillo's *Cristóbal Colón.* It is the theme of distance from human life, of a lament in space, the sorrow of a separation which can only be conquered by love.

The other day, driving from Berkeley, I heard the Debussy Sonata and again I wept as I have always wept at this music, experiencing the wildest and fullest sorrow. It always depicted for me the duel between earth and spirit, the conflict between isolation and con-nection with the earth, the need to fly, and the need of earth, the struggle between the solitary chant of the violin and the heavier, stronger piano.

Varda no longer lives in the barn at Monterey. He has moved to a big loft, a vast space in which he both paints and lives. He has arranged in one corner a shower like those in the army. When I arrive he is pulling the string which will cause the pail hung above his head to spill water over him. In another corner he fries huge pans of potatoes, and serves them with red wine.

I visit him with Paul Mathiesen.

Another time he invited me to go sailing on a boat he repaired himself after finding it in a junkyard. He made a colorful Greek sail for it. San Francisco is cold and I dressed like an Eskimo, with a hooded parka over my head, and everybody laughed at me. Because the weather was rough we could not visit the half-sunken shipwreck as he had promised me. In rough weather it might sink altogether.

[Summer, 1949]

New York.

In the Village I heard the One-Man Band. He is a Negro and he has an outfit made of:

one gasoline tin
one hot-water bag
one rubber mouse with a squeak
one frying pan
one doorbell
one whistle.

With a pair of sticks he manages to sound like a jazz band. When he gets wild he ends up drumming on parked automobiles, on the sidewalk, on the fire hydrant.

Because E. P. Dutton said that they could not publish *The Four-Chambered Heart* for several years, I made a contract with Duell, Sloan and Pearce.

I made friends with William Kennedy, who tells me all the magnificent things he will do for *The Four-Chambered Heart*.

Changes in Acapulco. There is now a long walk along the Bay, and a two-way road divided by acacia trees so cars won't collide. No more dust roads, no potholes, even the little road by the small restaurant is macadamized. Bad changes are that the Mexicans now bring radios as well as guitars to the beach, and they chew Chiclets while they dance. But they kept the little cabañas where one eats fish, and merely brought the sand right up to them, so cars are parked behind and out of sight and the beach is prettier. They planted flowers everywhere.

Spent Sunday on Varda's ferryboat, and sailing on his sailboat. So beautiful. A newspaperman entitled his book on San Francisco *Baghdad-by-the-Bay*, and it was not so far-fetched an image. It was a day of utter peace. The intense brilliance of the light, which Varda compares to the light of Greece, is what makes this Western life so joyous. And even when the fog comes, and you sometimes

49

drive right through it, and it envelops you on the bridge, suddenly you will be out of it, struck by the sunlight like lightning.

I am working intensely and writing a great deal.

[October 20, 1949]

San Francisco.

My father died this morning, in Cuba. The hurt was so deep, the shock so deep, the sense of loss so deep, it was as if I died with him. I felt myself breaking, falling. I wept not to have seen him since Paris, not to have forgiven him, not to have been there when he died alone and poor in a hospital.

Joaquin sent me a telegram. I wept and felt the loss in my body, this terrible unfulfilled love. Never to have come close to him, never to have fused with him. The cursed distance which is the greatest sorrow which can befall a human being. I saw him asleep, as I saw him when he fainted after a concert. The death is there inside of you. Certainly a part of one dies with those we love. You feel it but you cannot believe it. The pain attacks the body. I should have overlooked his immense selfishness. I should have sacrificed my life to him as he wanted me to. I fought not to be as he was, disconnected from human beings. I fought to reach all those who were like him disconnected from human beings. That was the mystery of my relationship to the closed, the cold, the remote ones. I fought to be near, to fuse, to achieve the opposite, communion with others. I cannot accept his death. It will never heal. Because it was an incomplete, an aborted, an unfulfillable relationship. One can accept death when it comes as a culmination, a natural death. But something here, this failure, was like an artificial surgery. Amputation, not natural death.

What I cannot bear is that to survive the destructiveness of others, we rebel, strike out, harm them, turn away. I wish I had been a saint.

Joaquin, who is a saint, writes me: "I tried to get close to him, and failed."

So many memories. Why did he build a wall around himself? Why did he always seek the flaws in others, why were his blue eyes so critical? No memory of tenderness or care, and yet my mother tells me that he took thousands of photographs of us, naked. He was full of aesthetic admiration for his children. It was the only moment in which he showed interest. Or was it interest in a new hobby, photography? I do not know. But the moment of photography was the only moment we received attention. I wonder if my dislike of photography came from that. Children are vain, and are aware of being admired. Did I repudiate this kind of admiration? Was there something else I wanted, not enjoyment of our bodies, but noticing what we felt, thought, displayed in our games. Our childish need of a secret house within a house. Why? Our own, distinct from the parents. We created it under the round library table covered with its long, heavy, fringed green cloth.

Did he bring out the woman's coquettishness in the little girl? Eyes of the father behind a camera. But always a critical eye. That eye had to be exorcised, or else like that of a demanding god, pleased. I had to labor at presenting a pleasing image. Of course, that is where it came from. Not to displease the Photographer God and Critic.

Joaquin wrote me about our father: "I tried to be friendly but he had already locked himself away from everybody. He was lost in the pit of his own loneliness and frightened at the sound of his own voice."

He had discarded all photographs but those of himself which were hung around the walls.

[Winter, 1949-1950]

Los Angeles.

Jim Herlihy is working at the Satyr Book Shop, and I paid him a visit in his small Hollywood apartment. The Pasadena Playhouse put on his play about a cripple, and he stayed on.

Whether it is depression, anxiety, or nervousness in him, it is all converted into a lively, tense, swift speech which in itself, by its rhythm, is elating. The dark bottom never shows. His persona is what is expected of a handsome young man. The glimpses I have of his darker side, we seem able to talk about without heaviness or oppression.

We have phosphorescent talks because of the buoyancy of his responses, his quick displacements, a quality born of American restlessness and migratory habits. He is like a chronic hitchhiker ready to go in any direction.

His friend made a mobile for me. We talk about books, Erich Fromm, psychology and religion.

New York. A maelstrom. Party for *Four-Chambered Heart* at Duell, Sloan and Pearce very sincere and successful. Then party at Lawrence Maxwell's bookshop. Everywhere friendly people. Kennedy leads me around, from bookshop to bookshop signing books. I have six lectures to give.

My adaptation of *Four-Chambered Heart* into a play for Irene Selznick did not satisfy her. [Max] Pfeffer sent it to Margot Jones and Cheryl Crawford.

I wanted to design a lamp which would throw colored lights or slides on the walls as it turned, but of course lacked the technology. But an old Spaniard, a friend of my brother, took up the idea and began to design a rotating lamp in which one could use film or slides. He will mail it to Los Angeles when it is done.

Harper's Bazaar lost my story on Weeks Hall with photographs by Laughlin.

In San Francisco I gave a reading at an art gallery. I met Bebe and Louis Barron. They wanted to make recordings of my readings.

They came to the white apartment. Bebe was pretty, with large dark eyes and floating black hair, and a gay, smiling nature. Louis was more reflective and hesitant. They carried the heavy equipment. We worked for hours, reading stories from *Under a Glass Bell*. They had already recorded Henry Miller and Aldous Huxley. They were starting a series called *Sound Portraits*. They were skillful and lovable to work with. We ended up friends. Josephine Premice walked in, and we tried one record with her voice and drumming in the background creating rhythm sounds for *House of Incest*. It was strange and dramatic.

A friend is concerned with the fact that great and powerful America has not produced a great and powerful American novel. He says the theme of the American novel should be that of its scientific and industrial energy. I said it should be the human drama of man collapsing inwardly under the outer pressures and forces of science and industry and the drama of man seeking to control them with an equivalent inner force. The real tragedy has been the dehumanization of man, his inner collapse.

Only the Negro has not collapsed humanly. Possibly the only expression of American energy will be scientific, industrial, and the only vital art which can match up to it will be jazz. Possibly the American novel will never be written, certainly not by the new novelists who instead of maturity portray hysteria, brutality in place of feeling, clichés in place of revelation, obscenity in place of sensual vitality.

But William Goyen writes *House of Breath*, a beautiful, sensitive novel, subtle and like a waking dream.

Wallace Fowlie writes a book on surrealism and comments on the poetry in Henry; but not a reference to me, when it was he who had invited me as a surrealist writer to read at Chicago University.

But then there are so many unnoticed writers: Djuna Barnes, Anna Kavan, Isak Dinesen.

I finished a book of two hundred pages which is a full-length portrait of Sabina [later titled *A Spy in the House of Love*].

Everyday I type from the original diaries to preserve the hand-written notebooks, and have the typed script to refer to when I need notes or reminders for my novels. My writer's notebook. It is changing from diary to notebook. I do not feel the same need of continuity and completion.

Notes for lecture:
Our senses tend to be dulled by familiarity, tend to become mechanical and automatic. What the artist or writer seeks to do by exaggeration, or distortion, is not only to make us notice a difference but to reveal a new aspect. Brancusi's sculpture revealed a new aspect. He emphasized the speed of flight of a bird by eliminating details which catch and retain our eyes and distract us from the pure sensation of speed and flight. If the most significant experience a bird can give us is the experience of flight and speed, it matters little if the artist sacrifices a bird's spit of color on a wing, the texture of feathers, the design of his beak and feet. This principle should apply to modern writing.

One reason why, for example, we may not care to live in the house of, or with the furniture of, our grandparents, is merely because they tended to create an atmosphere which subtly affects us and makes us recede into the past and lose contact with the present. The artist seeks not to continue to reproduce a familiar experience but to bring us a reflection of a contemporary one, to capture changes of rhythm, an increased awareness of aerodynamic forms, et cetera. So he may assume you are quite familiar with the form of the George Washington Bridge and seek to break it down into composite fragments so that he will reawaken or sharpen your vision of its details.

Even in reading literature we shift our emphasis according to our period. We read new meanings into Shakespeare. This is the rule of the artist, to seek to renew and resharpen our senses by a new vision of the familiar. In the novel, the same thing should take place. If I create a character which reminds you of an uncle of yours, your mind will quickly say: Oh, yes, that is like Uncle Philip, and you will rush to complete the identification by superimposing the image of your uncle's character over what I had intended. I had intended to reveal an aspect of this character not perceived before, but the basis from which it sprang made you situate him in *your experience* rather than in an unfamiliar one uncovered by the novelist. Therefore, to be able to reveal my new insight into such a character, I have to try and make one who does not resemble your uncle, so that you will not superimpose your image over mine. I have to do what Brancusi did with the bird, remove recognizable details so you will concentrate on a new element. This cannot be done without eliminating the familiar. In other words, the lens of this camera eye, our subjective vision, each time catches new aspects, new territories of experience. That is what I call the adventure of reading, the research, the innovation. For that reason alone I discard trite words. Not out of literary snobbishness but because they are overused and often dead. A trite word is an overused word which has lost its identity like an old coat in a second-hand shop. The familiar grows dull and we no longer see, hear, or taste it. The artist sacrifices a great deal of security, peace of mind, for the perpetual adventure, for the discovery of new colors, new words, new horizons, new territories of experience.

Perhaps behind our occasional hostility toward the artist and writer there may be a slight tinge of jealousy. The man or woman who for the sake of family life, children, takes up work he does not like, disciplines himself, sacrifices some fantasy he had once, to travel or to paint, or even possibly to write, may feel toward the artist and writer a jealousy of his adventurous life. The artist and the writer have generally paid the full price for their independence and for the privilege of doing work they love, or for their artistic rebellions against standardized living or values.

We must protect the minority writers because they are the research workers of literature. They keep it alive. It has been fashionable of late to seek out and force such writers into more popular channels, to the detriment of both writer and an unprepared public.

Educators do all in their power to prepare you to enjoy reading after college. It is right that you should read according to your temperament, occupations, hobbies, and vocations. But it is a sign of great inner insecurity to be hostile to the unfamiliar, unwilling to explore the unfamiliar. In science, we respect the research worker. In literature, we should not always read the books blessed by the majority. This trend is reflected in such absurd announcements as "the death of the novel," "the last of the romantics," "the last of the Bohemians," when we know that these are continuous trends which evolve and merely change form. The suppression of inner patterns in favor of patterns created by society is dangerous to us. Artistic revolt, innovation, experiment should not be met with hostility. They may disturb an established order or an artificial conventionality, but they may rescue us from death in life, from robot life, from boredom, from loss of the self, from enslavement.

When we totally accept a pattern not made by us, not truly our own, we wither and die. People's conventional structure is often a façade. Under the most rigid conventionality there is often an individual, a human being with original thoughts or inventive fantasy, which he does not dare expose for fear of ridicule, and this is what the writer and artist are willing to do for us. They are guides and map makers to greater sincerity. They are useful, in fact indispensable, to the community. They keep before our eyes the variations which make human beings so interesting. The men who built America were the genuine physical adventurers in a physical world. This world once built, we need adventurers in the realm of art and science. If we suppress the adventure of the spirit, we will have the anarchist and the rebel, who will burst out from too narrow confines in the form of violence and crime.

The mismanagement of *The Four-Chambered Heart*.

What happened is that all my dealings were with Kennedy. He would tell me all he was doing to promote the book. As I was so rarely in New York I could not tell what was being done.

One day I walked into Duell, Sloan and Pearce and I was told Kennedy was no longer there and nothing had been done. And now Duell, Sloan and Pearce is merging with Little, Brown and I am left without a publisher for *Spy in the House of Love*.

Los Angeles.

Christopher Isherwood came to visit. He has an adolescent smile, a wonderful broad grin which seems to touch the tip of his ear, locks of hair which fall over his forehead like those of a schoolboy bending over his homework, something delightfully whimsical and youthful about him. He came to my mountain hideout. He lives near the beach and loves the California life. He is suntanned. He keeps a diary too. He did not feel that *Four-Chambered Heart* could be made into a play or a film. He wrote me later: "Because Djuna is a sort of a saint, and saints *are* comic, that's why they bother audiences. The dialogue itself is certainly not at fault. It sounds beautiful and natural, not in the least literary. (It is significant that, for example, Alyosha never comes over well in dramatizations of *The Brothers Karamazov*.) "

We promised to see each other.

[Winter, 1950-1951]

This year the diary almost expired from too much traveling, too much moving about, too many changes. I felt pulled outward into activity, I did not want to meditate or examine, it was like floating. Several trips to Mexico, several explorations of the West, several trips to New York for the books, a mood of instability and restlessness, and I wrote mostly letters. In Mexico I tried to like the bullfights because the whole town would go and I would be left alone all day, and when everybody returned they would talk about it endlessly, so I tried to share their enthusiasm. At first I was excited, but at the first wound, to bull or man, I felt the wound in my own body. I could not share in the excitement of danger, or a cruel game, the spilled blood, and I left before the bullfight was over.

In New York I found that although reviews were more civilized, Duell, Sloan and Pearce had done nothing to sustain or propel the book, thinking it was a "prestige" publication and would not sell anyway. They only gamble on books they are certain will sell. So *Four-Chambered Heart* quietly sank, and Kennedy felt badly about it after all his wild promises.

In the West I visited all kinds of places, the desert, small towns, the beaches, the canyons, the snow peaks. I even tried skiing and found I was more adept at sliding backward than climbing to the peak for the run downhill. It was like a nightmare, I would take two steps forward and slide back three.

As a result of several trips to Mexico, Ian Hugo made the transition from engraver to film maker. He followed the process of free association; he filmed whatever touched him or appealed to him, trusting to an organic development of themes. The results were an impressionistic interpretation of the universal story of mankind's voyage told without words through a kaleidoscope of color, through sound and images. Beginning while he and the animals sleep and dream of the past, man is taken through tropical lagoons from birth, through childhood, adolescence, pain, struggle, old age, death, and burial in a mouth of a volcano in the clouds. Ozzie Smith improvised drumming and chanting as he watched the film unroll. Ian Hugo called the film *Ai-Ye*.

At about the same time he filmed some footage of a shipwreck on the beach, of the sea's constant tumult, which he later edited, inspired by the prologue to my *House of Incest* and the line: "I remember my first birth in water." The film [later called *Bells of Atlantis*] evoked the watery depths of the lost continent of Atlantis. It is a lyrical journey into prenatal memories, the theme of birth, and rebirth from the sea.

Ted Ruggles and Sylvia Spencer came to my bookshop party for *Ladders to Fire,* but we did not become friends till later.

Sylvia comes from the South. She has a lovely luminous face such as one sees in miniatures, always illumined by a touch of humor in her eyes, a smile. Her Southern accent gives a softness to her speech, which is a delight to hear in brash New York. Her erudition is disguised in airy graciousness and becomes entertaining. Her poetry is both sensitive and witty.

Ted is a silent New Englander of Scottish ancestry, but his warm dark eyes and warm smile convey empathy and responsiveness. He keeps a diary and I am certain it is a rich one because he does not disperse his ideas or feelings in conversation.

Sylvia has a gift for friendship, an openness and receptivity to all life. They are both engaged in a difficult profession, public relations, and both travel constantly. Sylvia is on many important committees and is always off to Washington. Ted travels, too, raising funds for colleges and universities.

In between we have these marvelous moments of meditation upon books which have disappeared from our modern life. We sit and have tea by the fireplace in their apartment, which literally overflows with books, with books on the piano, books on the tables, books in the entrance hall, books in the kitchen. We talk about our recent discoveries. We both haunt rare or secondhand bookshops. We share a passion for biography. A passion for people. In a society growing more and more indifferent, they both practice a most unusual kindness and thoughtfulness. In a time when gossip has an intent to kill, they maintain an interest in everyone's achievements which is devoid of judgment.

Their professional work makes them experts in obtaining grants and fellowships, and everyone wants their help. Very often Sylvia is involved with a theater, an orchestra, a dance group, a new children's school, or with the government and the United Nations.

If Ted hides his thoughts in his diary, Sylvia hides her poet self, until one day I discovered it and was delighted with it, and feel it must be sustained. She is a witty and sensitive poet.

Ted's first story was this: "Fresh out of Harvard, I got a job with a famous and wealthy psychoanalyst who was writing a book—a study of Bonaparte. He was given to plagiarism, and I was employed to deplagiarize his books. We lived in a sumptuous apartment overlooking the Park, near the Zoo. He liked to get up early, but I didn't. Not wanting to be too direct about it, too gauche, he never made an issue of this. But when he took his early-morning walk around the reservoir on his way home he would stop at the Zoo and rouse the lions, who roared angrily and so loudly they awakened me."

Ted brought out the separate chanter on which the Scotch practice for the bagpipes and showed me his clan colors.

Sylvia showed me an anthology of *Garden Poems* she had gathered together.

It was through them that I discovered an ironic absurdity. The big grants and fellowships demanded a professional presentation, elaborately set up, of information, budgets, recommendations, et cetera, which could only be properly done by professionals. If the artist cannot afford such a presentation his chances of obtaining grants and fellowships are very slight. I saw a presentation made by Sylvia, sixty pages of careful statistics and information.

Sylvia's description of events, places, and people always delights me. When I return to New York all I have to do is see them to be in touch with the pulse and center of New York activities. But all of it always bathed in an atmosphere of enjoyment, appreciation, and human involvement. We share many friends, and ultimately in every life I find traces of Sylvia's or Ted's kindness.

New York.

Peggy Glanville-Hicks, music critic of the *Herald Tribune,* and composer. She is on the music committee board of the Museum of Modern Art. She is small, very slender, very quick, with eloquent hands designing patterns in space to illustrate her talk. She has a small, impish face, with innocent, sharp, focused eyes, a humorous uptilted nose, a dimpled smile. She is decisive, sharp-witted. She wears her hair short, like an adolescent, brushed upward. She is a witty polemist. It does not appear at first like a battle. Her swordplay is invisible, it is done with a smile, but the accuracy of it is deadly. She mocks the composers and the critics who interfere with the development of a woman composer. She is asked to recommend, to bless, to support lesser composers, to introduce them, help them on their way. But this help is not returned. It was the first time I had heard a brilliant, effective woman demonstrate the obstacles which impaired her professional achievement because she was a woman.

I gave her all my books.

She wrote me a letter:

I am so glad you have written these things, personally glad. I found myself marking passages that expressed so implicitly things and thoughts that have been to me burning ineloquence all my days. Music is less precise, it embodies the feeling content of things rather than the significance and intelligence, and though this too has its great advantages as a form of expression, I often miss the greater precision of rational thoughts, or what you have miraculously done, brought the levels of super-rationality within the confines of the rational mind. How rare a thing it is when such radiant participation in life is balanced by inward penetration, and the ability to effect the equation in expression.

From then on she treated the characters in my novels as persons, already incorporated into her own life, existing.

"Paul in *Children of the Albatross* is Paul Bowles, isn't he, and Zora is Jane Bowles?"

"No, I never knew them."

"Of course, you are a jump ahead, you know, and you will have to wait for the others to catch up. It is a private world completely familiar to me."

We only disagree on psychoanalysis. She calls it the work of the devil. And she mistrusts science. She is on the side of the mystics. But because of her own climate, its elevations, I felt I would rather have her praise than a million other acceptances. She restored my spiritual pride, lost in a maze of humiliations.

Peggy had surgery. Her sensitiveness was violently jarred by the callousness, noise, and vulgarity of the hospital. Nowhere is inhumanity more revealed than in hospitals.

She came back to her apartment on Sunday. Sylvia Spencer and I took shifts to take care of her. At six A.M. Peggy telephones in a small voice: "Nin, please come." I put on black wool slacks, a black wool blouse, a heavy black coat and wrap my head in a shawl. It is bitterly cold. At her address I insert the key. First of all I smell the flowers sent by Yehudi Menuhin and Carlos Surinac.

I taped the windows against the cold, brought up the mail, watered the plants, gave her medication. I stayed until Sylvia came. We were very professional and left notes on what we had done, as nurses do.

I was giving back to her all the care I had received from others, passing on all I had been given.

Aside from the critical moments of pain, she was cheerful and ate with pleasure. Slowly this energy which seemed only intellectual and spiritual returned to her body, and she began to sparkle again. All her strength is in her spirit, to sustain a hypersensitive body. Doctors are blind to treat such a person as they would others. A finer specimen, more complex, and needing careful handling. She is convalescing now. For four days I lived only for her.

We talked quietly while I sewed. Touching lightly on our lives. Not too deeply. She is shy of the personal.

I teased her about wanting her in the family. I wanted her as a wife for Joaquin. But Joaquin found her "prickly."

"But I am part of your family without benefit of legalities," she said.

When Sylvia or I arrive with food she says: "How is the commisary?"

She is full of drolleries.

One morning she asked for the return of her birds, and the cage sat on her bed. Yellow and blue parakeets were chirping and flying about the room. The two lovebirds quarreled, so Peggy had bought a cage with an attic where Fiasco could go and sulk.

The room was full of sunshine. She told me about the lapwing bird: "It erases its tracks as it makes them, brushing the sand with its tail wing. When I travel I feel that is what I am doing, erasing my tracks."

She loves the clarity in Joaquin's musical writing.

I wanted to live on the outside, to see how it was to stay outside and never re-enter the cave of the interior life. I stayed outside, in cars, in buses, in planes, and never stopped to write in the diary. I did work on the novels.

Stanley [Haggart] set up a Negro cleaning woman as a night-club singer in Harlem, and we all went to hear her, out of loyalty, but she was not a good singer. I asked Stanley why he did that. He answered: "Because I did not like her cooking."

―――――

Joaquin is now Chairman of the Music Department at Berkeley, appointed by unanimous vote.

Took photographs of Cornelia Runyon's work to the Museum of Modern Art, to Philip Johnson, the architect, who is one of the directors. He gave them to Mr. Ritchie, in charge of sculpture. Johnson was impressed. He invited me to visit his glass house at New Canaan, Connecticut.

Philip Johnson's glass house was interesting. A feeling of living completely out of doors, set in the middle of twenty-five acres of forest. The only enclosure was a big round towerlike construction for the bathroom. But strangely enough, I missed the sense of shelter. I could not have gone to sleep without a feeling of protection, a wall, a tent, a corner somewhere. Also there was no room for books or paintings, as they would interfere with the view. So he had to build another building behind the house to contain records, books, paintings. Sculptures look well, his Giacometti beautiful silhouetted against the forest.

New York.
Tennessee Williams gave me tickets for *The Rose Tattoo*. Maureen Stapleton was wonderful; she acted a wild primitive Sicilian very much like a stormy Anna Magnani, utterly convincing. Play very moving, humorous, and hysterically emotional. I was surprised the American audience took it, as they dislike displays of emotion. It could have been an Italian play. I wonder if Americans find relief in letting foreigners emote for them. They do come to see it. Such a mixture of poetry, sensuality, and vigorous naturalness.
A friend called me in desperation because he had no money and wanted so much to see the play. I mentioned him to Tennessee. He called me again to tell me he had been given the goat to take care of every night after the show.

Met Robert Flaherty. A delightful old Irishman, preparing to go around the world testing a new camera. He was suffering from the many injections he had received but in spite of that was cheerful, told delightful Irish stories connected with his film-making. The barrels of beer he has consumed have become a part of his anatomy.

My deep admiration for *Nanook of the North* made this a momentous visit. I can see why people loved to work with him.

I was told that in one instance he was pressed to give the producer a script, and he sent in a sheaf of blank pages. For both Serge Eisenstein and Robert Flaherty financial backing was difficult to get. They both suffered from interference and lack of confidence in their spontaneous way of working. They never found a generous, lavish backer.

A young woman strongly objected to my writing: "Boulevards throwing off erotic sparks."

In New York I met Maxwell and Anne Geismar.

Our friendship started inauspiciously. I protested a review Maxwell Geismar wrote about Tennessee Williams' play in which he made the narrow-minded statement I had so often heard: that Williams did not belong to the mainstream of American literature because he was writing about neurotics, a peripheral, special, and limited minority.

I wrote to Maxwell Geismar that the writer is a prophet, and that Williams is feeling the deep currents of neurosis which run under the surface of American life, and that one day what seems to be a study of a segment becomes the diagnosis of a much vaster illness.

He responded mildly, conciliatory. We agreed on a visit. Personally the Geismars are brilliant, witty, and mature. We had a gay evening. I did not know then, as I found out soon after, that Max is a Marxist critic, and sees all literature only as a function of politics. Thus the depiction of neurosis is directed at a few individuals. The "people" are free of taint.

[Spring, 1951]

I decided to call this trip to Mexico the Journey of the Neon Cross. For the first time, the crosses on the Catholic churches appeared in all the shoddy splendor of neon.

In Mazatlán the carriage ride took me back into an atavistic past. The top of the carriage is of canvas with fringes like the carriage in which I drove with my parents in Evian when I was six years old. The houses are pink and turquoise. The windows are always either shuttered with green shutters or protected by grilles.

There was a boa constrictor on the road, dead, being eaten by vultures.

In the hotel the water closet was inside of the shower.

On the road a cow skeleton was propped against a tree.

A peasant house where we stopped for beer. Cool, trellised shade created by bamboo and palm leaves. A crib hanging from a ceiling. The floor was of dirt, but neatly swept. The walls of bamboo reeds placed not against each other but with a space in between to let the air through. The young woman wore a dress like a nightgown, the Yucatán white dress with embroidered sleeves or neckline. She wore a white handkerchief over her head. In the evenings we saw them eating out of doors, by candlelight, the entire family. The oven for breadmaking outside, round, like a giant anthill.

Oxcarts give a biblical flavor to the fields, the white Brahma bulls. Some chariot wheels askew, as if drawn by a child.

At Mazatlán we saw the traveling circus. It was so small, and the trappings seemed so frail and worn that I felt a constant anxiety about the frayed cords, the corroded ladders, the rain coming through the roof which could make the aerialist slip. The feeling of weary, overworn clothes, of worn ropes for the acrobat on his bicycle, of flimsy cages for the lion, of unsteady ladders, and nets with unrepaired holes in them. The whole circus was an act of triumph over matter, a greater challenge to human agility.

In Tepic vultures sat around the cemetery walls. In the north of Mexico the cemeteries were black stones piled up with unpainted crosses. In Mazatlán the tombstones were painted in joyous greens and pinks. The plastic flowers were in pastel colors.

The ferry was called *chalana*, a word which has a biblical flavor like *chalote* for shallot. To watch the dark people eating water-melon was a feast for a painter. The watermelon, at times as delicate a pink as the heart of a shell, and sometimes vivid with its black pits like eyes.

Tepic was festooned with blue and white ribbons of paper cutouts for the Virgin Fatima, the dark-faced Virgin. There were castles with towers of fireworks. Wheels of fire tongues dashed like wild comets among the people. Showers of purple sparks, which the children sought to be drenched in. People were chanting Ave Marias while walking, carrying lighted candles. The young women in white dresses. Outside the church were stalls selling sacred blessed trinkets, and people brought pictures to be blessed by the priest, crippled children, very old people on stretchers. It was like Lourdes, and the expectation of miracles was strong. The Neon Cross had not lost its magic power.

The churches of Mexico are their only Oriental splendor. Their own shacks so poor, but they delight in the Scheherazade ornamentation of churches. Their dream suffices them.

The hotel room so shabby in Puebla. Large and high-ceilinged, but with peeling plaster, cement floors creviced from the numerous earthquakes, a hard bed, and water trickling constantly from the leaking plumbing. The electric light was put on by making two naked wires touch. Under the bed a chamber pot. The water closet so far away and impossible to find.

I saw one of the oldest trees in the world, two thousand years old. A juniper called *sabino* in Spanish.

Like Islamic people, at dawn they cover their mouths, from a fear of early-morning fogs.

In Zihuatanejo the *catre* (army cot). No sheets. Communal washbasin and towel. Half mirror.

At Lake Pátzcuaro all I remember is the somber dignity of the men in their heavy woolen ponchos. In Tehuantepec the cotton ball trees. The mauve sandstone. The women's dresses, the heavy velvet skirts and lace blouses and lace headgear, the gold-coin necklaces, the lace petticoats showing at the edge, the hair braided high, interwoven with variegated cotton ribbons. The gold earrings. The heavy, flat-soled walk of the gypsies, proud and arrogant, even while watching their stands, selling fruits, or ribbons for the hair, or textiles, or pottery. The women handle all the markets, own the property. It is a matriarchy. The men are smaller than the women.

They sit in cafés and play guitars. At the market, besides the large black cauldrons of wonderfully spiced food, around which they sit to eat, one also sees these astoundingly beautiful women combing each other's hair, which often reaches to their ankles.

Lake Chapala. The graceful sailboats of the fishermen. The delicate tracery of the fishing nets. The devilfish they say comes from the lake and which they sell dried out, and which does look like a miniature devil.

With all its charm, San Francisco was damp and cold most of the time, and the doctor advised me to find a warmer and drier climate. Sierra Madre, near Los Angeles, seemed ideal. I had driven through it and smelled the orange groves, and the place I chose at the foot of Mount Wilson was still visited by forest animals. It was sunny and dry. It had very beautiful and very old eucalyptus trees, and seemed like a wonderfully peaceful place in which to work.

[June, 1951]

Back in New York saw a new ballet by Jerome Robbins which reveals woman as a terrible spider eating the male. Will we ever see the day when men can eat women with equal delight?

I felt that my frustration about the publication of my work was doing me harm. It sapped too much of my energy in fruitless anger. I could not resort again to publishing my own books, as I knew this took so much time that it would prevent me from writing. I felt the anger corroding me. I turned once more to psychoanalysis.

I had heard about a woman doctor who had come to America during the war. Several persons talked about her in a way that appealed to me. I had already proved to myself that I was more honest with a woman, because I was not preoccupied with charming the doctor. At times my life seemed to lack cohesion and synthesis, and it is difficult to live with dualities. My novels had caused an estrangement from people which was painful to me.

I visited Dr. Inge Bogner and liked her instantly. She seemed to fuse two qualities: acuity with sympathy. She was extraordinarily alert and intuitive.

She is small and very slender, wears her hair short and tousled. She has a lively manner, dark eyes and a warm, expressive glance. Her attitude fluctuates from a soft, steady sympathy to sudden elucidations. One has a sense of serenity and balance from her.

First talk with Dr. Bogner.

Just to see her sitting there, neat, dainty, collected, smiling, creates a moment of peace.

At first I feel a constriction of the throat which I have often on such occasions. I place my hand there. Am I trying to restrain what I want to say? The throat tightens. Do I want to keep myself from saying all I want to say, from weeping, from being angry? Am I afraid of irrevocable words?

"I can't explain why, but I know what I feel. I feel suffocated in my life, overwhelmed by the demands put on me. I feel I have no control over my life."

Life in Sierra Madre, or activity in New York. There must be a third way of life which I have to create myself.

I cannot devote myself to moneymaking and that makes me dependent.

I must create my own life.

Dr. Bogner works on making me objective about criticism. She makes me question the identity, the quality, the knowledge of the critic. When I examine that, I understand why they *cannot* accept me.

But when I imagine the kind of life I like best, it was my bohemian life on the houseboat in Paris. The boat cost ten dollars a month. I could have lived there for one hundred a month. Or Varda's life.

Malraux says art is our rebellion against man's fate.

La condition humaine is what I have never accepted. That is why I tried to create my own world.

Today I discussed with Dr. Bogner the increase in my courage to be myself rather than disguise myself.

How wrong it is for woman to expect the man to build the world she wants, rather than set out to create it herself. It is the source of woman's rebellions, her helplessness and dependency. I am setting out to create my own world, not to expect man to create it for me.

Dr. Bogner said: "You have always lived for and through others. You placed your angers upon Gonzalo, he acted them out, lived them out. You placed your own withdrawn shy self onto Leonard, the parts of you that freeze with vulnerability. You always forget it is you, you who are either frozen, withdrawn, or angry, or rebellious. You displace all you feel onto others. Long ago you became convinced that if you were yourself as you feel in reality, it would be destructive. You would not be loved. Now at last you are asserting what you are."

For this, woman must achieve economic independence. She cannot live and act vicariously in the world.

Talk with Dr. Bogner.

America is cold and hard, and has treated me badly.

I remember my life in Spain after my father left. This brought a flood of tears. It seemed all warmth, affection. Enrique Granados was protecting us, and my mother taught at his Academy of Music. The maid, Carmen, sang all day, the nuns were always leaning over and embracing me. At night before going to sleep, I heard the *sereno,* an old man with the keys of all the houses, carrying a lantern, who sang a reassuring little couplet: "Go to sleep, all is well, I am watching."

I waited for his song and then went to sleep in utter trust.

Dr. Bogner thought this was a projection. Spain was a continuation of my relationship to my father. We were near him, staying with his parents, seeing his sister, his nephews. I may not have believed in the loss. But coming to America was the break, and the fatherless child looked for an exteriorized warmth which is not typical of America.

I try to explain my feeling. In Spain everybody seemed connected to everybody else. Here I feel there is no contact, between people, with their inner selves, or with people from other countries.

I remember individual acts of kindness. My American uncle, a Navy man, helped us. Having seen me sweep the rug with an ordinary broom, he came one day with a carpet sweeper. The Irish doctor who took care of us never sent a bill.

[July, 1951]

In Sierra Madre I hear the train whistle at night and the coyotes in a pack with their thin wailing cries answering the train, mistaking it for the cry of another animal in the night. The first night I thought it was a woman in labor pains. Train whistles, like foghorns and ship's whistles, give me a feeling of distance between places, and the loneliness and void in between. Nature in Acapulco was mixed with smiling people, it was the background for people, people at work in the fields, selling their wares, fishing, planting, carrying wood, washing clothes. Walking and swimming and dancing at night. In America the vast spaces accentuate the vast spaces between people, deserts which stretch between human beings. It is a void which has to be spanned by the automobile. It takes an hour to reach a movie, two hours to reach a friend. So the coyotes howl and wail at the awful emptiness of mountains, deserts, hills.

The art of writing. Will it become obsolete? Libraries are getting rid of books to make room for films. Publishers are failing. The paperbacks are succeeding, but because they only deal in second-rate writers, people throw them away, like magazines. It is not like the French paperbacks which offered the best writers and if one wished to keep them one could have them bound. I find a danger in watching films. It is like passive dreaming. It requires no participation, no effort. It induces passivity. It is baby food; no need to masticate, no need to carve. There is no need to learn to play an instrument, to learn to read a book. People stretch on specially inclined chairs and receive the images in utter, infantile passivity. Speech, already inadequate in America, will soon disappear together with the ability to derive significance from the printed word. This is as radical a change as from monkey to man, it is an evolution from man into automaton.

Because my father was an erudite musician I believed he would understand my particular form of music, but he did not. Because Lloyd is an original and imaginative architect, I believed he would understand the architecture of my writing, but he does not.

[Fall, 1951]

El Mirador Hotel, Acapulco, Mexico.

At La Perla now they have a gypsy violinist married to a home-loving Swiss girl, who is so homesick she talks to me by the hour about Swiss butter, Swiss landscapes, Swiss snow. She is hysterically afraid of scorpions. It is so comical, this longing for Switzerland in the heart of the tropical beauty of Acapulco. If it were Christmas she would be singing "Jingle Bells" on a tropical night.

I met Dolores Del Rio, so beautiful, with her enormous slanted eyes. She is simple and direct. Was wearing shorts and a checkered shirt like her lover's. She was off to work on a film in Yucatán. Her bodyguards and retinue were mostly bald and wealthy.

The church is not yet reconstructed and repainted. The corner where the Post Office once was is still being torn down. The electric lights still go out just as you are making up your face for dinner or while you are in the shower. The stamps still don't have any glue on them.

Letter from Max Pfeffer:

I just spoke to Charles Duell who told me that he received Sabina [*A Spy in the House of Love*] about a week ago, read it and thinks it is a wonderful script. He personally likes it very much. He thinks it is grand and was much impressed with it. He really loves it, but there are plenty of problems involved. It will take another fifteen to twenty days for the other people in the firm to read it because the commercial possibilities are an important factor to be considered and practical points of view may not be ignored nowadays.

To me Acapulco is the detoxicating cure for all the evils of the city: ambition, vanity, quest for success in money, the continuous contagious presence of power-driven, obsessed individuals who want to become known, to be in the limelight, noticed, as if life among millions gave you a desperate illness, a need of rising above the crowd, being noticed, existing individually, singled out from a mass of ants and sheep. It has something to do with the presence of millions of anonymous faces, anonymous people, and the desperate ways of achieving distinction.

Here, all this is nonsense. You exist by your smile and your presence. You exist for your joys and your relaxations. You exist in nature. You are part of the glittering sea, and part of the luscious, well-nourished plants, you are wedded to the sun, you are immersed in timelessness, only the present counts, and from the present you extract all the essences which can nourish the senses, and so the nerves are still, the mind is quiet, the nights are lullabies, the days are like gentle ovens in which infinitely wise sculptor's hands re-form the lost contours, the lost sensations of the body. The body comes to life. Quests, pursuits of concrete securities of one kind or another lose all their importance.

As you swim, you are washed of all the excrescences of so-called civilization, which includes the incapacity to be happy under any circumstances.

The healing process is complete. I am ready for the indecisions of Duell, Sloan and Pearce, for negative decisions.

Only in the language of astronomy can one describe the beauty of the tropics. Every evening it seems to me I see the Celestial Equator, an "imaginary line in the sky directly above the earth's equator."

And every night I see "aberrations of light, an apparent displacement of a star in the direction of the earth's motion."

Jim Herlihy took a bus to Pasadena, walked from Pasadena to Sierra Madre, took a taxi from Sierra Madre to my house in the foothills and said on arriving: "You live in the sticks."

He brings me a mobile of golden angels turning around a candle, and as they turn, small bells ring. I told him that was a symbolic gift, an inspiration to work, and that it would set the mobiles inside of my head turning again.

At the age of seventeen I loved the ordinary poplars which stood as sentinels on the path of our house in Richmond Hill. I addressed them as friends, conversed and sustained a whispering relationship, noted all the changes caused by the season. There was at that time an Anaïs who could love an ordinary tree which was neither symbolic, nor exotic, nor rare, nor historic, nor unique. This Anaïs led a timid life under the protection and control of her mother, absolutely incapable of building anything in life at all except one in writing, between the covers of a diary, nurtured on fantasy derived from literature and entirely separate from her life on earth, which consisted of playing the role of substitute mother for her two brothers, lighting the fire in the furnace with orange crates, planting seeds in the cellar for a lamentable bit of garden, cleaning and washing and mending a house so old that nothing one did to it made it look any better, for the wooden frame was gray and needed painting, the banister was shaky, the windows let in wind and rain. It was too big for me, two floors, three bedrooms, living room and dining room and enclosed porch, to clean. There was snow to shovel, and mud on the stairs to sweep.

Is this the Anaïs I am trying to find again among the simple, unadorned, unsymbolic trees of Sierra Madre? In San Francisco I spent weekends visiting the giant redwoods. In Mexico we took photographs of a juniper, one of the oldest trees in the world, two thousand years old. I learned about cotton trees, orange trees, jacarandas, palms, dead trees, burnt trees; I laughed at the obscenities of Latin names (*Pinus contorta*) for flowers and trees. I became acquainted with redwood trees, pepper trees.

Did I recover this Anaïs once lost among the symbolic trees and swamps of Max Ernst, the skeletal trees of Tanguy, the trees of Utrillo, Suzanne Valadon, Matisse, Rousseau?

I am surrounded now by men who risk their lives to save trees from fires which devastate the forest. Men who give up lucrative professions and accept less money than a postman, to fight fires and prevent them, to defend the trees from fire and human abuse.

Item in the newspaper: A drunk firebug at a bar repeating: "So you think those trees are beautiful, do you? Look at them well. They won't be there tomorrow."

When I look at trees which belong to a community which has no history, a community of faceless, anonymous, standardized people, look out at cypresses which do not orchestrate the lights of Fiesole, which have no history, no aura conferred by the soul's convolutions, I wonder what I am seeking in a nature which is not the landscape to great feats in art or culture, but simply a spectator to monotonous simplicity.

I wanted to return to simplicity after the infernal life of New York, the interviews, the pressures.

I dream of writing the final book which will break my ostracism from the world. I carry in my bag another rejection of *A Spy in the House of Love* from Pellegrini and Cudahy, this time insulting. Farrar and Straus rejected it. "A Tiffany jewel, not for everybody."

Letter from the Viking Press, from Mr. Pascal Covici: "I en-

joyed, as always, your sensitive lyric writing but I am quite convinced that your romantic fantasy is not for us. Because of its erotic
subject matter and the possible difficulties with the censors, it
would be best, I think, to have some small private press bring it out
in a limited edition."

Houghton Mifflin turned it down, and Doubleday (where I was
once introduced by Edmund Wilson himself). Scribner, Bobbs-
Merrill Company, Hiram Haydn. Mr. Theodore Purdy of G. P. Putnam's Sons wrote:

We have had several readings of the new manuscript by Anaïs Nin. It is,
as usual, an extraordinary and unusual piece of work and I can't think of
any other writer who might have produced it. However, it seems less sub-
stantial than her earlier books and some of the passages are of course almost pornographic. Altogether, the consensus of opinion here is not in
favor of our bringing it out, much as we admire the author's vivid writing
abilities.

The interesting fact was that, accustomed to hearing only about
the neurosis of the artist, I was not prepared for the shocking discoveries I made among the simple people. Among the foresters,
those who had practical training and no college training were
jealous of the "college" foresters. One old forester I heard
grumbling once after many cans of beer turned out to be the
leader of a group of young men; and whenever he led them into
fire fighting, there were accidents. No one thought of attributing
this to his jealousy, quite openly expressed.

Others entered the Forest Service already distorted; some were
firebugs, setting fires to be able to put them out and get extra pay.
Some were autistic, in quest of utter solitude among the mountains. Living close to nature, modest, accepting a limited life for
a romantic profession, they brought the same neurotic flaws I had
seen in the artists around me, and in myself.

I stopped at San Francisco for my mother's eightieth birthday.
Each year she seems smaller, and her hair somehow whiter and
lighter. Joaquin delivered a witty lecture on Weber and Brahms.
His symphony will be played by the San Francisco Orchestra.

Frances Keene is doing everything for *Spy in the House of Love*.
I am waiting for an answer from Random House.

I am in touch with the whole world, and by a strange irony, all the friends I nourished with descriptions of Europe are there now, Frances Brown, Woody Parrish-Martin, James Broughton, Kenneth Anger, Kermit Sheets. But not me! I connect with the ballet through George Amberg, I hear echoes of Tennessee Williams' neurosis and creation, I meet Alice de Bouverie of the Astor family, who made their fortune stealing furs from the Indians and killing them after they delivered their stock. Flavors and scents from many worlds.

[Winter, 1951-1952]

Mrs. Arabel Porter, of the New American Library, after considering *Spy* began to quibble about the lie detector. She said at a conference there was an objection to the lie detector as puzzling. What did it mean?

I had lunch with Victor Weybright, a very literary man. I explained to him humorously that far from being a mystery, the lie detector was a personification of conscience dressed in modern clothes and quite real as he followed Sabina about. Mr. Weybright laughed and said: "I'll be damned, I didn't get that. Maybe if you made that a little clearer at the beginning we might reconsider it."

In the face of so much rejection of my work should I abdicate?

When I was in New York Jim Herlihy telephoned me from Detroit, his home. He was in great distress. His father wanted him to deliver telephone books for fifty dollars a week.

I said: "Come to New York. We will find a way."

He came. My friends adopted him. He found a job. He met producers, and publishers and magazine editors. His play was produced. Stanley taught him how to arrange an apartment with very little money. Everyone likes him. He sold a short play to television.

Jim is twenty-six. He has the Irish gift of the tongue, the laughing blue eyes. Between love affairs, between jobs, he makes crash landings at his home and then yearns to get away.

He works for a paper-plate company, and so all of us are eating from paper plates he brings us.

His atmosphere is playful, but he has a serious core.

He fixed a cold-water flat with all of Stanley's prestidigitations. Even a closet lined with egg cartons. He gives parties.

Jim is a grave host. His finely drawn features and his lean body give him an elegance contradicted by his slang. The young man born poor in a tough neighborhood (his father was a policeman and his mother a show girl; at fifteen his nose was broken by a gang of boys) has by speed and smoothness made his slang a thing of style no longer resembling the speech of uneducated people but something born of agility, quick wits, great accuracy, and reminds me of jazz. It is the fast-moving rhythm that gives it character and vitality, it has style while bearing no relation to cultured speech. Instead of refinement it has slickness, clear-cut edges, it is streamlined. There is no slurring, no limpness, no drawling. He tightens his belt around a neat, slender waist, and has an equally neat and slender delivery. This nimbleness permits him to enter any world at all, and handle it with dexterity. Tension is part of his style. It becomes an attribute. He is as tense as a magician would be. You sense he will dodge disaster deftly, that he has erased all traces of doubt, hesitation, or bewilderment.

He is spiritually and emotionally an aerialist. He is agile and knows how to leap. It is agility which enables him to live, write, without any preparation for either. He is the self-made man. Will achieve a prominent place through prestidigitation. He is the superior, the talented, creative, self-created man.

Jim's party. A tenement apartment transformed by tremendous work of papering, painting, plastering, wall making, fireplace making, closet making into a place of beauty. Stanley, with all his experience of home making, helped Jim. His ingenuity in working with little money, his gifts for substitutes and effects.

David Man, a little man, face smudged, not sculptured but like clay worked by thick fingers, occupied in translating Genêt, condemned in the homosexual world to be unloved because he looks like a little French shoe salesman, when drunk became a lyrical Irishman: "I don't mean to be maudlin . . . believe me . . . but, Anaïs, I hate women. . . . But you . . . you who are the essence of femininity . . . I love you. And I will love you all my life and right now, when I see how you listen to me, never paying attention to anyone else, or anything else happening in the party . . . well, I feel like weeping. Give me your hand."

He closed his eyes, he was about to weep. I smiled. I let him spill his drink on my dress. I did not dare desert him because I feel such sympathy for the unloved. I knew the world he moved in, where beauty is a requisite, the ever adolescent, ever romantic life. So I let him remain adhesive and talk:

"Franklin, the boy on your left, is the cleverest, the most intuitive of all of us. He is a genius, and if Genêt had known him would have recognized him as such. Franklin lived with Harold in

Chicago, and I know he looks like a priest, but he was full of hidden cruelties. You can see Franklin's eyes are cold and murderous as I talk to you. Isn't there sadism in all of us? Surely it is not unknown to you. You have read Proust, the most sensitive, not devoid of cruelty, it is all around us, I am the only one who seems to love without cruelty; but then everyone is cruel to me. I can see you are getting restless. . . ." He was swaying, almost falling over me.

"*Décolle toi,*" said Franklin. "I want to talk with Anaïs about Baldwin."

David reproached me: "Why is it as soon as you tell a person you will love them for life they run away?"

It was true I felt enmeshed in his drunken world and sought escape.

Franklin helped in a cruel way: "You bore her." I wandered to the kitchen and talked with Pepe Zayas, whose paintings hang on the walls. "When the critics and people tell me my painting is good, I do not believe them. I feel they all conspire to encourage me, because they love me." (Persecution mania in reverse!) "You were the first one to awaken me in Black Mountain College and I feel now that just as I gave up writing after getting two stories published, I will stop painting too, even though I received good criticisms and sold paintings in Italy. Whatever happens, do not give me up."

After I left, Stanley read to them from *Children of the Albatross.*

You live in a certain world for a little while, you dramatize your adventures in it, and this world continues an existence of its own and you can never become completely detached from it because it returns to claim you, as the past returns even after your love of it, your illusion about it, no longer exists.

Carter Harman is now music critic of *Time* Magazine, composer of ballets.

Charles Rollo, intelligent and quick-witted but not deep. He has written delicately about the early books. But has reservations about *Spy in the House of Love.* Maxwell Geismar flares up with enthusiasm, over the telephone. Victor Weybright is still irritated by the character of the lie detector and offers me a thousand-dollar advance provided I remove him from the book.

I see friends from New Orleans, friends on their way to England.

Jim Herlihy asks me to look for black silk sheets, the latest in erotic decor.

I see Wilfredo Lam, Negro-Chinese Cuban painter, protégé of Picasso. He is plaintive, anxious to sell paintings. In talk he elaborates intellectual constructions and all his cohabitations take place in space, not on a level of human gravity. He wants to shine with meteoric lights. As a human being, he stands like a Giacometti statue, abstract and distilled, in violent contrast to Teddy Brown, the Negro dancer of seventeen who says all he has to say with dancing, whose body is charged with electric fireworks, a magnificent agitation of a million particles and cells. Every Negro who imitates our abstract mental language serves to betray its absurdity, and exposes its weakness by caricature. Unconsciously, Wilfredo Lam presents us with an intelligent burlesque of our theories of art, concepts of living, mathematics of emotion, and analysis of passion. The formulas and the empty jargon. He cannot dance. He is the modern painter of white ghostly puzzles, subjected to our dissociative forces.

"Did you see Madame Bouverie? Will she buy a painting?" Alice Paalen, meanwhile, looks worn and thin, a secret sorrow undermining her.

I read from *Spy in the House of Love* at Circle in the Square.

The danger of poetry, said Maxwell Geismar, is the risk of incomprehension.

I see the lighting effects of Rollo Williams, using electronics to change the tones and scales of lighting. I see *Head Hunters of the Jungle,* a strong film. I see the painting exhibition of Alice, full of mystery always, mystical, occult. Her cats are like Egyptian cats, like fates, or diviners.

There is a very real, very opaque silence around my work. Charles Rollo once praised *Four-Chambered Heart* and now tells me there are no good novels being written.

Victor Weybright is still not sure about *Spy*. He wavers, and Arabel Porter takes care to make his judgment negative by passing a moral judgment on Sabina.

Saw Tennessee Williams with Oliver Evans.

An evening with Stanley and Woody.

I feel a new kind of sparkle, not the poetic one of earlier years, the fireworks which strew ashes, but the sparkle you achieve when you conquer anxiety.

Paolo Milano, a great natural comic (introduced Dante in a Viking Press edition). I finally pry the secret underlying his buffooneries: his hidden, secret writings. We quarrel in a friendly way. He does not believe in the poetic novel.

Jim's novel given to a publisher. I mail Geismar's book to Mondadori.

Under a Glass Bell is translated into Italian.

Twenty-five years late America is discovering surrealism, its vitality.

Rejection of *Spy in the House of Love* by Harper Brothers. Mr. Simon Michael Bessie feels the material is more adapted to poetry than prose. Macmillan said it was *esoteric*.

I have telescoped the outer and inner reality into a special poetic phraseology, always a phrase that has a double meaning. There is a transmutation. The external and inner become one. You are a spy in the house of love, a cape is also the flag of adventure, a dress is becalmed, as feelings are, it is more than a symbol, it is the integration of the two into one. Meaning *within* the object, contained in the object, suggested by the object. Anyway, whatever it is, they do not like it. They won't defend it, or situate it or give me my place in literature. Considering total abdication, I weep in the restaurant.

A deep sense of loss, the loss of a beautiful language painstakingly elaborated, a language I evolved which contains the meaning as well as the aspect. Sitting in a Greek restaurant the image of myself giving up a writing nobody wants appears like a vast fracture of diamonds sinking into the sea. A great loss, I honestly believe that.

There are precious words (yes, I know, the word *precious* today is an insult) which have taken many of us a lifetime to infuse with irreplaceable meanings. No one else can do what I have done, I know that, because it took a spiritual vision allied to sensuality to clothe in flesh such deep meanings, and it took a life in hell and many lives of painful explorations, and it took even a dangerous sojourn in the world of madness and the capacity to return to tell what I have told. Centuries of civilization too, it took birth, tradition, it took my freedom from economic slavery, which gave me my integrity, it took a body to live it all out, a soul willing to burn the dross.

I wept over the Negro problem in Alan Paton's *Cry, the Beloved Country,* and wondered once more at the people who sacrifice their human life to create a constant proof of the eternal for other men, proofs of the existence of the spirit, cathedrals, pyramids, works of art, saintly lives.

An adolescent culture shows the adolescent incapacity to admire, to respect, or to evaluate.

I have raged at the wall growing denser between myself and others. I do not want to be exiled, alone, cut off. I wept at being isolated, at the blockade of the publishers. But then I began to ask myself how much I was responsible for; the expectation of miraculous understanding was childlike.

I chose poetry and the metaphor not for the love of mystery or elusiveness but because that comes closer to the way we experience things deep down. Explicitness and directness cannot be applied to our psychic life. They are not subtle enough.

What we cannot see within ourselves, what we cannot seize within ourselves we project outside. A great part of our life is an invention to avoid confrontation with our deepest self. So I cannot make Sabina aware of her own anxieties and guilts because that would be untrue.

For myself, I seek the inner knowledge, I struggle with Dr. Bogner not to see America as a symbol, or France as a generalization. But this is a long, arduous quest for self-revelation which few would persist in. For example, it is not America itself I am in conflict with, but the country to which I was brought against my will and which separates me abysmally from my father's values, even by way of language.

In myself I have struggled constantly to bring the two selves together, the direct human one of the diary and the poet who sees that we live by mythologies. As the mythologies dissolve, they harmonize. I see both the drama of what America symbolized (the surrender of my European cultural values), which would make reconciliation impossible, and the outside America I am discovering apart from that.

With life in the West, I come closer to the heart of America, not to its industrial dehumanization but its human way of life.

But I cannot make Sabina aware of her guilt. It would be false. I first saw this displacement onto others in June. June lived by displacement. One could never touch upon the center, because she did not create one.

It would be funny if out of my struggle with America's total lack of imagination (even in science fiction they can only conceive of technology, instruments, and in a film I just saw, they fly to the moon, but once there, cannot imagine anything happening, and they can only suggest hurrying back home to earth because of a possible fuel shortage!) what they would finally accept is the Spanish realist of the birth story. But they didn't. Giraudoux's *Madwoman of Chaillot* was a failure; they attack Ralph Ellison's marvelous symbolic passages, Truman Capote's fantasy and poetry.

Very proud of Jim's diary pages, a description of the party and one of a quarrel with a friend. Insight, power of feeling, and exactness. This came through his own willingness to suffer, his energy to struggle, to dig, to search. He absorbed pages from my diary and nourished himself on them, and he broke through the slick surface of his public writing and entered a rich world in which his intuition and articulateness came from the depths. His description of the party was sharper than mine. And when he was in the center of hell, almost driven out of his mind, I said write, write, write, write. I did not refuse him sympathy (he had agreed walking out was not good, each time he decided to walk out he had monstrous nightmares), but I incited him to write. And he did. And he learned to calm himself, he learned to objectify through art.

Today I teased him. I told him these pages were the best he had done (but they could only be done in the secret womb of the diary, the only laboratory of the truth) where insight, power, and economy were all fulfilled. But he will not use this dimension in his public writing. He had a description of his grandmother in his diary, rocking back and forth in her rocking chair, while he saw the multiple railroad lines which had crossed and recrossed the town where she had been born, changing it from farm to city, all in the duration of one lifelong rocking.

He always has a virile rhythm, but it is sometimes on the surface. The moment he broke through the surface in the diary, I knew he could do deeper writing.

Jim's anxieties compel him to do all things more deftly than anyone, to erase all possible traces of doubts, ignorance, fear of failure, bewilderment. Dexterity becomes a style, a form, an organic structure.

———

I applied for a Guggenheim Fellowship; it was refused.

PROJECT:

One half of this project has already been accomplished in three published novels: *Ladders to Fire, Children of the Albatross, The Four-Chambered Heart.* The second half and termination of this cycle is what I wish to work on with the help of the Fellowship.

The three first volumes cover a depiction of the contemporary neurosis in novel form. The next three volumes will cover what I consider a philosophic demonstration of the understanding and mastering of the neurosis. In other words, a guidance under the form of fiction, the way out of the labyrinth of what the poet Auden calls The Age of Anxiety.

My contention is that very few people have been able to obtain help from psychoanalysis, but many more can develop an understanding from the reading of my novels. This has already been proved by the keen interest of students in all the universities. I have not only been invited to lecture on the modern novel, on my own work in particular, but after the lectures I have been questioned for hours on intimate psychological problems which concerned the students.

I am well equipped to carry out this project by training in psychoanalysis at the Cité Universitaire in Paris under Doctor Otto Rank (1935-1936) and a year of practice in New York under Doctor Rank's control.

This project will take me only a year as I have all my material ready, my notes, outlines, and character sketches from a life-long diary.

I sincerely believe my work is a contribution to a psychological understanding of the character and experience of our time.

I believe that while we refuse to organize the inner confusions we will never have an objective understanding of what is happening outside. In this project the relationship between the state of the world and the inner psychological conflicts is proved. Until this inner confusion of values and insights is clarified we will not be able to evaluate historically, and consequently we will be incapacitated for action.

For a more detailed description of my intentions and attitudes toward writing and the work I am engaged upon I am enclosing my lecture on Writing published the first time by Dartmouth College.

This writing I can do anywhere, and with the help of the Foundation I will be able to give my full time to it.

Then I see Lila, always either in hell or walking out of hell, but unable to remain in any realm between. She has an ulcer, one more broken relationship, cannot write.

It was Lila's story about feeling watched by a detective which inspired the character of the lie detector in *A Spy in the House of*

Love. She told me that her father set a detective on the track of her sister when her sister ran away from school, and that she believed he had done the same to spy on her activities in New York. She told me she had seen him in the subway, or standing at the corner of the street where she lived, reading a paper, waiting. She saw him everywhere, at restaurants, night clubs, movie houses. She asserted that he followed her and made notes in a little notebook.

Her father was a very important figure to her. He loved her possessively and wanted her home. When he became seriously ill and she visited him she asked him if he had employed detectives to spy on her. He was shocked at the idea, and his denial seemed so sincere that Lila never knew if the detective was genuine or a fantasy on her part, born of the knowledge that he had once done this to her sister.

Sometimes I monologue on other writers: they never leave the ground; they don't know how to be the aviators of language, the air force of air-born words, the air squadrons of semantics; they cannot play with words and let them loose. I was reminded the other night of Henry's power in this realm of surrealist levitation. He who was immersed in earth knew how to fly above it.

Jim expects this of me so inexorably that he is sensitive to the times I fly too low, when I get caught in trivia, when I get earth-bound, when I am trapped in duties, suppressed or oppressed.

Dream: I am going to give a lecture and am reading. I have worked very hard on my lecture. It is written exquisitely in French. Then just as I am about to face my audience, I realize they do not know French. I try to translate the lecture as well as I can.

I left out the introduction to the dream. A huge tarantula, hairy, hanging on a thread from the ceiling, was moving toward my face. I killed it. It fell on the floor, burst, and shed black seeds like those of a watermelon.

The monsters I have dreamed recently, giant snakes, leeches, tarantulas, are my feeling about the reviewers, the critics, the people who have derided my work. They represent the dangers I incurred when I decided to expose my work to their criticism.

Return to France, impossible. I dream of it. (In my dream I write my lecture in French.)

Talk with Dr. Bogner. "The fraternal life I led with other writers in France is not possible here."

"Why?" asked Dr. Bogner.

"I am not sure. I did make many efforts to live with the artists here. I know them all. But it was not the same. When we tried to meet at a café on East Thirteenth Street, [Stuart] Davis, the painter, turned on a loud radio to listen to a prize fight in place of talking together. The fraternity is destroyed by competitiveness. The pressure from the outer world is greater. The pressure of economics, the problems of living. In France the problems were reduced by the fact that everyone helped the artist, the climate helped, there was no puritan censorship of the artist's life, there was no political pressure, there was individual freedom. Varda is the only artist I know leading a free life today. He has reduced his needs. He only needs to teach once a week. The rest of the time visitors buy a collage now and then. He has no jealousy, envy, or competitiveness. I find in American life an excess of harshness, criticism, little capacity for admiration."

Jim teased me about my animal dreams. He said they were not original. He said they were borrowed from a woman in Pasadena who dreamed of a very black snake sitting on a rocking chair in front of the fireplace with a bonnet tied under its chinlessness. And in the dream she reflected: "Well, all is well as long as it does not run wild around the house!"

"Pardon me," I said in an offended tone, "if I'm going to lift anybody's dreams I insist on choosing the quality. That's a puritan's dream. If I'm going to steal others' dreams I'll steal yours."

When I told him again the dream of the tarantula he corrected me: "The first time you said they were pomegranate seeds."

"I'm just trying to be folksy."

Saw Tennessee Williams' *Summer and Smoke*. Met the whole cast. José Quintero, the director, told me my work, which he read five years ago in Woodstock, was an initiation to his new life. Geraldine Page is so beautiful and interesting an actress, fully sensitive and aware, full of shadings and delicacies.

In the larger world I am not yet at ease. I find it a strain to meet the Geismars because they are brilliant and ironic. It is a strain to meet Anthony Tudor, to go to Charles Rollo's parties and talk with Luise Rainer, with representatives of Knopf. In myself, deep down, there is a great insecurity and an inclination to withdraw into a simpler, more innocent life.

When I returned to New York I had gained detachment from neglect as a writer, from financial restrictions, from relationships which had betrayed me (the transparent children).

Saw Martha Graham dance. In the dancing of Martha Graham I see the same interior world, interior tragedy which her body and face occasionally reveal directly, but more often obliquely in such mysterious, devious ways that when she dies her meaning will vanish with her. But not her greatness; her greatness achieved by depth and tragic intensity will be revered.

I read Truman Capote's *Grass Harp*. Will his sensitivity and lyricism survive the American life?

Martha Graham. This is one friendship I wanted and could not have. Because of the close relationship between her work and mine, I sent her books, a letter, met her socially at Dorothy Norman's, but she showed no interest. It is a mystery to me, except that I know how tragic her life is. I could have helped her, loved her.

One of the strongest examples I ever had of the influence of the past upon the present was my association with Max Pfeffer. Years ago he wrote me a letter offering to be my literary agent. Russell and Volkening had just returned my manuscripts, saying they could do nothing for me. I accepted Pfeffer's offer. He was authoritarian but I thought this would be good for my work.

Years later, on the occasion of the death of his wife, I kissed him on the cheek. I did not kiss the real Mr. Pfeffer, but a personage created out of the resonances of the past. He was a European (like my father) ; he was authoritarian (like my father) ; he lost his wife (as my father did, twice) ; he lost his daughter (as my father did) ; his daughter had just told him she would not work for him any more. He made mistakes, and I knew he was not the right person for my work, but he was devoted. He was grateful because I had invited his fragile wife to a party, and it was the last pleasure she had before her illness and death. I knew that he would look upon a professional break as a personal desertion (the third). For me he was another version of the father to be rebelled against, and ultimately deserted. I feared his anger as much as his sorrowfulness, which had the power to arouse my guilt. I would be adding one more crime to my Ledger of Guilts. I also put myself in his place, losing first his wife by death, then his daughter, who was his helper in the office, because of her marriage, and now me. The transposition born of a few points of similarities creates these illusory bonds between people. Everybody advised me to change agents, and I was paralyzed. I was bound to Pfeffer by a design which might be described as the original sin against the father. I rebelled and deserted once. Every rebellion and every desertion from then on bore the stigma, without consideration of whether or not it was justified. The first one was. So was the one of Mr. Pfeffer. I confronted in myself the unreality of the bond, the points of similarities as *echoes*. It is with this echo we have a relationship. In reality did I have to suffer as a writer just to console Pfeffer for the loss of wife and daughter (as I would have liked to console my father for the loss of his second wife and children) ?

Pfeffer quarreled with Mondadori because Mondadori had been a fascist. He quarreled with other publishers for other reasons.

My friends forced me into a break. I was introduced to René de Chochor, who was in partnership with James Brown. René was French, exceedingly charming, and had become interested in my work through his wife. I decided to make him my literary agent.

Letter to Jim Herlihy, who complained of restlessness:

Restlessness is no offense to the loved one except that the loved one considers it a matter of personal pride. He feels he should be the Sea, the

Mountain, the Exotic Islands, the Religion, the Food, the Stimulant, the Inspiration, the Provider, the TOTAL UNIVERSE to his love. Actually restlessness, you could explain to your love, is an outcome of *being in love*. Having the love one wants, one wants to roam, taste, enjoy, discover, explore. It is an extension and continuation of the love. Love is at the roots. We choose our jailers. Thou shalt be my safety brakes, my hand brake, my foot brake, my automatic brake, my BRAKE. Some of these brakes are very attractive to touch and to hold. Otherwise you would fall in love with wilder and looser characters. Nurture your restlessness. It is a compass pointing to mirages.

Quotation from an unknown source:

"The adventurer is within us, and he contests for our favor with the social man we are obliged to be. These two sorts of life are incompatible; one we hanker for, the other we are obliged to. There is no other conflict so bitter as this, whatever the pious say, for it derives from the very constitution of human life which so painfully separates us from all other human beings. We, like the eagle, were born to be free. Yet we are obliged, in order to live at all, to make a cage of laws for ourselves and to stand on the perch. We are born as wasteful, and unremorseful as tigers; we are obliged to be thrifty, or starve, or freeze. We are born to wander, and cursed to stay and dig. We are born adventurers. It is this double-mindedness of humanity that prevents a clear social excommunication of the adventurers. If he fails he is a mere criminal. One third of all criminals are nothing but failed adventurers. Society's benefactors as well as pests. These are men betrayed by contradictions inside themselves, a social man at war with a free man."

Up to date the diary comprises eighty volumes in handwriting.

The library at Evanston is buying, for an absurdly low sum, the original manuscripts of my first novel, my second novel, and the short stories.

Dr. Bogner understands that the diary saved me: it was my truth and my reality.

[Summer, 1952]

In Sierra Madre I rewrite *Spy,* because Victor Weybright, my agent René de Chochor, and Geismar were against the lie detector. Then I found out that it was wrong, that he was a part of my vision, absolutely necessary.

I kept him, knowing it meant no publication and no money. Worked *con allegro* and *vivace* on a simplified but still poetic version. Poetry is a mystery, and if you want to draw close to human beings you cannot speak in parables. I pondered on mystery and suggestion, on all that Djuna Barnes did not tell us, all that Proust did not tell us, and on what Henry James did not tell us. In poetry and the myth you avoid explicitness, but only to reveal another aspect, another life.

When Sabina telephones at random to the lie detector to invite him to track her down, inviting pursuit (as the criminal does sometimes), the lie detector becomes a reality for her.

I was shocked, shocked by the unanimous dislike for the lie detector. René de Chochor said: "He should not be a personage, even mythical. It is her guilt and should be inside of her."

But I know how often we project our guilt outside of us, to the policeman, father, confessor, husband, doctor, analyst, critical friend, or art critic! The projection creates the hallucination of condemnation in the eyes of others. Sabina being neurotic and primitive, or subjective, would see this outside of herself, personified.

Last night after much housework, much revising, much ordinary life, streams of cars passing because of the Fourth of July, empty faces, the usual fireworks, a visit from drunken friends, I fixed my eyes on the Varda collage. It was as if I had stepped out of my life into a region of sand composed of crystals, of transparent women dancing in airy dresses, figures which no obstacle could stop, who could pass through walls, beings designed like sieves to allow the breeze through. Through these floating figures with openings like windows, life could flow. Even the air and sand were mobile. The houses they lived in were only façades, with flags waving and windows open facilitating evasions.

I escaped from the confinement of four brown walls, small screened windows, duties, restrictions, into a world of sand-colored earth shining as the grains of sand shone on Mexican beaches, of women lightly dressed for continuous fiestas, flags waving for perpetual celebrations, transportable houses, the entire scene one of freedom, crystallized, so that I ceased to think of myself as a caged animal pacing in a fever against limitations and wanting the impossible, for I acquired in these moments of contemplation of Varda's collage the certainty that such a state of life was attainable, everything that man creates being attainable, for he has invented nothing, he has transcribed his moods and visions and vistas, experiences and images. Varda reached freedom and I did not, but only because his image, being visible to the human eye, was stronger than the moments I describe and enclose in a book.

Next door to me in Sierra Madre lives a six-year-old girl who stands behind the closed gate looking out with round, wistful eyes. She has a tiny, delicate face, big eyes. We made friends. I swim in her parents' pool. Christie said: "Today I will be *your* little girl."

She comes to look at the Japanese dolls. We opened my costume trunk and I gave her my Spanish dancing dresses. So colorful and comic to see her trailing the vivid dresses along the green lawn.

Another neighbor, a forester, comes to tell me his wife is expecting a baby. Would I take care of the two children, and cook dinner for all of them? At dinner I heard about the foresters' life, their training. The drama centers on fires, devastating, terrifying fires. When someone rushed in saying the baby was born, I was as happy as if I were a part of the family.

Simple pleasures, away from malice.

Here where I am surrounded by real trees, I learn that the abstract tree is equally necessary to man, as nourishing as the tree in the forest of human life, as necessary as the human tree. The artist paints the lookout tower, the oasis, the hidden treasures so that we may find them. Otherwise we cease to believe in them and then lose heart.

In Varda's collages I find a life which the actual sand, the actual trees, houses, and people cannot give me, because they only contain the present, and do not have the long-range vision of the artist, which throws a light on hidden treasures.

For the same reason, my companion is Proust. I immerse myself in his world. He is more alive through his senses, his passion for every detail of his life, than a thousand so-called realists, because it is passion which re-creates a flower, a leaf, a cathedral spire, a sunset, a meal. And how he struggles to give each object its meaning in the pattern. The colors of the bathroom rug in the Balbec Hotel are not only the colors of a rug, they are vision into color, the discovery of color, the awakening of the senses to color. And how lifelike is his cellular development of themes, organic as life, one cell leading to the next, cumulatively, until the entire organism is there.

I saw a film on the theme of a parabola. Ice designs, snowy vaults, evolving glass spires, fan openings of feathery meshes. The great mathematicians lose themselves in intricate calculus, the astronomers in observing space, the scientists in chemical discoveries, all the inventors can take flight with permission from the world because they will bring back visible boons to humanity, a discovery, knowledge, a cure, but the artist who brings us the deployment and flowering of a parabola teaches us to deploy and flower.

Letter to René de Chochor:

I tried to remove the lie detector but it ruined the whole concept. Sabina cannot return to her husband with a confession because he only loves one aspect of her and would not accept all of her. Her talk with Djuna (whose presence I explain clearly, they had met before in Paris) is the only way to reveal the kind of truth I want to point up. Any other ending such as the classical return to the husband you suggest would mean the refusal to solve the problem of a new kind of sincerity: which is to recognize the roles people play in regard to each other and how rigid these roles become. I cannot change a word of that ending. I cannot at this point pretend to be a naturalist. I am exploring the psyche, and here both plots and resolutions are quite different. If the novel fails now, *tant pis*. There is no place for the poetic novel anyway. I would rather sink with it as it is and with my feeling of integrity. I am being true to a new form which will evolve out of the new relativity of psychological reality.

Old Joe Clark walks down from Big Santa Anita Canyon to visit. He lives, probably on a small pension, in a shack in the canyon bottom, far from the road. He just sits in the kitchen to get warmth and comfort and a cup of coffee.

Everyone in the town wants to put him in a home. They think

he is too old to live alone. But like the Mexicans who refused to be locked up in hospitals, he prefers his log cabin, and even though he needs care, he prefers his independence.

He talks about his life. He was not educated enough to join the forest service, so he became a private ranger: he watched for fires, he lived by selling honey, he took care of as many trees as he could, in his own way. He gave first aid to picnickers. He cleaned up after them. The foresters knew him. He visited the woman on the lookout tower who spent hours looking through binoculars for signs of fire. One day he came in, bleeding from a fall on his way down. The people who bandaged his wound managed to keep him. I never saw him again. Joe Clark was a character from the old West, the nature lover never seen in Western films.

At my feet a fuchsia rug from Chinatown in San Francisco. The windows frame trees. My Japanese dolls on the dressing table. Sprinklers are my only fountains of the Alhambra.

Christie gives me ten of her watercolors.

Letter from Henry:

Dear Anaïs:

Was glad to hear from you. Heard about library business from someone at the library.

Things are quite different for me now. Schatz's sister has come to live with me, the children are back (I hope for good) and we have a real, full, happy life daily. After sixteen months of no work I've just begun to write again—*Nexus.* If you ever pass by this way do stop in. I think you'll like Eve. I expect to get a divorce soon in Mexico. We would like to go to France, all over, in fact, but there is no extra cash. I earn just enough to get by.

The Books in My Life is out in England but not yet here. Is your present address a good one to mail books to? *Plexus* came out in France (Correa, Paris) but no English edition in sight yet. Have you tried Denoel or Correa or Gallimard with your books? Girodias is out of the picture now—firm taken over by Hachette.

I still have a job squeezing in a couple of hours a day writing. So very much to do around here. All the best

Henry

P.S. June is still ill and broke always. But shows more desire now to get well. I've improved this place considerably since you were here. I really feel at home here.

The French radio (Paris) made a transcription of *Scenario* [from *House of Incest*] and it made a sensation, I am told. I sent the tape recordings to Powell to get changed to our speed. Cendrars gave it an "introduction" on the air. His last six books I find marvelous.

[Fall, 1952]

A high moment listening to Ima Sumac. The voice has all the richness, beauty, and range of a mythical woman. It does not seem humanly credible. She sings like a siren, a bird, an angel, some seductive chant never heard before, high and low, fragile and strong. With all that, she has the exotic beauty of a legendary figure. I could imagine her in Peru, but not accept that she is married to a composer and now sings his Hollywood-type arrangements in a night club.

New York.
Jim came, very pale, tense, waiting to finish a play for television.
He has the Irish gift for talk, nimble. I am baffled by the difference of levels between his writing for the world and his diary. His diary is like his talk, uncontrolled and revelatory. In his diary he has a fulgurant beat. It is phosphorescent and elliptical, but his writing for publication is conventional.

He is reading certain portions of my diary. His enthusiasm sustains me, keeps me from suffering from my ostracism from the American writing scene. I am left out of every anthology, every poetry reading, every magazine. The world is silent.

As a result of my effort, Jim's first story is accepted by Richard Aldridge's *Discovery*, a book which will reach millions in paperback. Such celebrations! Jim's delight. He has been writing for only five or six years.

Jim wrote a story called "Jazz of Angels." I say over the telephone: "Jim, write me some more jazz of angels." We talk in writer's language. I say "rhythm" and it means as much to him as it does to me: contemporary rhythms. He is the first who tried to describe my way of writing in terms of jazz: I state a phrase and then restate it in another key, reaching out for still another, like the horn player. Jim's understanding of improvisation. There is a jazz rhythm in my writing and Jim of the future heard it.

Last night at Downbeat, Candido, the Cuban drummer drumming himself into an orgiastic frenzy, his legs around the drum, occasionally lifting it from the ground as if they would both fly off, propelled by the violence.

Max Geismar listening to jazz. A timid smile. He has not been feted, he does not live in the present. He is a serious historian of literature and it carries him constantly backward. His work does not give him joy. He and Anne convert their unhappiness into wit and satire.

Christmas in the air. Buying presents and my ticket for Los Angeles.

The Picasso painting of two figures tied to one breathing tube slipped into my writing once. I see why. Vicarious living is dangerous. And to Jim I said less seriously: "It gives sinus."

Jim incites me to improvisation because he responds to it. He takes up the themes and goes forth on his own. I still prefer his diary to his public writing.

At Black Mountain College, Richard Lippold, who was teaching art, felt a friendship for Jim, and said that his next large work would be dedicated to Jim. In 1949 he created *Variation Number 7: Full Moon*. It is beautifully exhibited in a dark room of the Museum of Modern Art, with the light only on the silver threads. Whether Lippold intended it or not, I saw in it a portrait of Jim. It is the perfect irradiation of swift and slender threads vibrating in all directions. It is a tower of antennae. Jim's words are so volatile, so full of improvisations that I cannot retain them. It is in talk that he scales all the musical edifices, in writing he is constrained by comparison. In talk he reveals the perfect wave receiver. What his writing will become, I don't know yet. He is handicapped by the false virility of American literature, he has difficulties in plunging inward. He is further hampered by a sense of taboos.

Before I leave the United States, escorted to the border by extradition laws against fantasy, I am going to leave a textbook on modern literature.

Jim makes me feel like writing because he has the power of levitation.

Jim reads some parts of the diaries avidly, and starts an answering rhythm in the code of today's language, and it is in his youthful, perfect receptivity that I measure the life-transmitting power of my life and work.

Jim says: "It is the only book I can read which gives me not only life but the knowledge of how to absorb experience, the chemistry itself of love and art perfectly wedded and perfectly told. The interplay between all the relationships, and the audacities, the courage . . ."

We met at the Museum of Modern Art on a sultry hot afternoon. I wear the light hemp shoes I found in Yucatán, a chartreuse handwoven skirt from Cuernavaca, a black cotton blouse. I carry a wicker basket.

With the greatest of ease we gain altitude, whether we are staring at Giacometti's *Young Man* or at Dufy, who makes the darkest night airy and transparent. Jim's talk, febrile and highly colored, seeks to return to me the waves of illumination he has received due to his open receptivity. No drinking necessary. The entire framework, senses, the mind, are all revolving within him, and the pleasure it gives me to see these luminous fireworks caused by my own profoundly buried inner fire is a sweet compensation for all the hours spent upon the diary, because it means I have received life and I have preserved it so that now it can be transmitted.

Jim is my spiritual son.

"When I get money from my book's publication," says Jim, "I will go and buy that castle in Mallorca which you told me about."

Louis Barron is deeply versed in electronics, as well as psychology, philosophy, ESP. Always mellow and smiling, he conceals his learning behind a hesitant manner. After working with Bebe and Louis Barron in San Francisco our friendship grew. The Barrons incited me to record all of *House of Incest,* which I was reluctant to do. I thought I did my best reading for them, but hearing it played back I found flaws and worked to eliminate them.

But the Barrons had no capital, no distributor, and the records sold badly. No one knew about them.

When they came to New York, they set up a sound studio and *Sound Portraits* became a profession. They made sound tracks for films.

When Ian Hugo filmed the prologue of *House of Incest* [*Bells of Atlantis*], they composed the electronic score and it matched the fluid images and narration. The three elements, sound, image, and music, fused. It was an unusual collaboration.

Today I heard a piece they composed to be played in Paris at a concert of *musique concrète.* I compared it to a Miró painting. It was light, whimsical, and full of rhythm.

This innovation had its inception in France with Edgar Varèse. It was called "organized sound." It was first used in a play, *Maya,* which I saw in the thirties. Jean-Louis Barrault used it for his play *Columbus.*

Louis and Bebe explain their electronic music:

This music is electronic music based on Cybernetics, the science which sets forth principles of behavior which apply both to machines and people. Among the better-known products of Cybernetics are the computers, popularly referred to as "Electronic Brains."

In applying this science to our music, we analyze a film in terms of its thematic and emotional content, as any film composer would. Then, instead of writing musical notes to express our feelings, we design special electronic circuits. We feed instructions to these circuits. The instructions inform them how they should react and interact to the sensations they receive from other circuits, and how they should react to their own behavior, which they sample through feedback loops.

This means that these circuits have an awareness of what *other circuits* are doing, what *they themselves* are doing, and what is expected of them by the designer—in this case the composer.

Therefore, in this music, not only the sounds are entirely electronic in origin (no microphones, musical instruments, or live sounds are used) but also the rhythms and some of the melodies and counterpoints are electronically structured, under the control of the composer.

The front room of their apartment on Eighth Street is completely filled with equipment. It is a jungle of electronic instruments, knobs, wires, as complex as the control panel of an airplane. It is separated from the living room by soundproof glass.

They keep open house, and I met many people there, Joseph Campbell, Jean Erdman, William Styron, whose writing I do not like, Peggy Glanville-Hicks, Barney Rosset, who does not like my work, John Cage, whom I knew for years, film makers, and many others.

With Louis and Bebe I found an easy, human relationship. They work with intense caring, and live a varied, chaotic, fecund existence.

[Winter, 1952-1953]

Maxwell Geismar fails to understand all departures from realism. He is not willing to see that the realist did not give us reality. There has always been in my life a series of ponderous, earthy men whose seriousness attracted me while it caused me distress. Max does not understand either poetry or surrealism. Is it my effort to connect with the earth? Is it the image of my earthy mother?

It is a relationship I hear in the Debussy Sonata. I hear the violin as a bird making desperate efforts at ascensions, and the piano, by its denser substance, not allowing the volatilization to take place. The piano asserts a ponderous body, which the violin seeks to transcend.

Thus my ties with Henry, with Rank, with Jakob Wassermann, and now with Max. And on the other side of them are the poets, Djuna Barnes, Joyce, the surrealists, who used their imagination to transcend contingencies, to reach elevations and freedom. I feel that I partake of both of these divided worlds, that if ever I can integrate them . . .

Max said: "If a system is corrupt, such as the literary system, how can we go on with our work without taking a militant step to achieve the power to impose certain values? It is as in politics, if it threatens the survival of human beings who have not been militant, then the human being is forced to become militant."

Meanwhile it is Aldridge and not Geismar who is made the critic's leader as editor of *Discovery*. Aldridge is truly an adolescent critic seeking to give final stature to adolescent writers, some of whom are not yet born. There is a word for the love of the dead, but no word for the American love of the fetus in the arts.

At this point I see everything clearly as if I, not Maurice Herzog, had climbed Annapurna, and without loss of gloves, fingers, and toes, could remain there a few minutes while the sun goes down.

Relationship to the airy young men (unreal, remote, nonhuman) is over because it was my relationship to a volatile, airy, nonhuman father. I now accept my friendships with serious, earthbound men, my comfortable relationship with women (my mother having been the fixed, stable point of loyal love).

I carry my own weight, not of earth, but of guilt, the weight was in myself, not in the men.

The diary gave me a frightening mistrust of memory. Memory is a great betrayer. Whenever I read it, I find it differs from the way I remembered the scenes and the talk. I find scenes I had forgotten, thoughts I had forgotten, and precisions noted at the time have become foggy or vanish altogether.

Letter from Maxwell Geismar after reading a few volumes of the diary:

Yesterday and last night I read the last two sections with increasing admiration. I suppose, in spite of my laziness in things like friendship, my evasive generalities that allow me to avoid thinking, I will have to suggest why I think it is an admirable job, first rate, marvelous, in parts: impressive. The following points are only suggestions too: during the reading I had a series of things I wanted to tell you, good things, and which I should have taken down.

Along with my admiration for your writing, I have always had, as you probably felt, some reservations on the score of that *materiality* theme, which somehow I demand of the writers whom I admire; well, that count is removed, and how; you quite terrify me, and I suppose I was a little shocked, being conventional at heart, even while I admired the narrative in intellectual and definitely moral terms: moral in the real sense. What is fine really is not so much the purely physical descriptions but of course the descriptions of the emotional states that comprise the flux of love; these are absolutely brilliant. That is to say, both the description of the illusion or the exaltation, and then the accurate illumination of them, and why you originally felt them. . . . This is literature of the first order.

White Horse Tavern, New York. A truly Irish café with dark wood panels, mugs of dark beer and a mixture of artists and the underworld of the docks. Dylan Thomas frequents it. Louis and Bebe won a goldfish at an Italian fiesta and it swam in pink water. Peter Grippe talked of Willem de Kooning and Esteban Francis as painters and neighbors; of how after living for years in a basement, they were so happy to have found an apartment with a tree almost growing into the room that they forgot to unpack, stretched a blanket on the floor and got drunk in celebration of a tree.

———

Letter from Henry:

Dear Anaïs:

Just got your letter here in this strange place—Simon offered it to us in his absence. Met him in Paris for just a few minutes—and struck it off at once. Am going to Vienne (Isere) from here, then back to Paris and Brussels, then home. Frankly, I'm homesick. The first time in my life. There's nothing new for me in Europe and I don't want any more the cultural, intellectual life. Too too much talk, rehash, etc. Besides, I don't see how Europe can survive much longer. The whole system is now crazy— it must collapse. Nothing has changed here, as I see it, except the *fantastic* cost of living. It's incredible. Worse than you may think. I have been marvelously treated everywhere—no complaints. But I am a different person and Big Sur is where I want to stay. I miss the children too—they mean more to me than places and people. All that divorce business has been tragic.

No, I did not want to mention your other books [in *The Books in My Life*] because it was not the moment—only singled out special ones, do you see. And I can't expand too much. Hachette took over Girodias edition and prints me in English. But Girodias, who is starting again, may get *Plexus.* Frankly, I don't care much any more who prints and doesn't print. The whole bloody business is a farce. I even begin to question the value of writing itself. If my book is a "success" as you say, it must be *"intime."* I worked as hard to launch it as I did with *Cancer.* Just as though nothing had happened in between. I almost believe it would be more "honorable" to sit back and beg for alms. Of course here I am taken seriously and enthusiastically. But I don't need it. I have no vanity left. This sounds discouraging. Forgive me. And I do hope your star continues to rise. All the best to you

Henry

P.S. My best and most reliable (also intelligent) publisher is Edmond Buchet of Correa, Paris. He's Swiss. If only you could bring yourself to publish the diary! Or unmutilated big fragments of it. Also—I spoke to Michel Simon about you—the houseboat, the monkeys in Paris, etc. A wonderful warm being, he!

In the air. A new kind of plane which makes the trip to Los Angeles in eight hours instead of eleven.

A white world outside. Clarity. Clarity. Recently I cannot bear the white expanse of my lucidities. Everyone else around me descends into chaos, inchoate lethargy, into fogs of the mind, temporary releases from lucidity. Some links, some bridges sustained and maintained by great effort are slipping from me. No rest, no refuge, no escape, no pause from awareness. A diamond lodged in the head, the unblinking eye of the clairvoyant. But altitude and strain wear out the heart. As the white clouds pass me, I think of this void between New York and Los Angeles in which I sit alone, a neutral state, a bridge of sighs, white sighs. When I come down again I will resume my humanity.

On the plane I had to take my shoes and stockings off, soaked by the rain before takeoff. The large airport umbrella almost carried me across the landing field.

I carried *Spy* in its final form.

High above, every form of life seems possible, only at thirty-thousand-feet altitude. And in cabins built against pressure. Pressurized cabins. When will I feel free of pressures?

We visited Lloyd Wright's completed chapel at Palos Verdes, near Los Angeles. The sun was pouring into it like a million saints' halos, the sea was glittering beyond the glass, the redwood trees were beginning to peep into the church. The beauty of glass expanded the spirit, let it loose among the clouds and in nature. What a poetic concept of a church. Not to enclose, in dimness, in stone, in tombs, with votive candles burning, but to free the spirit, to follow the clouds, to glitter with the sea, to grow from the earth richly scented with flowers and leaves. Incense and earth smells, the earth smell stronger.

There is Christie next door, an elfin child, a child of poetry. She has sweet parents, and two smaller sisters. She is old enough to be set free and she comes to tell me: "Anis, Anis, look, today I am a cowboy." "Anis, do you know something? Today I am a witch."

I hang up her joyous watercolors on my walls, and bring her mobiles to make. But today I had a shock: the school is teaching her to trace her drawings, and she is wearing a uniform with hat and gloves.

When she found out I did not have a child she said: "Today I am your borrowed little girl."

[February, 1953]

This time on the plane from Los Angeles to New York I could not sleep well because of the pain in my hip. For years I have gone to some doctor and said: "I have a pain here in the right ovary." They would examine me and say: "There is nothing wrong." I would be ashamed, thinking as I did as a child, on my way to my appendix operation, *"Je suis une malade imaginaire."* This time the pain pierced my sleep and I said to myself I must do something about the pain. I went to Dr. Jacobson, who sent me to another doctor. He found a tumor as large as an orange. I was to be operated on Friday, January 29. I cannot have feared death for I made no preparations such as I always intend making about disposition of the diary.

Thursday I entered the hospital. Left alone, that night, I felt the loneliness, the stark humiliation and dangers. The nurse shaved me, which saddened me. I still did not know, did not want to know I could be cut. I thought the operation was going to be done through the vagina. Early Friday morning at six A.M. they put a homely white shirt on me. The New York University Hospital is dismal but medically good. I had a tiny room with two small, narrow windows. In extreme illness I get very passive, obedient, childlike, trusting. I surrender to others. The trip to the operating table which I am so familiar with was as usual accomplished in half sleep, half fatalistic submission. I felt sorry for the staff, having to get up so early in the morning, and told them so. "Doctor Anaesthesia" was the last person I saw. She said she had to give me ether instead of an injection because my blood pressure was low. I hate ether. But she helped me by saying: "I will take the mask off as often as you wish me to, until you feel comfortable with it. And first of all I will give you oxygen until you see how easy it is. And as soon as you make a sign I will remove the mask.' I was so grateful that she helped me, that she was not autocratic, that after two whiffs of oxygen I gave in, holding her hand. Mercifully at the second whiff of ether I was unconscious. How long . . . it is like death. Total absence. Hours later, it seemed to me, I heard my name called. It was the nurse. I made a great effort to return. The feeling of having been very far away. I saw the doctor's face. I asked: "It wasn't cancer?" "Too soon to tell, we won't know until the tests are made."

I had a bandage over my stomach. I had been cut open. I had another scar. How I hate this surgery, butchering of one's body, scars. After that, pain, pain, pain. The night nurse ghostly, but so kind. Days of weakness, pills to sleep. Intravenous feeding. My arms blue and black from blood transfusions and dextrose, because I could not eat. A feeling that I had committed hara-kiri. Visitors. Presents. Feeling so weak it was an effort to talk. Jim, Lila, Dr. Brichta, Lawrence Maxwell, Ruth Witt Diamant. Weakness, weakness. But now they make you walk on the third day, slowly. And as I walked slowly along the dirty mayonnaise-colored hallways, I saw the patients whose doors were open. One very scholarly old man, whose night table was piled high with art books. His beautiful profile and long white hair and the art books aroused my curiosity. The nurse suggested we visit him.

He is a German Jew. After we talked a while, he asked the nurse to leave us alone. And then he said to me: "I trust you. I don't know what I am doing here. I was in a concentration camp. Do you think they are trying to harm me? What is the meaning of all these contraptions around me?"

Fortunately the nurse had told me that he had had a prostate operation, and I was able to explain about the bag, the intravenous feeding. I was able to reassure him that this was a hospital, that surgery here was intended to cure, that he would soon be well.

But I could see in his faded blue eyes the remains of doubts and fears. His experience in the concentration camp had scarred him deeply.

When we talked about art, his mind was clear. He was an art critic and a historian. But every evening I had to come and visit him alone, to reassure him that no harm was being done to him.

When it came time for me to go to the hospital for surgery, a few people remarked, not without malice: "Now that is one event you cannot make exciting or glamorous." At last, they felt, I was caught in a brutal experience which could not be enhanced.

But my persistent desire to transform experience and not resign myself to its ugliness made me take with me my red wool burnoose. Wearing this while being wheeled to the X-ray room was enough to spread some rays of amusement in the hospital, to startle the other patients and cheer them. Then the gods, who sometimes listen to the defiance of the artists, decided to listen to my prayers for a little beauty to cover the stark events. The king of the gypsies was having surgery at the same time! According to their laws, the whole tribe must stand by, stay at his side. They planted their tents in a nearby parking lot next to the drab old hospital. All day they walked through the drab corridors, traveled in the drab elevators, squatted outside the king's room, and no amount of hospital discipline could drive them away. There were about six hundred of them. My whole stay at the hospital was changed into a spectacle of their faces, costumes, animated behavior. I was convalescing in a gypsy encampment. I read their history, and inquired about their life.

They were believed to have come originally from India, and their dress might confirm that. The long dress, and the sarilike head covers, the profusion of colors, and the dark skins. There are different legends about them. For centuries they were persecuted in various ways. They lived by reading cards, making prophecies, and stealing. They were inbred, for their religion allowed no marriage outside their own people.

In the south of France they congregated every year to pay tribute to a black virgin, the "weeping virgin" as she was called. Blaise Cendrars was one of the few white men they accepted as a brother. They lived near the ragpickers, outside the gates of Paris, in their wagons.

In America they say there are fifty thousand of them. In Greenwich Village, where there were shop fronts for rent, they would hang their rugs and tell fortunes. And in the hospital, for ten days I had the joy of their company and talked with them. They particularly loved my red wool burnoose, which I wore in the hallways for my walks. My recuperation was hastened by their presence. And by my plan to visit Yucatán.

When I looked out of the hospital windows at the end of the hall, small, narrow, and barred, giving on an ugly courtyard, I turned my mind and my will toward Yucatán. I wanted to see Chichén-Itzá. I was reading about it. My spirit was already there. All my body had to do was to pick itself up and follow.

As the physical body healed, I became aware of the psychic illness once more: the fact I cannot face is that I am a failure as a writer. The publishers won't publish me, the bookshops won't carry my books, the critics won't write about me. I am excluded from all anthologies, and completely neglected.

I had to pay for the printing of *Spy in the House of Love,* done by an inexpensive printer in Holland.

The artists know the secret of freedom. June only found freedom by living in a world of fantasy. But Varda made his fantasy come true. His life is the one I admire. When I left San Francisco he had already acquired a ferryboat from which the motors and wheels had been extracted, leaving a poollike center to look into. He was beginning to make windows for the deck. With time the ferryboat grew in beauty. It is moored in Sausalito, and attached to it is a sailboat. Everything is made with his own hands, with little or no money. He makes a little income by teaching at an art school. But he does not need much. He wears jeans, takes showers army bucket style. If money is low he does not hesitate to serve only fried potatoes and wine. He cooks in an enormous frying pan from the flea market, with enormous wooden spoons from Mexico. He is a poet, sublime ragpicker who turns everything into an object of beauty. He taught me, in San Francisco, to admire a chair which had been whitewashed by the sea to a pure bone color.

Another life I like is Len Ly's. He has a house by the waterfront in New York, on West and Tenth Street. It is an old house (1800). When they scraped the paint off they found beautiful wood underneath. He has his studio in the cellar, and plenty of rooms above. Several artists have bought houses on the same block. It is a community. It is near cheap workmen's bistros, Spanish restaurants, Dutch restaurants, Irish bars, and near the market where they buy fresh and cheap food. I admire those who live graciously with little money.

Convalescence. Such an utter weakness that you lie like an animal hibernating, playing possum. You float. You are adrift. Every current is stronger than you.

What I dislike in New York is that life is dominated by achievement, activity, and the constant game of personalities. They are all played in terms of: this is the playwright of the moment, acclaimed; this is the actress of the season, acclaimed; this is the best-selling author; this is the best composer; this is the notorious Z or the toast of the town proclaimed by *Vogue* or *Harper's Bazaar.* The others do not exist at all. What one *is* does not count.

What makes my work so difficult to understand? I do not accept ready-made patterns, I do not practice the accepted integrations, the familiar synthesis. I am evolving a more fluid, flowing life, living out each fragment, each detour without concern for the conclusions. And it all ends, life and writing, in a deeper correlation, interconnection, not synthesis.

[Spring, 1953]

Max underlines the "comedy" of love, as most cynics do, forgetting that the moments of illusion and passion are the highest moments of life, are those one remembers. To dwell so much on the disintegration of passion when tested by human reality is merely to assert that death ultimately triumphs over our bodies, but this does not mean that we should refuse to live or love. These philosophers discount the duration of the passion, its euphorias and ecstasies, to observe only its dissolution. If we are unable to make passion a relationship of duration, surviving the destruction and erosions of daily life, it still does not divest passion of its power to transform, transfigure, transmute a human being from a rather limited, petty, fearful creature to a magnificent figure reaching at moments the status of a myth. My moments of courage and divination were all born of passion. The deserts which follow I do not dwell on.

What everyone forgets is that passion is not merely a heightened sensual fusion, but a way of life which produces, as in the mystics, an ecstatic awareness of the whole of life, that it is in this way that poetry becomes the greatest truth, by intensification, condensation of experience. While poetry is considered by most as illusion and delusion, it is the only reality, the moment when we are completely alive.

The problem I have to solve is how Stella, Djuna, Lillian, and Sabina arrive at a moment of transformation of their personality, without describing analysis. It is the writer who must do the analysis. He must do it in such a way that it seeps into the writing separate from the personality of the analyst. Many confessions are made without priests. The difficulty is that nothing will give the awareness we get from psychoanalysis. No friendship or love, even when there is a vital exchange, can go as deep and have the power to alter the consciousness, or the power to alter the course of our life. I can tell Jim all about himself.

Relationships cannot reverse the process. To know is not sufficient to change, to act. What few understand is that analysis is not intellectual, it is a reliving of situations, like psychodrama, so that one re-creates the feelings, and confronts them. I can analyze others, or my characters, but the power to alter, to change and be transformed is not within pure analysis alone but the long psychoanalytical *reliving* of experience, so as to detect the feelings which created our tragedy. In the old classical novels deep changes did not take place, or they were hasty and unconvincing. There were reforms, abdications, sacrifices, renunciations, withdrawals, but few complete transformations. Oh, yes, from alcoholism to sobriety, from Don Juanism to monogamy, from one political affiliation to another, from bourgeois to man of the people or the other way round, but such changes were superficial, not profound, they were done by the will, through external pressures, not organically, from within, from an evolution. I am trying to say that changes by an evolution of awareness are rare in the classic novel.

If Lila decided with the help of AA to cease being an alcoholic, by a great, shared communal effort at discipline, it is not the same change as she is working on now with an analyst.

She confesses that when she read a few portions of the diary she realized that alcohol was only one of the ways by which she eluded experience (by anaesthetizing pain, reducing awareness, subduing hungers, dissolving activities). "I used to go dead for long periods, when I felt nothing at all and I see now what it is to be emotionally alive all the time, as you were, and aware." Sobriety was not enough of a change. It could have made Lila's life a simple dedication to rescuing other alcoholics, a world of service and sacrifices. But the other change is more positive, there is a Lila beyond alcoholism and sobriety, which neither alcohol nor dedication to the rescue of other alcoholics could give birth to, a Lila not yet born, one she may have caught a glimpse of in heightened moments of passion or awareness, aspired to, pursued. When so extremely ill with rheumatic fever, she sought my work through Gonzalo, reaching for other forms of expression.

In the unconscious lies not only man's demons (as we feared), the primitive, the instinctual, the uncontrollable forces of nature, but also this creative, expanded force which connects with the universe, found in such great figures as Beethoven, Einstein, in painters and writers of value. Man's love of these figures reveals his own dreams to reach the heights of man's achievement.

Dear Lila:

I had to wait for the right moment, and to read the manuscript twice. I think you have achieved exactly what you set out to do, to produce the mystery play, the intimation of truths by the most abstract process possible.

This creates what I call the diamond phrases, but must be read carefully. It is beautifully done, in language and in conciseness. It evokes a mood, the most obscure as well as the most precise happenings, ˉabstraction and, at the same time, impressionism of blurred emotions. It is, of course, the work of a poet. I pick out again the same perfect climax phrases: "All fertility rites begin in death," which in a way is the underlying theme of the whole. The shattering of the glass is a wonderful substitution for the shattering of the fortune-teller crystal, and a gesture against the intoxicants which no longer intoxicate. I like: "Not anybody . . . a watcher, writing a foaming history in her head." The poet-spectator, the essence of both. A wonderful image. You succeeded as in modern painting, in seizing upon the inner structural design, the premeditated and irrational, without subjecting it to a reorganization of experience by consciousness. It is a perfect image of the senseless, broken, shattered action which takes place between human beings, when all the threads are cut, and the substance corroded by neurosis. It is a very contemporary image of chaos, chaos designed and planned by a game which delights ultimately in confusing the issues, destructively so. It is true to that design of chaos, not a false one as we saw in Tennessee Williams. The game of scholars is the supreme irony, for the game turns to be a game of the irrational, arranged in a supreme disarrangement, and finally exploded.

Women are wearing short hair and huge Ubangi earrings, crinolined skirts, ribbons in their hair, ballet slippers, and shawls. A sleek model with heavily painted eyes wears a cotton dress and carries a country basket.

I wear a leopard-fur belt over my white dress and leopard-fur earrings.

Analysis is like a shock treatment, it throws you back into childhood in order to recapture the reparable elements, to reconstruct the personality. To reconstruct the personality it is necessary to find the original wound. You have to revaluate the past so it will not remain an incubus or succubus.

For example, I look at others with my own eyes, my own values, I evaluate them by my own standards, but when it comes to looking at myself, I look at myself through my father's eyes. I judge myself by his standards, and in his eyes I was not beautiful, I had flaws. He found and saw only the flaws. His standards were superficial, vainglorious, purely external. Varèse spoke disdainfully of the early days in Paris when they met at the Schola Cantorum: "He was obsessed with *le joli*, always *le joli*."

———

I feel dimmed and slowed down. Is it convalescence or a new state? There is too much to synthesize. Peggy was shaping geometric figures with her hands in space, to express the need of limiting, encompassing. I was amused by the comedian Garner spoofing an orchestra conductor and equally "boxing off" into squares, and circles, the flowing music. The emotional life cannot perhaps retain the old forms it once used as a mold any more than music or the novel can use the old structures.

There must be a new architecture for our lives and works of art as well. At one point no one knew whether Debussy had merely lost his way and dissolved. Now we know he was discovering the fluid quality of emotion, just as Alban Berg discovered the language of our nerves. And now, writing here, where do I go? Which way? From where? Relativity is the key word. Flow. Is it only in America that there is such a denial of emotion? The diary was held together, was given its unity, by my being at the center. The novels? In whose consciousness does the whole appear? Shall I be there as Proust was, but invisible as a catalyzer?

After convalescence I felt detached from everyone. But when Peggy says: "There is a synthesis in every line you write; there is no need of a final one, in the old classical sense; continue fluid, continue to flow," I feel she is talking about the kind of life I have chosen, by its immensity, its many extensions, fullness; its integration must happen in every moment, in every fragment, a truth and wholeness in the moment.

We have learned all the separate functions of the body's separate parts, but we do not know how they relate to each other, we cannot see them in interaction while alive. I have learned all the separate functions of our emotional being but I do not know how they can be integrated. Relativity theme. These are my secrets. We relive different ages. Karma, they call it in the East. But the truth is they happen in one life, not necessarily in afterlife. All of our experiences extend as far back into the past as into the present and future. I may stumble upon a secret of our unconscious in which there is no time; past, present, and future are superimposed. We set up a false rational man. We had to rediscover the denied and powerful irrational, and learn not to suppress it but to control it by understanding. Meanwhile we need good deep-sea divers, we need adventurers, we need explorers. Synthesis, integration, are often replaced by absolutes. There is no danger of dogmatism in the way I work, only in conventional summaries, not in the open, indefinite continuum I practice.

I left Sierra Madre for Mexico, on a trip to Chichén-Itzá I had promised myself when recovered from surgery. In a Juárez restaurant a party of eight Americans bewildered by the waitress who did not speak English: "They can't talk," said the drunken, older head of the group.

Through Chihuahua, on the way to Aguascalientes. Courtesy toward the Mexicans obtains what money cannot. They give each other courtesy and respect it, and it is the only currency most Americans do not know the use of, even among themselves.

Such good rice and chicken soup, good eggs and black beans and fresh tortillas.

Learning the names of new trees, new bushes, new flowers, new birds. Ocotillo. Hot desert drives. Crosses over mounds of stones by the wayside, as in the old West. Wonder how they died, those who died by the wayside.

Slept in a windowless adobe house which was once an oven. Hole in the center of the pointed ceiling. Granaries, cone-shaped. Whitewashed now, with dark Spanish furniture, and Mexican serapes on the floor. Dust towns. Deserted all day by the men working in the fields. A few women and children about. The women hidden in their shawls, in which they also carry the baby. Children curious and joyous. Streets of dust, which the wind blows about.

Vera Cruz. Shrimps sold at the café served on a piece of toilet paper. At the market an American girl asked for brains. The butcher took a cow head off the hook and shook brains into a market bag.

Squares, cafés, marimbas, bands of guitar players and singers all the way. Women with fans and red dresses. Even tombs are painted in joyous colors, laundry blue, pink, red. Waiting for the ferry on which the car will cross the river. A Mexican lies asleep on the seat of his truck. The same Oriental patience, quietism, facility for waiting, for reverie, I saw in Morocco. A philosophic acceptance of obstacles, delays, frustrations.

On the road to Coatzacoalcos. Little boys always seeking to earn a peso. We drive through jungle. Waterfalls. The thatched houses now have only roofs and no walls. They cook out of doors. They wash laundry by the riverside. Next to the huts, the rocks are painted yellow, green, blue for decoration. The laundry spread on the rocks and trees blooms like giant flowers of many colors. Strange, forlorn little hotel room. Shower inside of the water closet, shower drips on you, or when you take a shower it floods the water closet. Mirrors are cracked. The towels are so worn they cannot dry you. Beds uneven, tend to spill you. Mattress bumpy. Closets with nails which tear your clothes. Animals wander in and out of the courtyard, famished dogs and pigs. This in violent contrast to Chichén-Itzá. Stones hand-carved and laid by artists have a beauty that will outlive modern Mexico. We do not know their names. But we know, as we watch the proud, arrogant pyramids and tombs, buildings, courtyards, wells, arches, that this beauty will live forever.

Letter to Anne and Max Geismar:

Your escapist number one, Doctor of Philosophy of Escape, Bachelor of Art of Escape, Bachelor of the Science of Escape, Master of all Escape Territories, is writing you while driving at seventy-five miles an hour through Mexico. "When one is hurt one travels as far as possible from the hurt," wrote a writer nobody reads ("Child Born out of the Fog," in *Under a Glass Bell*), a writer we know too well and other people not well enough. Purple cactus, mountains shaped like Aztec temples, and children who think a Woolworth toy a supreme delight, all this and the contemplation of different kinds of troubles; such as droughts, or one's best cow killed by a foreigner's car, fevers, malaria from the lagoons, cataracts even in children, poverty; the hard rubbing of clothes in a cold river to achieve whiteness, the pride in whiteness which gives such arduous labor, destroys the validity of our sorrows. Why did the ancient artists not care about recognition and accept anonymity. Probably because they believed in celestial rewards, and we don't. I have come to learn their secret, and to learn to extirpate the ego, which is unknown here. Climate unfavorable. There are no egos. There is no respect for achievement, only for charm, wit, and other perishable products. Words are used for songs and court-ship. Of course, one does not get cured immediately. While waving back at field workers, consorting with children and emptying a trunk full of toys and oranges (the children lack vitamins) while awed by the work of the architects, I have written twenty pages of a new book. One consolation: that if I had lived in the time when men built Chichén-Itzá, I would have loaned my braided hair to the hauling of the stones. I would have painted unsigned murals, written unsigned charters, but what do we have that we could thus give ourselves to, that would engage our gifts, and our giving of these skills? We do not have fiestas in the streets, religious or pagan, we do not sing to each other, or court young women with poetry. . . .

I was still feeling weak when I was faced with the sharp ascent of the pyramid. The stones are placed so that the step you take is twice as high as for our ordinary stairs. But the beauty of this ascent, pyramiding in a point toward the sky, I could not forfeit, and I climbed it. At the top, the vista of the Mayan city was dazzling— the dome of the building in which they studied astrology, the courts in which they had their athletic games, the pools, the arcades, the sculptures, the huge stone snakes guarding the entrances, the slab on which the human sacrifices took place, the well from which so many treasures had been stolen by archaeologists, now lying in some university museum. Fallen statues not yet reconstructed, fallen columns lying half imbedded in moss, statues covered by climbing vines, stolen at night and taken to other countries. Nearer to the sky, and, because of the space, the symmetry, the proportions, nearer to the sky than one feels from the Empire State Building.

Two books which I loved and read during the trip: Sullivan's *Beethoven* and *Really the Blues* by Mezz Mezzrow. Two extremes, not only musically, but philosophically. One, supreme awareness and gaining altitude by suffering. The second, forgetfulness and gaining altitude by moments of fever, ecstasy. The first defines the role of art. The second the role of opium, drugs, musical jags.

Regaining altitude after the episode at the hospital, helped by those two books and by the sight of Chichén-Itzá, the Mayan city.

Climbing the pyramids with fevers and chills, but climbing, away and upward. Wrote a little in the car until fatigue and the strain of traveling silenced me.

From Yucatán through the Isthmus of Tehuantepec toward the Pacific Ocean. How strange it was to drive through the jungle, on our way to Tehuantepec, knowing that for six hours there would be no villages, no gasoline, no water. The top was down. We could see the trees with their tops interlacing, the ferns, the same parasitic lianas hanging from them like tattered lace. The air was tinted green from so much foliage, the sun could not penetrate except in shafts now and then. The smells were pungent, like a mass of odorous herbs pressed together, damp, exhaling strong vapors. Now and then we met two or three men on horseback, in white suits and immense hats, carrying their machetes like swords. They were hacking wood or seeking mushrooms, I don't know. They watched us pass with somber eyes, neither hostile nor friendly. One group waved us to stop, and asked us to take a boy who was about eleven or twelve back with us because he was getting tired. The boy was frightened of us and would not sit next to me. He settled on the back of the car, holding on to the spare tire. After a while he jumped off. We fear the jungle and the unknown, and never think of how they fear us. It was a dirt road. Aside from the men with their machetes we did not see anyone.

But the arrival at Tehuantepec was like entering a Gauguin world. Flowers, vines, rivers, and in the shallow rivers, nude women bathing. Women and children. We would have liked pictures of them but knew their hostility to photography. We went to the hotel, the usual rambling house with a patio, tile floors, and I had to beg for a room because I was exhausted by the six-hour drive.

But after an hour's rest we were out again, walking through the market. The same women who had bathed nude objected to my off-the-shoulder cotton dress and spoke of American lack of modesty. They were astoundingly beautiful women, six feet tall, often with hair touching their feet. They were dressed in long velvet dresses, with embroidered vests and lace coiffures (the baby's baptism dress they found on the shore from a shipwreck they turned into a headdress). They weave cotton of vivid colors into their braids. Dressed like queens at the Elizabethan court they sell their wares at the market. They wear their fortunes around their necks in the form of Spanish gold pieces strung together. They run not only the market but real estate and everything else. The men are five feet tall. They sit around in cafés, they play the guitar and sing. The legend is that the women came from elsewhere, having lost their men in a war. They look more like luxurious gypsies. They are physically unlike the rest of Mexican women, who are small and delicately boned, with small feet and hands.

The market was a feast for the eyes. Fruit and vegetables arranged in beautiful designs, like an abstract painting. Ribbons and colored wool and colored textiles hanging in the breeze like pennants. Big cauldrons of odorous stews cooking over braziers. Pottery of all kinds, water jugs in beautiful, graceful shapes, and also at times humorous, in the shape of a fat-bellied man or a woman with breasts or the whole curved jar painted like a woman's face.

The women sit on straw chairs combing each other's incredible hair. The mantle of Godiva is eclipsed by the dark raven hair with blue shadows in it.

A wedding couple passed, the woman tall and proud (for their carriage is noticeably proud), the man smaller and relaxed.

The legend tells, of course, that many strangers who wandered into the region were seduced by the beauty of the women, by a life of ease, and remained there.

They rebelled against photography and did not hesitate to throw pottery at the photographer.

The flowers were like the women, vigorous and colorful, and seemed arranged in baskets as if they would never wither. The perfume of jasmine and magnolia was overpowering.

New York.

A martini makes an ordinary glass shine like a diamond at a coronation, makes an iron bed in Mexico seem like the feather bed of a sultan, a hotel room like the terminus and climax of all voyages, the pinnacle of contentment, the place of repose in an altitude hungered for by all the restless ones.

Create space and order in the house. It is very important. It is like the empty room of the Japanese, ideal for the gestations of the imagination and inner visions. Uncluttered. Our clutter interferes with freedom of thought. Air and lightness.

Costume in New York is a white wool coat, a white dress, a white hat with two slim abstract birds in flight. A painter asked me: "Aren't you afraid the birds will fly away?"

"No, I always fly off first and they follow me."

Parties. Exhibitions.

You dream of the evening and of what it will bring at twilight, it is the hour I love best and which always saddens me. You cease the day's efforts, you recline, you bathe, you dress for some event. I love bridges best of all, planes, taxis, the diaries, the hour of dress, the in-between hours, the only moment when I exist alone.

Lila and I went to see *Camino Real*. We did not like it. It vulgarizes fantasy, it is a caricature of love.

Jim and I carry on a rapid-fire language of our own. His new novel, *Blue Denim,* is well done, firm, like a James Cain. But in his diary he transcends the direct action and produces what I call the equivalent of jazz in writing. He has rhythm and flashes of insight. The danger for him is one I cannot help him with, it is undetectable, it cannot be combated, even defined: the danger of the cliché. How does one evade it? By a knowledge of literature which Jim does not care to explore. He accepts the cliché. It seems, it appears, deceptively to be a universal language, but actually it is the disguise, it is the mask, it is the false language. It conveys nothing.

On days of anxiety he looks pale, rigid, frozen.

The most tragic moment in human relationships is when we are given to see, accidentally, by a revealing word, or a moment of crisis, the image which the other carries within himself of us, and we catch a glimpse of a stranger, or a caricature of ourselves, or an aspect of our worst self aggrandized, larger than nature, or a total distortion.

What most people do not understand is that there are escapes and flights which are constructive. There are those who, in self-defense, build a shell as they advance in experience. There are others who, instead of building a shell, take flights, find other forms of life, other richer places and people and return consoled and strengthened. The Geismars do not understand this. I do not like the crustacean type of human being.

I found *Under Milk Wood* childish, village gossip in nursery rhymes, pub humor, beer fumes, and Dylan Thomas himself looks like an overgrown baby.

I suggested to Brigitte Tishnar, who works for *Vogue,* a series of articles on women's dress according to various writers. No response.

I met Harold Norse, a poet who has great emotional power in a beautiful, disciplined form.

I saw an astonishing film, *Strange Decision,* by Curzio Malaparte. The disappearance of beautiful or stunning films causes me anxiety. Where do they go? They pass too quickly, and where are they buried?

Peggy Glanville-Hicks: she appears frail and small, but sharp and incisive bodily too, with a presence full of nervous energy and nervous fire like a bird. As she talks her focus is impeccable, her language subtle. Quick-witted and graceful. It was enchanting to find someone with such a luminous structure, a complete inner city of definite values. Living and feeling only from a core. Illuminations on music, on Paul Bowles (they were born on the same day and she has felt a twinship with him throughout her life). She made me regret the incident which estranged me from Paul Bowles. It happened when his wife Jane brought out her first book [*Two Serious Ladies*]. I remember I was so distressed by the tightness, the involuted quality, the constricted, coiling inward (not into an infinite interior but a tight one) that I wrote her a careful, gentle, warm letter warning her of the danger of constriction for a writer, and she took it as a condemnation (a wrong interpretation). She asserted it was that letter which arrested her writing. Knowing how tenderly I handle writers, I knew my letter could not have been harmful. The difficulties were in herself.

Peggy thinks I have explored new territory. She was convinced I had described Paul Bowles at seventeen in *Children of the Albatross*. That is how she saw him.

Visit to Max and Anne Geismar is another atmosphere. More earthy. A house in the country. Children. Dogs. A garden. Earth and mind. But no aesthetics. Max is laborious, Anne vital, small, assertive, but with a humor made of thrusts, an honesty like a child's, but satirical. Max is modest, self-effacing, and not as famous as he should be. Even though I do not see writers as he does (only historically and politically), he is still solid and sincere. Though we disagree on every subject, we respect and like each other. Anne's humor is a kind of courage. Max is warm and gentle. He is not contemporary, and certainly has no perception of future writing. He is moving backward into history.

I saw Anne's face on the Mayan sculptures; the Mayans are said to be the long-lost Hebrew tribe. Max's and Anne's humor converts their anxieties. They belong to a period of the thirties I did not know, because I was in Paris. Max was encouraged by Edmund Wilson when he was a young writer. They were friends of Max Lerner, of the left intellectual group around *The Nation*. When he writes about young writers he either does not know what to say, or he is destructive.

I have to face that I relate to my friends in a partial way. I observe, notice, enjoy what I love, and leave other aspects of them alone. I turn away, and what I cannot love, I overlook. Is that real friendship? I seek the love so eagerly that I don't want to see what might interfere with it. I am ashamed of that. It does not seem like loving enough; I should include all of the person. It is my major flaw.

Illusion. First there is the illusion of perfect accord, then revelation by experience of the many differences, and then I come upon a crossroad, and unless there is a definite betrayal, I finally accept the complete person.

During a country weekend, the host got dressed in the costume of a country gentleman, red shirt and shorts, and offered his legs to the sun's promiscuous rays. However, the sun is more selective than we think, there are some legs it frowns upon, and does not tan with graciousness. Those are the legs of the people we do not happen to desire. . . .

Double exposures, all during this month, with images blurred and running into one another. I started to copy original diaries, which meant several trips to the Pasadena bank vault, a hurried one-day trip to San Francisco to bring back half of the originals I had left in Ruth Witt Diamant's cellar, trips to Bekins Storage, Arcadia, where I kept the typed copies. It meant renumbering them, rechecking dates (there was an error). It meant copying the volume of life in Paris, the detachment from Henry, the meeting with Gonzalo. It also contained the trip to Morocco and Spain. First of all these images as they appeared upon the images of life in Sierra Madre created strange superimpositions. The description of Morocco, pure images, without political undercurrents, the poem and the music and the realism of its life. This floating world of beauty, mystery underscored by the harsh nasal voices of the radio commentators: "New riots in Morocco. Thirty persons killed. Arabs kill Jews and French inhabitants." And in the newspapers, only images of the dead and wounded lying in the streets.

Henry, in volume fifty, is concerned with age, certainly unreasonable, irrational, when twenty years later he has married a thirty-year-old actress and is obviously a satisfactory lover still. He was fading only in his own heart and body. A phase. And twenty years later he writes me: "I am writing about Moricand [*A Devil in Paradise*]. Do you remember the name of the restaurant on the way to the Porte d'Orléans, on the right, where I first met him? And who was the friend he talked so much about, not Blaise Cendrars—the other?"

Café Zeyer, Max Jacob. It reminded me of Proust's visits to ascertain the kind of flowers Mrs. X wore on her hat ten years before at a party. He even wanted to see the hat.

So while we correspond about Moricand I copy feverish pages about Gonzalo. Gonzalo was like a volcano on fire. This dark, fervent Gonzalo casts no shadow over the present. Fire consumes itself and all it touches.

Curtis Harrington has a new job with Columbia Studios. He wants to recommend books and plays. I suggest Jim's play and

Simenon, whose adventure books would make the most marvelous films. His books on Tahiti, on Africa, on South America.

Curtis also wanted to recommend me to work on an adaptation of Marcel Proust's work. He arranged an interview with Jerry Wald. The room was invaded with books. They lay in pyramids on the floor. Little white papers stuck out of them, usually near the beginning. I had a feeling none had been read completely. There was a secretary who taped our talk.

His questions, my answers, and the careful way they were being recorded made me uneasy. I had a feeling I was being exploited, my suggestions, ideas, references to recent books. There was talk also about *Jean-Christophe* by Romain Rolland, about my translating it and helping with the script. I love the book and felt it would be safer in my hands. But the way Jerry Wald talked, and his constant repetition of "you can't go wrong on the classics" astonished me. The books became merchandise.

Curtis suggested I get an option on one of Simenon's books. I wrote to his wife. I received a curt reply that only agents were given options.

That ended my working for Jerry Wald.

I often baby-sit for the three little Campion girls. They are delightful children, full of playfulness and fantasies.

I love the Campion family, I love Millicent, and yet I will never write about them because I love them as human beings only, they do not belong in the territories I am keen on exploring. The artist submits himself to adventures into the irrational. He is merely another type of adventurer. He does not climb Annapurna, but he risks both his human life and loss of reason or health as the mystics did who withdrew from the world to pursue a vision. The hells traversed by the artist most human beings are unwilling to traverse. When Jim accepts the demonic journey, he becomes more interesting to me, more interesting to write about.

I am reading *Psycho-Analysis of Artistic Vision and Hearing* by Ehrenzweig. It helped to confirm me in my pursuit of the inarticulate and in-depth visions and sensations.

It stresses the comparison between the psychoanalyst's method of selecting apparently unimportant details, the irrelevant detail, rather than the one which seems on the surface to be important;

similar to the modern artist who selects what appears to be irrelevant or negative or unimportant, in contrast with traditional painters. James Merrill accused me of "meandering," which corresponds to the word "roving," which is connected with all processes of free association. In Picasso's painting the body outline is also a guitar and the guitar something else.

What irony that Proust, who selected the most shallow of all people, the wealthy and the aristocratic, should have reached the greatest depths which a novelist has reached into the unconscious, and that he was accused of depicting only decadents. He created the best portrait of a servant, Françoise, better than that of any social realist, like Zola or Balzac. I can't remember any of Zola's or Balzac's characters, yet I know all of Proust's intimately.

Paul Mathiesen braved the distance and came to Sierra Madre. He talked about Renate, a Viennese painter, and her son by her first marriage, Peter.

He had changed a great deal, and I wondered how much Renate had to do with the change in him. He talked, he was expansive. The adolescent dissonances, like those of the adolescent voice before it settles, had disappeared. He was incarnated. He was physically present.

In this double exposure I saw what Dr. Bogner had tried to show me: that my duality and conflict were not with others, relationships, but within myself. It was not Gonzalo or Henry who were rebels, but I who did not acknowledge my rebellions. When Gonzalo's fires ceased to consume me and to consume him, I find my own fires consuming me.

In Paris I gave a beautiful Tahitian party, with real Tahitians playing and dancing, in the orange rooms decorated with lanterns, the windows open on the glittering Seine, my friends kicking off their shoes to dance in the soft summer night.

Renate and Paul, however, could have installed themselves in that moment with ease. They would have understood Moricand and Gonzalo, and easily become "characters" in the diary.

I blamed Henry, Gonzalo, and Helba for the destructive elements in my life, but when the three disappeared, I accomplished their roles alone. I acted out my own destructiveness. The image of myself struggling against Helba's and Gonzalo's destructiveness (an image I admired) was not entirely accurate. When they left, I enacted my own. In each case we fight the others when they are living out the role assigned to them.

How beautiful it would be if we recognized the hidden wish and when handing others the keys to the city we were not able to conquer, we also consented, adhered to the division we ourselves created.

I fought Henry's physical and mental promiscuity, when gregariousness was a fantasy I acted out at the age of five, inviting everyone in the street for tea.

I fought Gonzalo's irresponsibility when my own exaggerated responsibility stifled me. I entrust others with "safety measures," so I can live out my transgressions.

We fight this part of ourselves which is unknown, which we instinctively fear. Because it was feared we stifled it. Because it was stifled we must breathe it through others. (The June in myself? In other women? The Henry in myself, friendly to the whole world? The Gonzalo in myself, rebel and untamed?)

But the revelation of this aspect in those we love becomes the threatening enemy. We cannot come to terms with it. The proof of this truth is the reversals which take place. Henry and I are estranged, and I have to do my own living and writing. Gonzalo returns to France, and I have to achieve my own violence.

[Fall, 1953]

At Lillian Libman's party I met Cyrille Arnavon, a most sensitive and cultured man of letters, who translates American novels into French. His father was a close friend of Giraudoux. He was amazed that I knew Giraudoux's novels so deeply and said wistfully: "No one reads him any more in France. We are all in reaction against fantasy."

John Humphrey, professor at Columbia University, includes *Under a Glass Bell* on the reading list.

John Merrill, poet, finds *Four-Chambered Heart* not good at all, a "fairy tale, too naked," whereas a novel by his friend Bruchner has a "lovely texture" and *Chateau d'Argol* is enchanting. He invites me to tell me this, delivering these assertions as if he were handing me flowers.

I gave a party for Maxwell Geismar's *Rebels and Ancestors*. Thomas Ginsberg, James Herlihy, René de Chochor, Lillian Libman, Miriam Kreiselman, Miranda d'Ancona, Tony Richardson, Pepe Zayas, Larry Maxwell, William and Letha Nims.

I had his book on display all around the room.

Someone said to the painter Rousseau: "Why did you place a sofa in the middle of the jungle?"

Rousseau answered: "One has a right to paint one's dreams."

Max is struggling with his concept of poetry as artifice, my poetry in life as artificiality. What is natural to me, confuses him. Henry also once confused art and artifice.

But when I read *Rebels and Ancestors* I felt a genuine respect for what Max has done. I sent a telegram from Sierra Madre, in total acceptance of the task he set himself:

YOUR BOOK A UNIQUE BLENDING OF DEEP PSYCHOLOGICAL INSIGHT AND HISTORICAL EVALUATION WITH THE NOVELIST'S POWER TO DRAMATIZE, HUMANIZE, REVIVIFY SO THAT IT READS MOVINGLY, CAPTIVATINGLY, LIKE THE BEST NOVEL OF OUR TIME. MOST CRITICISM IS VIVISECTION. YOURS BRINGS AMERICAN LITERATURE AND CHARACTER INTO WARM,

VIVID LIFE. RECEIVED IT ONLY TODAY. PLEASE MAIL THIS TO HOUGHTON MIFFLIN WITH MY DEEPEST ADMIRATION.

I do not agree with the basis of Maxwell Geismar's criticism. He never asks: "How is it written?" He considers only the contents. He approves the contents of Dreiser's novels, and does not see that the man is a clumsy, heavy, journalistic writer. He gives us a social document, a card index, annotations, marginal notes, a photograph, and none of these is writing. There is in Geismar's historical point of view a complete lack of the aesthetics of writing.

The liberation of a free association accomplished by Joyce gives us the content of a scholarly, explorative mind. It was Joyce's private inner comedy, the limitless expansion of a vast imagination. Can we seek to enter another's mind as fully? Joyce attempted to distribute inner monologue among his characters, but in the end it is his voice we hear. If each one of us were truthful about the content of one mind, our own, the only one we know in totality, we would achieve a unity of knowledge. Other minds we only know by flashes, intermittently, and having won our consciousness, we can only descend into the subterranean chambers of our own unconscious.

Jim's play will be given at the Theatre de Lys. Jim flies in and out. His black withdrawn moods concern me because I cannot reach him then. Lila explains why on one side of himself he writes like all the sons of Hemingway and James Cain and in his diary and in his talks with me he manifests a more subtle, poetic self. But this side he will not give to the world. He thinks of it as his vulnerable side, to be protected from the world.

We went to see Beauford Delaney's studio, which Jim may want to rent. Beauford is going to France to live. It was a vast loft, with his paintings turned against the wall. It was here I came to see him years ago at Henry's suggestion, and had a very strange visit. He had covered (in my honor, it appeared later) everything with white sheets, which gave the studio a funeral quality. He spoke with slowness, and gave such formality to the occasion that I was frozen. He sat down at the piano, lit two candles, and sang a religious song. I felt oppressed.

This time the visit was lighter. I feel a painter should live with his paintings around him, visible, part of the air he breathes.

———

Letter to Max Geismar about *Rebels and Ancestors:*

The first time I read the book for pure enjoyment, quickly, and to give you a general impression of my feeling about it. Now I read it again more carefully, and I still have the feeling that I am reading a work of fiction because you have made such an interesting drama of the conflict between the writer and his work and the world and his relationships. It is the complete dynamic analysis which gives it that living quality of a drama. I am amazed how fully you can evoke the times, the atmosphere, the history, the intimately personal environment, so that both the work and the man are balanced, fully known. I have learned in the process the history of America as well as all the psychological quirks of its individuals, the deformations and what caused them. The history is beautifully told. About your language I repeat myself, because I have said that about the other books. In fact, it is unfortunate, for your novelists, that your own language is so accurate and varied that when you quote them, they sound poverty-stricken and bare like twigs. That is the creative part of your work, to enhance, and glitterize . . . ! That is the captivating quality of the book. Actually, I never would have read all that history of repression, of greed, etc. except told by you. In other hands it would be rather awful.

About the psychology, here I know what I am praising. I believe it is exceedingly accurate, the personal and the relation to the world and other individuals. Also the exact knowledge of the power of each, the ability to measure the chemistry that took place, that I think you do like an analyst of the first quality. Cause and effect on the writer, and then as it is manifested in his work, etc.

You fulfill the role of illuminator, so rarely carried out by the critic, which is to reveal what others have not seen. Here is where the critic plays a role similar in value and very much needed by the world, in revealing what others cannot see or feel, in expanding our vision of the world and of character. Your statement on the problem of the life of the passions in the United States was also very startling and well said. Personally I like best the Stephen Crane section, but that is purely personal. Probably because you could allow yourself more personal and individual lyrical flights in writing about him, and it showed your understanding of the more subtle, more intricate and difficult evolutions in this "odd halfway house of modern realism." Your understanding of the "wounded, lyrical and humble." For that it is more moving perhaps. But while this one was studied with utmost delicacy, you managed to give a fine portrait of the brutes too, with the necessary strong brush strokes, the Jack Londons and the Norrises . . . incredible people, but how well you handled them, all that blood and thunder and blind actions, and the false pioneers . . . the ones who did not create the country but who plundered and quarreled.

I admire and respect your core, the fixed core from which you operate, evaluating all fairly and equably. The core of values never oscillates, yet the human sympathy does, toward values you do not truly admire but do understand, which is as it should be. I would say (that is the way I see it) that you achieve the full painting of the large mural, the universal one, like the immense Orozco paintings, while being able to focus with gentleness on the smallest detail, the fallacies, the failures.

Above all the sense of truth. The summary in "Years of Gain" is truly profound, in the exact weighing of the spiritual values gained and lost. "And don't the ultimate insights about human behaviour proceed most surely from the submerged portion of human activity? The hidden life of the great artists is probably their truest life—if we could only discover it." Well, Mr. Geismar, by implication, divination, interpretation of outward facts, you have certainly done just that, as well as exposed the secret life of American letters and American character. So many novel themes, the study of the virility complex through the violence, the study of the implications of a break from the "cultural heritage," the final emphasis on Whole Vision, a plea for it. I do think you have achieved a beautiful structure of synthesis of a most difficult and unstable material, that you have lighted up a massive chaos, and established values in a moment when all values are nonexistent. It's a valuable work, which took great care and skill and thought. I see now how right it is that you should work at this and nothing else, because in remaining out of the ugly and deafening currents of present activities, you have conserved your energy for the very clarification and guidances most deeply needed. In a moment of great confusions in all values, to write about literature as you do is actually applicable to all the other activities and should influence and seep into all the realms of darkness in which most people live. I tell you, what is most needed is not more murky novels, but more understanding, more wisdom, more humanity like yours.

The value of any individual development, research, or experiment is regarded here as antisocial, but I believe that until the individual is developed he is useless to society. His function in the whole may not be immediately apparent but it is essential. I know that I am contributing to our awareness, not mine alone.

In *Spy*, I am not sure I did the right thing in presenting the men only at the moment they passed through the intense searchlight of Sabina's desire or vision of them. I purposely chose to intensify both the limitations of passion and its quality, intensity instead of completeness in relationship. I reproach Sabina at the end for loving only one aspect created by illusion. I feel this might have been lost if I had done the men more fully. And anyway, this is a novel from the point of view of a woman. In this realm I am exploring;

I may make errors due to the search for other *truths,* other than the obvious ones. One may gain one truth at the expense of another. I was being true to Sabina's inner screen and inner lighting. *So that one might know her intimately.*

For the same reason, I leave out many of the minor characters that usually pad other novels. If I do this, it is for the sake of concentration, not because I do not value them. I do feel that this terrible standardization of character by which Americans reach economic security is dangerous to whoever seeks individual patterns. When doctors or scientists go far out in offbeat research, no one troubles them or tampers with them because they believe they will benefit from them. But they think they have a right to tamper with the artist because they are not convinced that he is necessary to them, unlike primitive societies far more civilized than ours, where the prophet, poet, and singer were exempt from fishing or hunting because they had other contributions to make.

Of course, I could say that what is left undone now in the novels may no longer seem to be so when the novels are completed. Sabina is not finished, nor Djuna. I'm working on completing them all.

I stressed the neurosis as the impediment to growth, then at the end of the tunnel change and freedom from it, I hope.

René de Chochor returns from France and tells me of changes. "There is too much suffering, too much tyranny, too much tension between Russia and America. The youth spend their time jazzing and they read Mickey Spillane. The people who grew up with me, who were students with me, before the war, I have seen them every year, I have seen them change. They are bad-tempered and bitter."

Usually he is light-hearted and witty. He is dark and handsome, with soft eyes and a shy smile but with poise, and we have charming business lunches. He throws publishers' letters in the scrap basket before my eyes. He treats me like the Queen of Writing, but he cannot help me. *Spy* was turned down many times. He tells me about a publisher who accepted a beautiful book, was wildly enthusiastic, but when he discovered the author was forty years old he canceled the contract. *Paris Review* does not want Maxwell Geismar on their editorial board because he is forty years old. Yet Geismar is responsible for the discovery of William Styron, who is one of the editors.

I went to San Francisco to stay with my mother while Joaquin took a three-day trip for the University. My mother sits in the house with the shades down shutting out the sun (a Cuban habit), rushes out to scold dogs and children for making noise, works on lacemaking, reads detective stories, observes her swollen legs and feet, and waits. The horror of aging, the deafness, the false teeth, the more and more restricted areas of life. She can no longer enjoy films.

I condemned my father once more for being vain and proud of qualities which are not humanly valuable. Why be proud of being a Spanish aristocrat, for example? At the same time I became aware of the irony of this situation, for I have been more identified with my father than with my mother because he was the *artist*, and my mother's human qualities (generosity, motherliness, devotion, sacrifice) seemed to me then to be a submission to the *condition humaine* rather than a re-creation of it. For every day I rile at the human condition, which means domestic life, chores, nursing the sick, marketing, mothering of others, and I have a secret inner religion of art, a wish to transcend the human, to be able to bear the human. I associated human with slavery, and the artist with the one who escapes slavery through *another life*. It happens that my father fits into this image of the artist: his music, his musical friends; music in the house was the only joy of my childhood. It was not the cold aristocrat I loved, but the aesthete who enhanced and transformed reality. "Your father," said my mother, "had such a power of illusion that I could never love anyone else, they all seemed so prosaic and plain and homely beside him."

My father, by deception, lies, inventions and a gift for illusion improved upon reality. It was my mother's acceptance and resignation to the human condition which I feared to espouse.

From taking care of my mother, I returned to caring for Reginald after his operation.

Then I realized the vital necessity of art. Human life, yes, you nurse people, you clean house, you market, but then comes the moment of solace and flight. I sit and write and summon other friends, other forms of life, other experiences, and the voyage and the exploration, the delving into character, the vast expanse of life's possibilities and potentialities, contemplation of future travels, of dazzling friendships, all this then makes the chores and the sacrifices beautiful because they are diverted toward some beautiful aim, they become part of the structure of a work of art.

The day I went to see Renate for the first time, her ex-husband had just been there and Renate was disturbed. I entered saying: "We will exorcise him," and a half hour later we were laughing. Renate has the most inventive of vocabularies, her insights are so vivid and dramatized, there is a tragicomic quality to all she tells. At the door, what I first noticed were her eyes, at times blue, at times green, very large, with a full round orb so that when she looks down the eyelids appear very rounded as they do in Da Vinci's *Saint Anne*. Her skin has a warm, almost ruddy color; it is highly sensitive to change; the aliveness quickens the blood and gives her a blushing tone, or else the circulation is arrested by emotion and she turns pale.

She laughs as she lives, openly and freely. Her anxiety propels her outward, into action, imagery, and fervor. Her emotional gyrations are full and complete, like a state of euphoria so natural it does not leave a hangover. At first I saw no descents, no lows, but soon I divined them. The price of flying over obstacles; and then collisions take place for which one is unprepared. She is illumined with high feeling and a capacity for empathy.

Renate can penetrate any experience or role without dissolution of her self. They are extensions, dilations, expansions, not dissolutions. She can play various roles with none disconnected from each other. She is as fluid as mercury, which can move in all directions and yet not be divided. She paints, she decorates, she sews, she builds her own house, she nurses, cooks, analyzes, and incites others to create. She is a fecundator. Her ebullient and imaginative energy is contagious. No part of Renate has died under experience, she nourishes on it, and converts it to gold or honey, as you wish.

Her house in Malibu is high on a hill, overlooking a wide expanse of sea.

Her walls are hung with paintings by Cameron. Curtis, Kenneth, and Paul talked of Cameron as capable of witchcraft. She was the dark spirit of the group. Her paintings were ghostly creatures of nightmares. In connection with her, this was the first time I heard about Aleister Crowley. There is an aura of evil around her. Her husband was a scientist who delved in the occult. He was blown up during an experiment in his garage.

Renate told me about her early love of animals. As a child she opened the cages of birds, of chickens in the marketplace, unleashed dogs. She felt affinities with them and abhorred domestication. This has become the major theme of her paintings, the coexistence of woman and animal.

Renate's gift is a heightened mood which communicates itself to others. She creates a state of natural intoxication.

Conversations become vertiginous; she gives wings of humor to all events, even the most tragic. One day her fireplace smoked and we were driven out of the house. It was raining. "I always dreamed of a picnic in the rain," she said.

One of her greatest preoccupations is not to be dominated by man. She approaches love warily, as some jungle animals approach a suspected trap. She has a horror of being counseled, advised, instructed by anyone. Her independence is fiercely defended. Her impulses, thoughts, opinions are spontaneous and always a surprise. Nothing seems to have patterned her, and she grows like a wild flower, in any color or form she pleases.

The only factor I can find which may have influenced her life is her love of her father and his words to her: "No man will love you as much as I do. Do not trust man, and above all, never depend on him. We share one soul."

Renate's story:
When she was five or six years old her father took her to a doctor who had invented a psychological test, the precursor of the Rorschach test. He put on a record and asked Renate where the music came from.

Renate meditated a moment, then pointed to her heart and said: "From here."

Another story. At sixteen she wanted to be an actress. Her father took her to a famous teacher, who was also a famous Don Juan and taught his pupils far more than the art of acting. Renate knew this, and knew specific instances of seduction. When he saw her he said brutally: "You can't be an actress. Your mouth is too small." At this Renate grew very angry and she began violently to accuse him of all his seductions of his pupils. He grew red and was about to burst out in self-defense when Renate stopped herself short, bowed, smiled, and said: "Wasn't that good acting?"

Paul. Angelic blue eyes, and a young boy's mouth. A little animal whose wish is to go around kissing everyone. But this nestling is homosexual. Renate suffers from his promiscuity. He does not protect her from the knowledge. He said: "A man must have cruelty."

Once when Paul Mathiesen had a fit of asthma he asked Renate to read to him from Lady Murasaki's *Tale of Genji*. Knowing the book, I could understand how it took his mind away from the present into a life of great beauty in the year nine hundred in Japan. The book itself by its symmetry, order, and stylized presentation of events created air and space to a degree unknown in the modern or Western novel. Every scene, every event is treated like a painting; it is a series of tableaux; even when the events are violent or treat of death or illness, there is something in the unity of tone, in the calm telling which gives a sense of harmony and peace. It must have been an extraordinary effort of art to contain the savagery of life in such a way that it appeared, to our eyes at least, to be controlled. It was in this strange isolation of the court, because the rest of the country was impenetrable, dangerous, filled with bandits and wandering predators, that they turned their energies to creating all the culture which we know of Japan, poetry, pottery, costume, the tea ceremony, painting, music, dance. I could well believe the *Tale of Genji* could be a cure for asthma, could make us forget that today we live openly in the jungle without such a secret haven of beauty to restore our battered selves.

Paul and Renate thought of a masquerade to which we would come dressed as our madness.

I wore a skin-colored leotard, leopard-fur earrings glued to the tips of my naked breasts, and a leopard-fur belt around my waist. Gil Henderson painted on my bare back a vivid jungle scene. I wore eyelashes two inches long. My hair was dusted with gold powder. My head was inside of a birdcage. From within the cage, through the open gate, I pulled out an endless roll of paper on which I had written lines from my books. The ticker tape of the unconscious. I unwound this and handed everyone a strip with a message.

When we arrived the entire house was softly lighted with candles.

Renate met us at the door. She was wearing a merry-widow hat, a waist cincher, and a black leotard. An iridescent scarf enveloped her. She carried two death masks on sticks. As she removed one mask, a second, identical mask was revealed. Her costume was inspired by José Guadalupe Posada's portrayal of voluptuous females with skulls for heads. Her madness was a conflict between sensuality and death. Her madness was: she *is* what she pretends to be.

Paul's madness was to escape his angel blondness. He died his hair black and wore a black mustache. He appeared half pirate, half Spanish Don Juan.

My escort was in a black leotard covered with plastic eyes. He carried two eyes on the tip of a wire projecting from his forehead. He had two eyes pinned on his genital region. He was all eyes, the spectator, the shy spectator.

As I entered I found the walls covered with sumac branches, which made the bare rooms look like a forest. On them Renate hung Mexican masks of people and animals. They hung like strange fruit, and at times, in the shadows, the masks and the people's painted faces were intertwined and could not be distinguished. Incense was burning and people seemed to issue from smoke and vanish into smoke and shadows.

Kenneth Anger was not there when we entered. He was waiting in the bedroom with a lighted candle and had asked Renate to let him know the propitious moment to make his entrance. Busy with guests, Renate forgot him. When she remembered, the candle was burnt halfway. But Kenneth Anger made his propitious entrance and everyone stood still to look at him as they had stood still when I came in.

He was dressed as Hecate, goddess of the moon, earth, and infernal regions, sorcery and witchcraft. Only one heavily made-up eye was visible. His long black fingernails were made of black quills. The rest was all a towering figure of lace, veils, beads, and feathers.

Curtis Harrington was the somnambulist from *The Cabinet of Doctor Caligari*. He walked with his hands in front of him as if he had been hypnotized, and, slim as he was, looked the part. His madness was to be caught in an archetypal figure.

Samson de Brier's madness was identification with an Eastern potentate. He was absolutely covered with jewels, and his fine dark Oriental eyes suited his fantasy.

John Reed divided his body into two colors, white and black. Even his face was half white and half black. The madness of duality.

Three persons I did not know stayed together all evening, sharing in one madness. One of them lay on a stretcher and was carried about.

Kate Kadell came as Cleopatra, and she looked the part with her straight nose and slanted eyes. She was a gay Cleopatra, mischievous and witty.

One woman held an open umbrella over her head, over which fell layers and layers of veils, scarves, jewels, like a waterfall. Her madness was the need of a secret hiding place, her need of security.

Renate was dancing with Kenneth Anger. She stopped suddenly, out of breath, and said: "It is so tiring to dance with one's madness."

At this I said: "You talk just like the women in my novels, and people still insist such talk does not exist."

Happy because *The Four-Chambered Heart* was sold to a Swedish publisher.

Talk with Geismars about problems of publishing the diary. Aside from the human problem of those who have to be protected, there is also the problem that the diary is not finished. The condition of its continuation is secrecy. Exposure will kill the diary itself just as the exposure of a spy will put an end to his activity. My identity cannot be exposed or the diary ends. The public eye and spotlight will kill it.

I discussed with Dr. Bogner the increase in my courage to be myself, rather than disguise myself into what others needed and wanted of me. The dilemma of opening the diary is a part of this need.

An old friend said: "You have changed so much that for years I felt I did not know you, I felt I was not related to you."

But that is because he refuses to make friends with the Anaïs of today. He still thinks of me as the Anaïs he first knew.

At the Fourteenth Street Spanish shop I buy guava paste and a mantilla for my mother's birthday.

Relationship with Jim Herlihy endangered because I cannot love his play *Moon in Capricorn* and he needs my total admiration. The slightest hint of unacceptance disturbed him deeply. The dialogue ceased to be sincere.

During several trips to Venice, Ian Hugo again filmed everything which moved him, without any preconceived plan, and when he edited it he achieved an image of Venice never attained before, as it included the past, the present, the fantasy and the reality of Venice, in layers suggesting infinite dimensions.

We are living in the age of the image but this means not only that we can register more perfectly with cameras the external image, but that we can now also penetrate and photograph our inner life as if with an undersea camera. Our unconscious life is composed of free associations of ideas, fragments of memories, musical flow of impressions, or symbolic scenes. In our dreams and in our fantasies we are all surrealists, impressionists, abstractionists, symbolists. The camera more exactly than words is capable of reflecting this inner life and revealing the metamorphosis which takes place between a realistic scene and the way our moods color, distort, or alter the scene as through a prism.

The freedom of improvisation expressed in Ian Hugo's films corresponds to our emotional life, which is continuously projecting and retaining on our inner screen previous images. A face we are looking at will suddenly recall another face out of the past by way of a slight resemblance, and the image from the past will blur and interfere with the present face. As James Joyce tried to capture the form of our inner monologues which accompany but do not match the flow of our talk, Ian Hugo emphasizes the simultaneous levels of experience: a mixture of dreams, memories, and immediate impressions. He also seeks to capture how our thoughts jump from scene to scene in an *apparently* unrelated way, to better match the structure of our emotional life, which is fluid, symphonic, and composed on several levels at once. In this way these films do not represent merely the personal vision of Ian Hugo, his impressions of Mexico or Venice, but a way of seeing and remembering common to all of us if we caught our first flow of impressions before organizing them into an artificial chronology and pattern. A conventional rational sequence does not necessarily correspond to the way we feel or remember a journey or the events of our life. And if these dark and wayward realms of the heart seem dark and confused at times, it is only because we have not yet thrown enough light upon them. For example, we do not remember journeys or the events of our lives in chronological order, but as in the film *Ai-Ye,* the death of a man evokes the memory of a dead tree, and the dead tree evokes the image of a dead dog, until, as in a musical composition, the theme of death is completed. Placing images in this order, the order of feelings, brings out their inner meaning. Thousands of tourists have photographed the Mexican boys diving from high rocks into the sea, until that image becomes trite and dies. But when Ian Hugo places it as a recurrent motif it acquires a symbolic meaning and reminds us of our repeated plunges into the mysterious depths of our own selves as well as into the sea, the origin of life. By following such improvisations, assembling images according to the design of our emotions, we also enter this region below consciousness where experience actually takes place directly as music does, without interference from artificial cerebral patterns.

Becoming more and more aware of this inner unconscious life we need a corresponding change in our art forms. The realization that fantasy and memory are not separate activities but the basic key to our secret life demands a change of focus, a freedom from old molds, a technique to encompass new dimensions of character and insight.

The music, too, has to extend beyond familiar sounds and free itself of past structures, has to seek sounds which match our contemporary moods and sensations.

The experience of Venice was captured by layered sequences of images, superimpositions, which combined memories of Venice's past with personal dreams of Venice, and the constant presence of today's Venice in all its moods, working, cleaning, laundering, daily, homely Venice. Over all this the poetic, mythological tragedy of Venice as the bride of the sea (a ritual performed at the beginning of its history was the throwing of a wedding ring into the sea) and this sea perpetually striving to drag Venice back into its depths.

[December, 1953]

Kenneth Anger felt that the masquerade "Come as Your Madness" resembled a dream he had, which he had painted and which hung in Samson de Brier's studio. He decided to make a film of it [*Inauguration of the Pleasure Dome*]. We were to come in the costumes we wore. He said to me: "I want you as Astarte, the goddess of light. You are a magic person. I want to capture that luminosity which startled everyone at the party. It is an inner light and so difficult to capture."

We filmed in Samson's apartment from seven o'clock to one o'clock in the morning.

Part of one room was painted, gold ceiling, black walls; another room was made to look like a cave, all gold and red, with beaded, iridescent curtains. There was a backdrop painted to represent a Venetian scene. Most of the colors were intensified and created by the use of gels. Under the floodlights, Paul looked like a blond Nordic god.

Samson's apartment was ideal for the film, for he had trunks filled with costumes, textiles, costume jewelry, fans, lace, old photographs, gloves, scarves, veils, feathers.

Kenneth was working in the same way as Maya Deren; he wanted to capture elusive aspects of our personalities, undirected, spontaneous, accidental. Renate stood in front of the backdrop with her large hat, looking very beautiful, laughing, laughing as only she can, so fully and unrestrainedly, abandoned and total.

Peter as a little prince, shy, daydreaming, as if he were walking through a fairy tale. Peter, the gentle, dreaming boy, like a child from another planet. I thought of him as Saint-Exupéry's Little Prince. He has beautiful, liquid-blue eyes, a wistful face, and a manner so remote that he seems to be sleepwalking.

Cameron, with a frightening mask of dead-white, chalky face and ink-black eyebrows and eyelashes, looked as if risen from the dead. A large voracious mouth and narrow slanted eyes. She is surrounded by an evil aura, which fascinates Paul, Curtis, and Kenneth.

We worked all through a weekend. We all felt we needed to know the meaning of Kenneth's dream, so that we could act in it.

But he did not confide in us. The scenes seemed disconnected, and the characters changed costumes and personalities. There was chaos because the theme was unknown. I stepped into the room through a window. Paul had wrapped me in yards and yards of blue muslin as in a cocoon. My head was in the birdcage I wore at the masquerade. My lace-stockinged foot slowly descended on a fur bench which seemed to bristle at the touch. The contact with the fur was sensual, the fur seemed to raise its hairs to encounter the foot.

Paul said: "In the film Samson is the false man, the man of many faces, that is why he changes costumes and make-up all the time. The various women, Renate as sensuous romantic love, Joan as the virgin beauty, Cameron as the satanic woman, and you as the woman of light, all offer him gifts which he rejects. Curtis brings him the wine of ecstasy from the caves of the unconscious. They all drink and are transformed. You, Anaïs, refuse the drink. You have no need of it. You are Astarte, goddess of the moon. I, the romantic lover, reach in vain for the unreachable moon."

Cameron sat on a thronelike chair and took out a lifeless breast.

There was a cave, weblike, labyrinthian, in which I danced, in the light of red gels. Samson ate pearls, Paul drank from a goblet, Kate acted a Cleopatra gone mad.

Beads fell off one of the flapper costumes. We were cutting our bare feet on them. I picked up a broom to sweep them and Kenneth would not let me.

"You are Astarte," he said.

At first Astarte was illuminated in the film, shed her light, but Cameron became a stronger figure as evil, a hypnotic figure, and the mood of decadence and destruction won out. Renate, with her Austrian beauty, very much like Luise Rainer but more voluptuous, represented the joy of sensuality. I, the ecstasies of the dream. Paul struggled out of the grasp of orgiastic women to reach for Astarte.

Renate had made Samson up to look like the Great Beast. His mouth was made invisible by paint and another mouth appeared on his chin. A duplicate mask was designed on his chest. His nails were a foot long, made of lacquered cardboard. He shook them in people's faces and the threatening gesture frightened everyone. He frightened himself too. As a degenerate potentate greedily swallowing all his jewels he was the best actor among us.

Curtis Harrington was serving the drink which created ecstasy.

Kenneth Anger asked Peter to dip his finger in the goblet, touch his tongue with it, and fall into a deep trance.

Renate suddenly felt she did not want to see her child poisoned. She rebelled against this scene. For her it was not a symbolic act but a real danger. Kenneth argued that it was symbolic and that he was merely asleep. Renate was deeply disturbed and no one could convince her that she was confusing symbolism and reality.

After a long battle, she surrendered. The scene was filmed. To see Cameron sitting with one breast uncovered and Peter tasting the elixir was to feel a chill of fear that her witch's milk might be the source of the goblet's content.

Renate's interpretation of Kenneth's film was that it was an extension of the masquerade. It was a portrayal of people's madness. The reality and the madness mingled and that made chaos and confusion. The links were missing, as in madness.

There was a distortion. Love became hatred, ecstasy became a nightmare. Those who began with a sensual attraction ended by devouring each other. The elixir, which Kenneth said came from the unconscious, Renate saw as coming from infernal regions, whipping the madness to dizzying heights from which it would collapse. The whole feeling was out of balance.

I am making my peace with the earth.

What new loveliness is there in Molly carrying a bottle of milk which is half of her own size and knocking gently on my door for me to make her a chocolate drink. And how she sits under my arm to show me a bruise on her incredibly small elbow. The mother, I love too. She is sensitive, humorous, and thoughtful.

Loneliness increases as you ascend into a rarefied atmosphere. I am now able to live in both worlds, the human and the imaginative.

When it is too cold, I go to Sears Roebuck at Pasadena, to the tropical-birds department. They keep the place very warm; it is full of bird chatter and tropical plants and flowers. It reminds me of Mexico.

Renate and Paul invented another masquerade. This one was to be "A Thousand and One Nights."

It was a story-telling party, gentle and soft.

I came as Scheherazade and told stories. I wore a nylon

iridescent dress that seemed like water, and, as a headdress, a Christmas-tree ornament that looked like a fan, from which the waterlike, floating, transparent texture fell like a waterfall.

Samson dressed as a Persian potentate and read from the *Kama Sutra*.

Peter was dressed as a Persian prince from miniatures. He wore a turban with an ostrich plume, blue trousers, and boots. He wrote a special story for the evening.

Renate was a Persian princess and acted out the drowned women of the Sultan's harem whom he had thrown into the Bosphorus. It was from the story told by Lesley Blanch in *The Wilder Shores of Love*. Two hundred women he had grown tired of were tied together and pushed into the river, but the bodies did not disintegrate, and years later a diver found them standing, with their long hair undulating in the current.

Paul was a grown-up prince.

Rudi Gernreich and Galianos came in business suits. We were disappointed, because Galianos was a famous designer, and Rudi was already known as the first West Coast designer.

Renate and Paul designed a lantern of black paper with geometric cutouts, inset with many colored gels. They twisted the cord which held it to the ceiling, and as it untwisted it rotated and threw flickering colored lights on the walls and on us.

For the Roman masquerade party Renate and Paul set a huge center banquet table covered with geraniums, with pillows on the floor. There were candles, incense, and flowers and tin plates from Mexico. Each guest brought a Roman dish. We were expected to have read Pliny, the Roman naturalist of the year 23 B.C., and Pliny the Younger, who was a Latin author and orator.

Renate and Paul gave up all activities for survival and devoted three weeks to the preparation of the party. Paul painted a Roman mural of a belvedere. Renate baked a huge loaf of bread in the form of a phallus, stuffed with sausages and eggs. Many of the dishes were decorated with flower petals. Someone else brought dishes of jello containing insects.

I brought wine and said it was an aphrodisiac. Renate believed me and was afraid to drink it, fearing her passions would get out of control. We reclined on the pillows like real Romans while Paul lectured as if he were Pliny and demonstrated posters we had made of Pliny's anatomical theories. The lecture was a mixture of fantasy and fact. One was that brave men's hearts were covered with hair.

Because I came to the first masquerade with bare breasts, Joanne Carson said then: "I wish I had thought of that." So she came to this party bare-breasted and we all admired her gorgeous breasts.

I wore a pleated-nylon nightgown shaped like a Roman robe. Sprayed gold on my hair and dressed it in Roman style.

My handsome escort was dressed as a Roman soldier and the two of us took poses of Roman friezes against a white wall.

Someone else read about Heliogabalus, describing one of the parties he gave at which the ceiling opened and tons of flowers were poured over the guests. Four hundred persons suffocated.

Raimunda, a descendant of the Orsinis, brought ricotta and said it was made of the milk of the mythical wolf who nursed Romulus and Remus. I refused to eat it.

Samson de Brier, Curtis Harrington, Joanne, and Renate acted a mock orgy.

Each time the orgy seemed about to become too real, jealousies would flare up.

Raimunda played the guitar and sang Roman songs.

With Renate's childhood obsession with animals, and her desire to free them, it was natural that she should devote her painting to portraying the friendship between woman and animal. She paints a luminous woman lying peacefully beside a panther; a woman with blue-tinted flesh floating on the opening wings of a swan, a woman and a turtle, a beautiful naked woman reflected in a mirror and watched by a raven. She paints a woman feeding a flower to a goat, a woman on a beach watching a beautiful fantail pigeon with his wings spred; he is larger than she is.

It is the mythology of woman in relation to animals, wild or domestic.

All of them are figures from dreams. They are interwoven with nature, as the woman wrapped in a cloud by the seashore, this cloud covering three older women (duennas, ladies-in-waiting, mothers?) , and the tip of the cloud sweeps the sky to touch a face reigning there.

The landscapes are lunar, or from other planets. In one a hand appears, alone, a death's head, a lake above the clouds.

The sun is a fiery figure with a sword who does not destroy the woman consumed by light.

One of my favorites is the actress. Her chest is a cagelike stage, in which three faceless figures appear in roles waiting to be performed.

I appear as Pisces, enwrapped from shoulders to feet by bands of paper with quotes from my work written on them, the ticker tape of the unconscious which I designed for the masquerade. I am surrounded by a collage of my book covers, and by Pisces fish swimming around me.

Renate's motorcyclist does not stay on the road, he drives with the hounds of heaven. Her women do not sit on the edge of the sea, they are born of it and take their skin colors from the shells.

[Winter, 1953-1954]

A man rushed in to announce he had seen smoke on Monrovia Peak. As I looked out of the window I saw the two mountains facing the house on fire. The entire rim burning wildly in the night. The flames, driven by hot Santa Ana winds from the desert, were as tall as the tallest trees, the sky already tinted coral, and the crackling noise of burning trees, the ashes and the smoke were already increasing. The fire raced along, sometimes descending behind the mountain where I could only see the glow, sometimes descending toward us. I thought of the foresters in danger. I made coffee for the weary men who came down occasionally with horses they had led out, or with old people from the isolated cabins. They were covered with soot from their battle with the flames.

At six o'clock the fire was on our left side and rushing toward Mount Wilson. Evacuees from the cabins began to arrive and had to be given blankets and hot coffee. The streets were blocked with fire engines readying to fight the fire if it touched the houses. Policemen and firemen and guards turned away the sightseers. Some were relatives concerned over the fate of the foresters, or the pack station family. The policemen lighted flares, which gave the scene a theatrical, tragic air. The red lights on the police cars twinkled alarmingly. More fire engines arrived. Ashes fell, and the roar of the fire was now like thunder.

We were told to ready ourselves for evacuation. I packed the diaries. The saddest spectacle, beside that of the men fighting the fire as they would a war, were the animals, rabbits, coyotes, mountain lions, deer, driven by the fire to the edge of the mountain, taking a look at the crowd of people and panicking, choosing rather to rush back into the fire.

The fire now was like a ring around Sierra Madre, every mountain was burning. People living at the foot of the mountain were packing their cars. I rushed next door to the Campion children, who had been left with a baby-sitter, and got them into the car. It was impossible to save all the horses. We parked the car on the field below us. I called up the Campions, who were out for the evening, and reassured them. The baby-sitter dressed the children warmly. I made more coffee. I answered frantic telephone calls.

All night the fire engines sprayed water over the houses. But the fire grew immense, angry, and rushing at a speed I could not believe. It would rush along, and suddenly leap over a road, a trail, like a monster, devouring all in its path. The firefighters cut breaks in the heavy brush, but when the wind was strong enough, the fire leaped across them. At dawn one arm of the fire reached the back of our houses but was finally contained.

But high above and all around, the fire was burning, more vivid than the sun, throwing spirals of smoke in the air like the smoke from a volcano. Thirty-three cabins burned, and twelve thousand acres of forest still burning endangered countless homes below the fire. The fire was burning to the back of us now, and a rain of ashes began to fall and continued for days. The smell of the burn in the air, acid and pungent and tenacious. The dragon tongues of flames devouring, the flames leaping, the roar of destruction and dissolution, the eyes of the panicked animals, caught between fire and human beings, between two forms of death. They chose the fire. It was as if the fire had come from the bowels of the earth, like that of a fiery volcano, it was so powerful, so swift, and so ravaging. I saw trees become skeletons in one minute, I saw trees fall, I saw bushes turned to ashes in a second, I saw weary, ash-covered men, looking like men returned from war, some with burns, others overcome by smoke.

The men were rushing from one spot to another watching for recrudescence. Some started backfiring up the mountain so that the ascending flames could counteract the descending ones.

As the flames reached the cities below, hundreds of roofs burst into flame at once. There was no water pressure because all the fire hydrants were turned on at the same time, and the fire departments were helpless to save more than a few of the burning homes.

Because all the men were away fighting the fire, I was asked to help answer the phone at the Ranger Station. I became annoyed at callers laughing at my French accent and started answering, "Foreest Serveece—Paris branch." A woman with a very thick French accent called to ask, "Eeze zis zee place to geeve clothes for Zee Zuni Indians?" (By this time many different Indian tribes had been brought in from Arizona and New Mexico to fight the fire). I answered in my best Parisian French, "You had better speak French as I cannot understand your English."

The blaring loudspeakers of passing police cars warned us to prepare to evacuate in case the wind changed and drove the fire in our direction. What did I wish to save? I thought only of the diaries. I appeared on the porch carrying a huge stack of diary volumes, preparing to pack them in the car. A reporter for the Pasadena *Star News* was taking pictures of the evacuation. He came up, very annoyed with me. "Hey, lady, next time could you bring out something more important than all those old papers? Carry some clothes on the next trip. We gotta have human interest in these pictures!"

A week later, the danger was over.

Gray ashy days.

In Sierra Madre, following the fire, the January rains brought floods. People are sandbagging their homes. At four A.M. the streets are covered with mud. The bare, burnt, naked mountains cannot hold the rains and slide down bringing rocks and mud. One of the rangers must now take photographs and movies of the disaster. He asks if I will help by holding an umbrella over the cameras. I put on my raincoat and he lends me hip boots which look to me like seven-league boots.

We drive a little way up the road. At the third curve it is impassable. A river is rushing across the road. The ranger takes pictures while I hold the umbrella over the camera. It is terrifying to see the muddied waters and rocks, the mountain disintegrating. When we are ready to return, the road before us is covered by large rocks but the ranger pushes on as if the truck were a jeep and forces it through. The edge of the road is being carried away.

I am laughing and scared too. The ranger is at ease in nature, and without fear. It is a wild moment of danger. It is easy to love nature in its peaceful and consoling moments, but one must love it in its furies too, in its despairs and wildness, especially when the damage is caused by us.

[February, 1954]

New York.

The plane landed in a snowstorm. It was six A.M. I wore no rubbers. I shared a taxi with several passengers; it was unheated and had a difficult time getting through the snow. All night I had felt such pains in my chest that I thought I would die. I was surprised to find myself alive in the morning. In the cold taxi I felt so weak I thought this was truly the end. I took a hot bath to warm myself. In the bath my sense of illness and weakness overwhelmed me. I wept. I went to bed. I got up at eleven to see Dr. Bogner. We arranged for a medical checkup the next morning. No heart trouble, no tuberculosis or cancer, just a low functioning of the thyroid. I was given pills. The pains continued for a few days but the anxiety disappeared. Once more I was repaired by doctors.

With analysis there is the pain of breaking through, of pushing out. It is a rebirth. Only it has to be done by one's self, not the mother. All the efforts come from one's own self. And there is the same shock of light, cold, when you thrust out too far into the world, take too many risks.

Party for Cornelia Runyon. As she is sixty-eight and belongs to one of the best and oldest families of New York, her friends and relatives appeared as if they walked out of a Henry James novel. I saw for the first time the Village's oldest inhabitants, who built the graceful, solid, small houses, sat under crystal chandeliers, and possessed courtesy and wit. A good vintage, a mellow wood, a mostly vanished civilization. The qualities disappeared as the old houses on Washington Square crumbled and deteriorated in the hands of fake bohemians, who painted the beautiful natural wood with slick, garish paint, who painted over the marble fireplaces, who let the backyard gardens dry up. The Stuart Montgomerys, who founded the Seamen's Bank, the Danas, the Alexander Bings, the Lewins, the Whitmans, the Hoffmans. They all owned the houses that now encircle the square. Great polish, mellowness, and grace.

The better artists scraped away the layers of paint, rediscovered the pure wood and the original fireplaces.

Santha Rama Rau came in her purple sari, saying she had shaken and trembled over the film *Bells of Atlantis:* "I re-experienced the birth of my child, even to the sounds I heard under anaesthetic."

Her husband, Faubion Bowers, writes beautiful books on the dance.

Suddenly I was in a mature world again, and its charm rediscovered. I was weary of children and their vulnerabilities, the fevers of adolescence.

I would have liked to know the real drama behind Mr. X, who "accidentally" fell from the fifteenth floor of the Gotham Hotel.

I no longer see people as the classified façade they wear: this one is a banker, this one a director of the opera. I see a human being who might have been anything else, one of Simenon's characters, with fears, doubts, regressions, defeats, sorrows.

It is difficult to live with the pure. They do not condemn you; they forgive you. This forgiveness is more terrible than a judgment. The lapses from purity seem then like a crime against one's child or innocent self. Against one's own soul. And then one has the terror of being struck down with death, or old age, for in maintaining the soul's clear vision lies youth. Age is astigmatism, near-sightedness, a cataract of vision, born of impurities.

Met two remarkable taxi drivers. One a very slender, youthful but gray-haired man who said: "I am very thankful to have a passenger who adorns my new cab."

Surprised by his language, I made him talk. He was captain of a ship during the war, but his career meant separation from his wife and he preferred happiness and freedom. He intended to own a fleet of taxis and at the age of sixty to retire and write a book about his life and the people he met.

I suggested he start writing his book now, as he worked. I said we must fulfill ourselves in the present and that he would be happier in his taxi-driving work if he also accomplished his literary ambition. I complimented him on his literary language.

The other was a magnificent old man of eighty-two, with a weathered red face, fat and jolly. He told me that he drove a taxi in the winter and a horse and carriage in the summer. He was one of the oldest of the Central Park carriage drivers. He had adapted to modern life. But he was happiest in summer: "I miss the smell of the trees, of the grass and of my horse."

At the Public Library at Forty-second Street I saw the room of manuscripts. It looked like a jail cell. It was locked, and not only locked but it had a heavy iron-grille door like that of a prison. It was more terrible to me, this burying of manuscripts, than the burial of a body in the earth. Perhaps because I have been tormented by the ethical conflict of the diary. Should I destroy it for the sake of human beings it might wound, or keep it because it has value for human beings. I received my life from books. So I would be killing a life-giving creation, to save a few from the truth. But who saved me from the truth? No one ever spared me that. The world needs the truth. No matter how painful. Because when people bury the truth it festers. The grilled, locked room of the Public Library is also the tomb in which we lock the dangerous truths.

I cannot imagine my diaries there. Read in gloom and darkness, not in the sun and by the sea.

Letter to a writer who asked: "Why does one write?"

Why one writes is a question I can answer easily, having so often asked it of myself. I believe one writes because one has to create a world in which one can live. I could not live in any of the worlds offered to me: the world of my parents, the world of Henry Miller, the world of Gonzalo, or the world of wars. I had to create a world of my own, like a climate, a country, an atmosphere in which I could breathe, reign, and re-create myself when destroyed by living. That, I believe, is the reason for every work of art. The artist is the only one who knows the world is a subjective creation, that there is a choice to be made, a selection of elements. It is a materialization, an incarnation of his inner world. Then he hopes to attract others into it, he hopes to impose this particular vision and share it with others. When the second stage is not reached, the brave artist continues nevertheless. The few moments of communion with the world are worth the pain, for it is a world for others, an inheritance for others, a gift to others, in the end. When you make a world tolerable for yourself you make a world tolerable for others.

We also write to heighten our own awareness of life, we write to lure and enchant and console others, we write to serenade our lovers. We write to taste life twice, in the moment, and in retrospection. We write, like Proust, to render all of it eternal, and to persuade ourselves that it is eternal. We write to be able to transcend our life, to reach beyond it. We write to teach ourselves to speak with others, to record the journey into the labyrinth, we write to expand our world, when we feel strangled, constricted, lonely. We write as the birds sing. As the primitive dance their rituals. If you do not breathe through writing, if you do not cry out in writing, or sing in writing, then don't write. Because our culture has no use for any of that. When I don't write I feel my world shrinking, I feel I am in a prison. I feel I lose my fire, my color. It should be a necessity, as the sea needs to heave. I call it breathing.

I enjoy breakfast, the morning light on a church steeple, or on a modern building which looks Grecian against the sky.

I arrived in New York in a black coat and black dress. I left in a white coat and white dress.

[Spring, 1954]

Spent twenty days in Acapulco.

Never has a period of my life seemed more like a dream, a dream in which I wept with joy. Acapulco is the place where my body and spirit are at peace. Everything contributes to its dreamlike atmosphere.

The drive from Mexico City on Sunday. Cuernavaca was festive, it was overflowing with visitors, the cafés were crowded and animated. The Mexicans, when not at work, dress as for a fiesta. There is always a fiesta, always something to celebrate, a saint or a revolution. Ribbons, red and yellow, in the black hair. Starched white dresses, red, green, yellow, purple, or light-blue ones. The little girls with short black hair and bangs wear butterfly bows of satin in bright colors, the same butterfly bow that as a child in Cuba I was so eager to have tied so it would stand like a butterfly about to take off.

A heavy rainfall came suddenly and drenched us, and everybody scattered, laughing at the rain.

The drive to Acapulco is harsh and difficult. The new road is not yet ready and the old one torn up. We drove over rocks, through clouds of dust, through dry riverbeds, new tar and gravel. In spite of this the sight of Acapulco around the bend of the road, from the top of the mountain, is like a mirage long desired. No place in the world where the mountains, rocks are so awesome, the vegetation so abundant and fecund, the air so soft and caressing, the people so human and natural. No need of painters to paint a world, no need but of eyes to see. The dresses of the women blend in colors with the flowers and the fruit. Their dark hair is adorned with ribbons and colored wool. Their hair is glossy, their teeth dazzling.

After the heat and thirst and weariness, Acapulco in the sunset seems like a balm; it enters the blood like a drug after one inhalation of the scent of flowers, one glimpse of the bay iridescent like silk, the sunset like the inside of a shell, so much like the flesh of Venus. The coconut palm with its naked elegance which makes other trees seem fussy like a woman with over-curly hair, gossipy and chattery. The palm with its stylized body, lean and pliant, nude, throwing all its adornment into one luxuriant head of hair of plunging feathers and plumes which sweep the sky gently.

The poets of India were always comparing palm trees and women. A child can draw a palm tree easily, a sensuous feather duster ever dusting a tropical sky of clouds and mists and keeping it brilliant day and night.

At the hotel we ask for ice and remember that impatience is a major *faux pas* in Mexico, a breach of taste, a futile gesture too, which is inevitably frustrated by the Mexican, just as tyranny is resisted by other races. It awakens the most solid resistance. It is the major sin against timelessness. How dare we enslave men and women to clock time, to seconds, minutes, hours, when they have succeeded in eluding time, in living in the moment at a natural rhythm.

I learned this from an old photographer on the beach. There are several very old men carrying old-fashioned cameras covered by a black cloth. They take a photograph which they develop on the spot. This particular old man was very beautiful. The wrinkles had not changed the lean shape of his head and his smile was as open as an adolescent's. The friends we wanted to group together took a long time to gather themselves in one spot. I was pressing them for the old man's sake. As he watched me shepherding them, saying: "The old man is waiting," he said to me with a full smile: *"No se apure, no se apure. Hay mas tiempo que vida."* There is more time than life. There is time. Time and timelessness.

Our days are spent at the beach, swimming, and our evenings, dancing.

Awakening is slow, breakfast is slow, the beach is slow to awaken.

From swimming to eating to dancing. *La Ronde, la ronde* of Max Ophul's film, a series of love affairs circling, interweaving, cycles without a break. *La ronde* of body rhythms. Wild waves at Revolcadero. Wind which makes you feel like a sail, or a bird. You forget your feet. Suntanning. The sea is warm like a womb. How soft the night, and music is the net which catches all the acrobatics of love, of dreaming, idleness, pleasure, so we are never allowed to drop to the ground.

The gentleness of the Mexican voices dissolve one with trust: gentleness exists. From the songs I am carried by aerial musical notation to a harp being played while we eat on the square, to the marimbas, to the jukeboxes filled with Cuban mambos, to a street singer, to a night-club singer, and always to the sea, a sound of being washed, or being lulled while never more alive, drugged, yet never more alive, alive with the body only, warmth, sea, sun, all interwoven by the breathing of the sea linking dancers, swimmers in a rotation so sweet that I sit and weep with joy.

One night club is an African bamboo and palm-leaf hut on the beach. The tides wash your feet as you dance, the ancient Ondinean theme upon which mambos and American jazz play their accelerations of the pulse, in the same quickening of desire and completion which love-making practices upon our bodies.

Another night, at another hut high above the bay. The spotlight from the night club lights up a leafless jacaranda looming like a giant Japanese design against the dark purple mountain. The necklace of lights around the bay has a texture of velvet tonight. I weep with joy again, not only at the still, serene beauty but at the soft, tender breath of the tropical night so rich in tones, perfumes, and textures that it seems to caress you physically, to whisper to the cells of the body to match this voluptuous existence.

The way the waters of the bay lie, like a capricious bolt of silk unraveling its sinuous reflectiveness to light, sometimes reflecting, sometimes elusive, at times ruffled and contradictory, opposing green to the mountain's heavy violets, asserting turquoise obstinately against an overly orange sunset, or like tonight, asleep, having enfolded in itself all the colors of the day in the ineffable colors of sleep no painter can ever reproduce. My body photographed this night for the days of deprivation.

The first time I wept I thought: only the Latins and the Negroes are right. Happiness is in the physical life, and sorrow in thought. At least I can say I have possessed all physical life. But I wish I could devote myself to it, live only for it.

I envy the Mexican babies carried within a wide scarf around the mother's body. When I look into Mexican eyes I wish I had been born here, in the warmth and emotional richness of their nature, with feeling at the core.

That is why I wept. Because my hunger for this had been so often unsatisfied. And now the fullness of the gift melted me. This was my home, the home of beauty and feeling.

Los Angeles. A night at Zardi's to hear Shorty Rogers' Band. We are sitting at a table right beside the band, where we are drenched in the jazz that sparks from the trombone, the clarinet, trumpet, piano, bass, and drums. The subtle, the incredibly developed variations of these accomplished and dexterous players. The increasingly accelerated rhythm of the blood, the mounting ecstasy. I felt that next to the wild moment of passion, I loved this jazz, and then the sea, and then more music.

Jazz is the music of the body. I wish I could give back to the jazz musicians the joys they have given me. I feel jazz in my blood, in my nerves, in my flesh. I receive the drumming right on my body. I didn't say all this well enough in *Spy in the House of Love*. I have so much more to say. I can't catch up with all I know. I hope I will be given time. Sometimes when I think of death, I think merely that it would be too bad, for I have not yet yielded up all the treasures I have collected. The chemistry I am producing of turning experience into awareness is not yet finished.

The contrast this evening, sitting in the large hall of Cal Tech, listening to a Brahms quartet, the spiritual continuity, the eternal quality, the deeper layers of the soul and feeling. The jazz musicians are the Dionysian people, seeking fire and impulse and ecstasy from drugs. There is such a subtle way of metamorphosing one's life. Art is the method of levitation, in order to separate one's self from enslavement by the earth. The earth demands servitude from us, menial tasks, earthy tasks, every day, every hour, and only at this moment at which we discard the servitude and enter the world of the spirit through music or painting or writing are we free. It is the only genuine freedom. Once acquired it is deep and permanent.

In every book I have written I was faced with the painful conflict of protecting someone. How can I tell all without damage, betrayals, murders?

In jazz there are the volcanic explosions of the drums, the wails, the moans, the sensual vibrations, and above all, in bebop, the curious mystery of the withheld theme, known only to the jazz musician but kept a secret and then given to us in the variations, free associations, the peripheral explorations and improvisations.

This is so close to my own destiny. I too withhold the theme (diary) and play all the music permitted me to play outside of that.

For the novel with Mexican background I have created a character named Lillian Bey. She is the daughter of an American who lived and worked in Mexico. She was born in Mexico and was influenced by its warmth and expressiveness. Then at sixteen her father was sent back to the United States and she had to adapt to life in America. She was an excellent musician but hated concertizing in a formal way and gradually drifted into night-club playing. Her engagements kept her traveling.

When I start the book she feels estranged from her husband and children, restless, and wants to be alone for a while to understand what is happening to her and whether this is a permanent estrangement.

She is caught between nature (and her nature) and the city, between life of the body and synthetic life, between nature and the distillations of art. Were the swamp, the lagoon, the jungle of Mexico less than Max Ernst's swamps, lagoons, jungles? Was the desert less than Yves Tanguy's deserts and its ruins less beautiful than Chirico's roofless and solitary columns?

So much to tell. Lillian leaves her husband, finds him again and relives the beginning of her marriage and her errors.

Lillian deserts her husband and children, but finds extensions of them in her voyage because our actions are not always in harmony with our psychic inner life, and in the sincerity of her quest for self and for others, she rediscovers her husband, the key to his behavior and the key to the reunion. I gave her some of my experiences in Mexico, but she, because of her pattern, interpreted them differently and learned different lessons from them.

The dirt floor in the huts, the crib hammocks hanging from the ceiling, and, as in Oriental homes, the minimum of possessions, one trunk of goods, one set of clothes, one shawl—this reduction appeared to Lillian a great simplification by poverty.

Discovery of her inability to be alone. First of all a feeling of desertion when people did not invite her, even when they were people she did not want to be with. Worse even when she forced herself and went out with a man who owned a stockyard in Chicago. She called him Mr. Spam.

I am writing about Lillian in Mexico while the musicians are playing chamber music. They are scientists from Cal Tech. The open cello case stands in the corner and looks like one of Henry Moore's sculptures.

I pursue my adventures in Mexico, and Lillian's adventures. When Paul Mathiesen came, he seemed too mystical, and Lillian feared he would destroy her carefree sensual mood. He was to her the pale dreamer, ill at ease in frivolity. She eluded him as she was eluding her own interior life, fearing he would guide her inward again and she wanted only the sun, the sea, and forgetfulness.

Dios ganas. Gonzalo used to explain that the word *ganas* meant "I feel like it, or I do not feel like it." The Peruvians ruled their lives by *Dios ganas.* And the Mexicans too. It was a fully justified attitude: you either felt like it or did not feel like it. No one questions the integrity of such decisions.

[May, 1954]

New York.

In Acapulco I did not remember. But the serpent which lay coiled awaiting the moment to inject his poison was patient. I knew its name. It was the need to write, the need to be a writer, the curse of it, the unrequited gift to the world. I knew what awaited me: the enormous, stark, harsh failure. The party at the British Book Center for *Spy in the House of Love* to which none of the invited critics came. The puritanical, tight-lipped reviews.

America tried to kill me as a writer, with indifference, with insults. I can name the offenders. But they cannot kill the life and beauty of my writing, of my life, they can only strangle the books. Even Maxwell Geismar with his lukewarm words. And then the irony of his words over the telephone: "The book is so alive, so alive."

I answered: "Why didn't you say that in your review?"

"You have to remember who you are writing for."

The review of *Spy in the House of Love* [in *The Nation*] by Maxwell Geismar:

TEMPERAMENT VS. CONSCIENCE

Anaïs Nin is as well known to literary circles here and abroad as she has been little known to the general reading public. Her unpublished diary is something of a legend, and the present book is the best of her series of novels published in this country. The craft moves directly toward the area of psychological realism; the prose is a pleasure to read. This is, in short, a sensitive and discerning fable of a woman's love life, which manages to compress within a very brief compass some of the rewards and almost too many of the anguishes of passion for its own sake. It is almost a terrifying book—saved by the humor with which Miss Nin endows her theme, which raises it finally to the level of an artistic tragicomedy. The story concerns the amorous exploits of the heroine, Sabina, a veteran of these battles, pursued by her own guilt and fears, caught between her temperament and her conscience. In the symbolism of the narrative she is pursued by the "lie detector," a sort of F.B.I. of the heart. (This figure is an amusing mixture of psychoanalytic technique and conventional morality.) The heroine evades him, and we begin to realize that Miss Nin is one of the few women writers in our literary tradition to affirm the centrality of the biological impulses for her own sex, and on the same terms as for men. The point is that she is also prepared to describe these emotions from the feminine point of view with the same ruthless honesty that marked a D. H. Lawrence or a Dreiser. And what a price is paid by the protagonist—or the victim—of the present story for her moments of ecstasy and conquest! She must move on a superficial level of lies, tricks, evasions in each new case of love; the tactics of feminine deceit are all exposed here in a manual of love's subterfuges. On a deeper level of genuine affection she must still prepare to wound before she is wounded, to betray so that she may not be betrayed, to make her escape before the lover makes his. The price of impulse is eternal anxiety, Miss Nin implies. This spy, like all spies, must be prepared for treason, for flight, for ignoble death. The theme is dramatized in a series of separate episodes with rather shadowy masculine figures who operate mainly to project the various roles a woman also plays in love—or is forced to play. In the end Miss Nin's heroine turns for comfort and wisdom to another woman, Djuna, who has figured in the previous novels in the series. Friendship is the solace for passion, perhaps, as art is the crystallization of imperfect human desire.

I thought Acapulco had anaesthetized me against all this. But the anaesthetic wore off as soon as I landed in New York.

Nobody lifted a finger, not Edmund Wilson, not Wallace Fowlie, not Charles Rollo, to defend me against such obvious prejudice.

Peggy Glanville-Hicks, music critic for the *Herald Tribune,* is the only one who evaluates the book. She says: "It is the only new writing. It is what writing will be. It is a perfect work of the intuitive intellect."

She believes it is the intellectual who blocks the way by his subjection to tradition. But I feel it is also the anti-poets, the moralists, the anti-emotional and the anti-human.

Peggy also feels I cannot return to the European source of my work because I have gone beyond it.

What is so strange is that I have faith in my work. I reread *Spy in the House of Love* with severity, and become aware that it is a piece of music, and that it is full of awareness. I am proud of it. It may be that Peggy hears it because she is a musician.

So I have to learn to live and work not only as an outsider, but in opposition to the trend.

Peggy's voice is like the small finger cymbals used by the gypsies, like the tinkle of gold-piece necklaces worn by the women of Tehuantepec. It is aerial too. A filigree of a child's laughter, a *jeune fille*'s smothered laugh. The thorns are visible too. The frail body and the powerful incisive mind. But the scars I can guess. Her prestige is great. But her compositions are not performed widely. The bias against a woman composer?

Letter to Maxwell Geismar after his review of *Spy in the House of Love:*

You're right, of course, that friendship does not break down because one does not understand the other's work. There is a lot in your work that I may have failed to get too. But now that time has passed and we are both more objective, I do want to explain what bothered me, in spite of the fact that I know you meant well. It was not what is called a rave review I wanted from you. But I felt you did not understand the novel. Faced with a theme in which the problem was to go deeper into the motivations of Don Juanism, to go beyond the usual story, to go deep into its meaning, dissociation of the personality, the break into the wholeness of love, to rewrite, in our modern terms, *Madame Bovary*. You, I felt, are embarrassed by open sexual themes, and so were flippant, in the use of [a phrase like] "amorous exploits," taking away the gravity of the neurotic conflict. That was one point. Another is that Sabina sought man's liberation in separating the pleasures of sensuality from the pains of love *but failed to do so.* To win your heart and your respect one has to write a novel against [Joseph] McCarthy, even a bad one such as the one you reviewed so favorably. And that makes me sad and divorced from America, that literature as an art has nothing to do with themes, actuality as the only mainstream of life (which we quarreled about before) ; but that is your sociological point of view, irreconcilable with the point of view which builds for eternity, not the small circle of family, country. That is why I no longer want to talk this over, because they are opposite points of view. I am continuing the work of Freud, which I believe more valuable than the work of Marx. If we had gone deeper into Freud we might have emerged wiser and nobler politically than we are. Freud knew what lay behind all these wars and concentration camps and cruelties and was attacking the very source of the evil at its inception, whereas sociologists are merely trying to remedy the hostilities of human beings. Freud, well understood, would have cured us of hostilities and prejudices. We are always tackling the evil from the outside and not tackling the source of it. That is what I believe. Our failures (wars, racial prejudice, greed, corruption) prove the error of Marxism. But in the end you have to go on with your work and I with mine. I want to change human beings at the source. That means psychological deep-sea diving. Sometimes one option such as mine may seem out of time and out of pace with the present, but it may be because I see further. I see the dismal failure of literature here (because of its purely functional, journalistic point of view) and the failure of sociologists to get us out of hell, and I put my faith in Freud and those who developed and expanded beyond him. It is puritanism which has delayed the effects of psychology. There is in the work of Freud, Rank, and Jung an understanding of symbolism which is basic and vital, not mere poetry. In Sabina it is not passion for its own sake, it is passion for the sake of wholeness through intensity. She does not "turn to another woman for comfort and wisdom," but for more than that. Djuna is a symbol of the woman who is aware rather than blindly impulsive, as Sabina is. The disregard of symbolism (of the split atoms in music, split atoms in painting, fragmentation of all feelings), which was intended to emphasize neurosis, makes you consider the story as a banal plot of a woman who has lovers. That is due to your disregard for the art of writing as a transposition from realism to emotional reality, which you do not believe in. We talked about this in your garden once, referring to Miller who you thought had lost by his surrealism the realist he might have been. The time will come when we will learn to balance true psychological realism with external realism. Meanwhile you, who are the best and sincerest exponent of the latter, still represent what I have to deny in favor of psychological research into the motivations of human beings, experimentation and exploration of new frontiers. Of course, you win. I am the loser in the present scene, the failure, until we weary of Huxley's *Brave New World,* its automatic and functional writing, its one-dimensional writing. American writing is committed to its false realism, and until neurosis is recognized as a negative proof of the presence of a powerful unconscious which can be converted into positive use, we will continue to refuse the inner voyage I believe essential to the wholeness and whole vision which will humanize us faster than new systems. I am sure of my faith, but lonely. You are lucky, you think with the majority. Your point of view is shared. Frances Keene did her best to complete the onslaught on the concern with growth of the self. I don't believe that social awareness will destroy the McCarthys but psychological awareness of our leader's characters. I'm workng from the other end, and it's a damned lonely one, with everyone feeling virtuous when they write about political themes and disregard individual hostilities which are projected onto the vaster issues. It is like waiting for the world to realize that instead of more jails they should create psychological help for children *before* they become delinquents.

I have a long wait. But I will inherit the kingdom of Freud, and Freud's wiser and deeper contemporary kingdoms too.

Annette's dream was to build a house in Acapulco. She did, on a hill behind the Mirador.

No sooner was the house built than she came to New York with a journalist and took an apartment on Third Avenue. I met her in the street. I could not understand finding her there.

She took me to the apartment. We walked up the stairs. Instead of a plain outside door like those of the other apartments, she had erected a trellis covered with vines and hung with birdcages and singing birds. The gate was painted bright yellow. She had transported Mexico to Third Avenue. She had her serapes, her Orozco and Diego Rivera paintings, her ethnic jewelry, her bright woolen scarves, her ribbons and colored wool for the hair, more cages with singing birds, gay bottles and pottery bells.

She wore an orange dress. Beautiful figurines and heads from Mexican ruins were set on stands, textiles from Oaxaca on the windows.

We shared a passion for Acapulco, and the same dream of having a home there. But before I had a chance to ask her what had made her give it up, Charles appeared. He had turned up in Acapulco to report on fishing and on the boat races. He was a childhood sweetheart. Annette had made a wide circle into sophistication, internationalism, exotic lives, to return to New York where she was born and had gone to school.

With much Mexican panache she had returned bravely and gaily to a smaller, less romantic life. She did not surrender the beauty she had found in Mexico, beauty of background, and dress. By now her jewelry was very successful and was exhibited in museums. Her gaiety was irrepressible, and her magic transportable and effective anywhere.

Felix Pollak writes:

A Spy in the House of Love is deeply, almost desperately serious, and the reviewers' plea of unintelligibility seems quite intelligible to me as a rationalization of their subconscious resistance to it. For being solely and exclusively concerned with the individual (and not even a typical and certainly not a conventional one), being, moreover, concerned solely with the most secret and disturbing aspects of life, the subterranean territory, "living as others live only in their dreams at night, confessing openly what others only confess to doctors under guarantee of professional secrecy . . ." it runs head on against all the taboos of a middlebrow mass civilization that can view man only from a sociological point of view and find on its scanty scale of values good and evil determined only by what is beneficial or bad for "society." The novel's whole theme must be anathema in a country that, despite its hectic overcompensations, is still laboring under the Puritan strain; for even in the sexiest novels produced here, sex is always treated functionally; a recurrent need, leading to recurrent acts, to concessions, whether deplored or affirmed, to natural functions that must be fulfilled so that they can be forgotten and make room for higher things. While in your books, and most clearly in the *Spy*, sex is exposed as the ever-present life force, the life of the senses as all-pervading. Eros, sensuality are shown as the spark plugs that set the whole machinery in motion, as the source, the spring, the key, the Mother in the Goethe sense. Unity in manifoldness, no tortuous and artificial duality, no Christian rift between mind and body, no sterile divorce of emotion from reason, but reason and emotion as inseparably mated and molded together as effect and cause; instincts, drives, seen as what they are: the wire pullers of even our most rational thought processes. The tremendous hidden portion of the tiny iceberg visible above the waters.

Such a concept brings with it the inescapable problem: the exposed, the confessed schizophrenia of the internally rich and honest and complex personality, the immorality of the ethical, the agonizing search of the possessor of a self for the selves that comprise it; the lust and torment of the compulsion of living each of these selves; the fears and flights from super-egos and lie detectors; the deceits necessary for being true to one's being; the clashes of the outer and inner reality. The novel's essential theme seems to be the deeper variations of a sentence from Hamlet: "This above all, to thine own self be true." And the quest for the recognition of these selves, the old question: Who am I? altered with deeper insight into: Who are I? Only he who has selves, has self, and only in being true to one's selves can one be true to one's self.

Let me say again how captivated I am with your forte: your language. Its lucidity is all the more astounding as you are setting out to express the almost inexpressible and thus have to prestidigitate more in between the lines than into them. This makes for difficult and exciting reading within simple sentences. Your rhythm and your music, your probing for meaning and nuances, the blood-beat and the tart sweetness of your prose cast again the old spell over me. You have the foreigner's prerogative of seeing and hearing and sensing every word as if it occurred for the first time, you know and use expressions I seldom encounter in native prose, you taste their sounds and shadings with a sensitive and sensuous passion, a nervous aliveness that is superb. The erotic fluid emanating from all your books stems not in the least from your erotic relation to words.

Musical delicacies like the juxtaposition of moulted and moulded in two closely welded sentences, passages like "who can never reach termination as ordinary people reach peaceful terminals . . ." and many other poetic excursions into the depth of language parallel to deep-sea diving into the unconscious of the soul leave me time and again with one adjective which to me best characterizes your writing: exquisite.

These are the letters which have kept my writing alive.

Felix Pollak was a librarian at Northwestern when my early manuscripts were sold to them. He became interested and began to write me. He is an Austrian poet, literary, a fine letter writer, and we corresponded fully and richly. He asked me to read [Herman] Hesse. He had known him.

When *A Spy in the House of Love* came out, Mary Green was employed by the British Book Center to help with publicity. The only thing she did for me was to accept a malicious review in the magazine she edited and to take me for an interview with Barry Gray. This took place late at night, about 11:30, and I was to be thankful for that. She admired him because he had once been beaten severely in a fight for the unions. As if this equipped him for discussing a literary book!

I was waiting for my turn and watched him interview a beautiful, dignified Swedish woman, the head of the Society for the Protection of Unmarried Mothers. His crudeness was revolting but there was worse to come. He asked about her father (a minister with thirteen children) and commented: "I wonder when he had time to pray." She talked about her work. He was not interested. He repeatedly asked her why she had given up her career as a pianist to open this shelter for unmarried mothers. She evaded the question. He persisted. He asked her what was the matter with her hands. Finally, in desperation, she said bitterly: "My hands were burned in a fire, that is why I had to give up my career as a pianist." She was humiliated. I was angry. I said to Mary Green: "I'm leaving."

Mary Green said: "He won't do that with you. We are friends." His first phrase was: "You wrote a novel. I fell asleep at the first page. So you tell me what it was all about."

I do not remember the rest. I went home at midnight, hoping no one had heard the interview. I felt immensely lonely in an ugly, hostile world. These were the people who judged bullfighting barbaric and outlawed it.

He is still on the radio. Why does no one rebel? Why didn't I walk out?

To me people with intuition are like wall-less rooms, like ballets, like abstract painting, like music. They are transparent, and you are never in danger of breaking your head against a brick wall. With intellectuals there is an interference with penetrative or absorbent activities. They cannot receive, feel directly. Herlihy, with little literary training, is more absorbent, has more natural antennae. He has an alert agility of mind which I compared to Lippold's mobile. Jim's lyrical improvisation about my writing comes closer to what I want to hear: it is the response in equivalent terms, it has to do with freedom, the freedom similar to that in jazz, in the unconscious, in the poet, in children. So that without the equipment of maturity they seize upon the evolutions of experience better than the Edmund Wilsons and the Maxwell Geismars.

Mary Green felt bad about the episode with Barry Gray. "I have felt uneasy, unhappy even, about getting you in the hands of such people, wondering if it was not a kind of crime to expose you to that, whether it would not be best to leave you in your literary world."

But in the first place, my literary world has not treated me any better. *Partisan Review* allowed Diana Trilling and Elizabeth Hardwick to tear me to pieces. *Kenyon Review* published one short story in fourteen years, and that was all. I was not asked to contribute to *Perspective*. I am not included in *New Writing* or in *Discovery*. The intellectual critics have not even read me. I am left out of magazines and anthologies. So what I feel is this: naturally I do not expect to be a popular writer, but there is a world in between, of people I want to find, who are not intellectual or political snobs, those who have feeling and intuition. I know they exist because they are the ones who write me letters, simple emotional letters. I want to find them, make my bridge with them. The literary poets have betrayed me. Auden asked Ruth Witt Diamant after hearing me read: "What's with Anaïs Nin?" and Ruth answered: "She is a poet." Auden should have known this. Dylan Thomas, Tennessee, Truman Capote . . . what support did they give me?

[Summer, 1954]

Sierra Madre.

Mourning days for failed friendships are over. I am not victimized by neglect, less prone to earthquakes of the soul, to tidal waves of anguish. Quarrels at one time were prophetic of separation, loss (since the largest quarrel of all led to the separation of my parents and the loss of the father, country, a musical world). Jealousy was once a messenger of divorce (my mother's jealousy of my father). Today I can live for months without the strangulation of anxiety. I have occasional minor attacks of nervousness, or panic; no nightmares, less guilt for living my own life according to my own nature. Very little of that excruciating fatigue which tightens my neck like a vice until I do not rest, nor eat nor sleep well.

An evening with our neighbor Forest Rangers. The little American room, like a motel room, impersonal, barren. The innocuous books handed out by the Book of the Month Club, the absence of paintings, the functional home and the maintenance talk, about gardening, plumbing problems, community trash problems, dumping, smog, incinerators.

The people around me are so standardized that they are colorless, anonymous, and have no distinguishing characteristics. Their talk is fundamentally unrevealing, functional. I have as much difficulty in telling one face from another as I have one house from another, one set of children from another. I feel I know what they are going to say, what they say to each other in intimacy, I feel it is a formula, and I wonder whether a society as conscious of its social life can become so uniform that a personal, intimate relationship becomes impossible. Once, a neighbor came, and in the middle of a colorless talk, broke down and wept: "I am so unhappy with my husband." I responded immediately, and we discussed the situation. But the next day the door was closed again and she talked about the weather.

We were invited to the home of Bob Balzer. He is very wealthy, he travels, he is a friend of famous people. He built himself a Japanese house. It was situated on top of a hill overlooking Hollywood. Three young Japanese men in white kimonos met us at the door. We took off our shoes and were given slippers. The house was beautiful. It was a copy of the most beautiful of all styles in architecture. It has a sense of space, serenity, and stylization. The sliding panels concealed closets, screens, and statues. The simplicity, and the separate and unique beauty to be contemplated deeply. Even a reproduction of a Japanese house, too new, too lacquered, too glossy (I am sure the genuine ones are soft and muted in texture and tones) was an aesthetic experience.

On the terrace, after the music, we drank champagne. But just as the beauty of the canyons, the sea, the chaparral is still so obviously external and does not contain the flavor of legends, a mythological essence, so this evening, while offering an aesthetic experience, gave but a shell which did not move me deeply. It gave me the feeling of a stage set, because the man of wealth who was satisfied with this reproduction was like the man satisfied with the reproduction of a painting. There was no deep bond between the purchaser of an imitation and Japan. Imitation is not a proof of love but of the satisfaction with semblance rather than creation.

At Bob Balzer's party Lloyd Wright was there, capable of creating an original home, native to America, indigenous. But because Lloyd had not received the approbation of fashion, the blessing of popularity, society would not let him create works which would have been original American architecture.

During the music, I meditated on my personal death. I realized I must complete my work, because I am an instrument for human consciousness and an instrument constantly disciplined to create, not to imitate.

But if I should die, music, painting, literature would always continue, but not my particular awareness caused by the intermingling of two cultures, of the differentiation between creation and imitation.

I drank the champagne, and with the illusion of beauty shed by the reproduction (an illusion strongly aided by the three young Japanese men in their white kimonos), the summer night, and my ability not to hear trivial conversation, I went into a spatial flight and reached enjoyment.

In the car, driving back, I consoled Lloyd. "Yes, we know the difference between original creation and imitation. We have the original with us."

Still under the euphoria synthetically created by a synthetic beauty, I had met and conquered the fear of death by discovering a realm which does not die, the highest moments in art which alone are perpetuated. I had discovered the realm in which I am at home, and glad to be buried in, the pyramids of art. And there at least, I would never feel loneliness.

Let us suppose a person is made up of four colors. Let us suppose we respond intensely to one color in him—the tone of voice or the expression of his eyes. We will continue to respond to this particular trait rather than to an image of the total personality. We have a continuous response to fragments.

Only analysis inquires into these automatic responses and seeks to alter our reduced circuit. It exposes its mechanical character, and seeks to open all the circuits to include a total vision into others' personalities. It seeks to open us altogether to new impressions and more complete receptivities.

I was invited to East Hampton to celebrate the Fourth of July.

It was a family scene which to a passer-by might have seemed touching, and which, if pasted in a family album, would have shed sweetness and nostalgia like pressed flowers. The scene from the outside was painted in trite but familiar colors, the kind that long-lost adventurers or men at war dream of returning to.

Three generations had gathered outside where the garden met the beach. They sat in the garden, at dusk, awaiting the darkness to set off fireworks. Grandmother lay in a chaise longue, discoursing on the evils of sunbathing, as if the sun were responsible for the withering of her skin. The flowers all around her seemed to shed their perfume dutifully at her bidding, listening with bowed heads to her addition of the hours spent on caring for them, as children listen to their mothers describing what a difficult childbirth she had endured for them, quietly amassing a reservoir of future guilt. "My geraniums," said the grandmother, "my rhododendrons," as if this roll call would make them stand in tidy ranks ready to march against the weeds.

Her daughter was expecting another child, and because of her boyish haircut, her very long legs, and heavy earrings, looked like a Ubangi woman of royal descent.

She was explaining how she managed to get evenly tanned while pregnant: "I dig a hole in the sand, and rest my stomach in it, and that way I can expose my back to the sun."

Grandmother turned to grandfather then and said: "How I wish you could dig a hole in the sand and hide your stomach there for a while."

At this, grandfather, who had been about to lie beside her on the double-sized lounging chair, moved away as if he had been stung by an insect and went to sit as far away from the danger as possible. He also drank his highball a little quicker, as if to accelerate the state of anaesthesia.

There were two married couples. The Ubangi woman wore a bathing suit, the other woman a cotton dress. As if there were not enough flowers and vegetables and fruit around, the dress was also covered with them. The flies, butterflies, and bees were often deceived.

"I always wanted to work hard," said the grandfather, "and then go around the world."

"But I can't travel now, because of my arthritis," grandmother said.

"Arthritis can be cured," I said.

Then the truth appeared, which the arthritis disguised. "At my age! When I look at myself in the mirror I can't imagine traveling now. I used to have the smartest figure."

"Happy birthday to you, grandmother," sang one of the children, bringing her one of the flowers which had fallen into the pool and carried a bee attached to its humid pollen.

"Think of having a birthday on the Fourth of July! I used to think that the fireworks were for me. A little boy who adored me used to say to me: 'Why, Edna, nobody else but you has fireworks for her birthday. You must be someone special.' I was fifteen before I discovered that those marvelous fireworks were not in my honor. From then on I have always hated them. Besides, they always dirty the beach and ruin my hydrangeas."

"The fireworks tonight are in your honor," I said.

"Can we start the fireworks?" asked the seven-year-old grandson. "It's almost dark enough."

"No, you can't. None of you children must touch the fireworks."

"But why?"

"Because they are dangerous. I knew a little boy once who had the whole side of his face burned off. And another little girl who lost a finger. Fireworks are unreliable. They sometimes backfire, or they set fire to the house."

And so all her anger to have discovered that fireworks had not been set off in her honor was passed on to the children, an inheritance of terror which affected them for the rest of the evening, so that when the fireworks started, they were in a state of anxiety and all their pleasure was marred.

A red-haired boy moved his small mouth like a fish looking for nourishment among the weeds.

"What I like best about my family," said the grandmother, "is their kindness. Kindness is very rare and I always brought up my children to prize it above everything else."

"Open your presents," cried one of the children, "open your presents!"

The first package contained an electric vibrator which everyone began to use playfully, amused by its soft purr and electric caresses. Everyone but the grandmother, who knew it was intended to relieve her of pain but who wanted these pains unnoticed and was impatient to conceal an object which underlined her humiliations.

The second box contained a hand-knitted bed jacket for her need of rest and which she did not like.

The third was a book on Valentino's life, which recalled to the grandmother the passing of a period she had lived in, and wanted to forget, as it made her feel old. As a teen-ager she had worshipped Valentino. She laid the book aside.

The two young husbands began to light the fireworks in the middle of the beach. One of them seemed to choose instinctively the ones that did not go off properly. They would sputter, and go out in his hands, and he would stand there feeling somehow personally responsible, standing there like a young lover suddenly deprived of his potency.

Grandmother was still worrying about her garden: "Tomorrow I will hate you all."

While some of the effective fireworks were illuminating the beach, the grandfather suddenly went into the house and after a moment several shots were heard. There was a minute of frightened silence. Then grandfather reappeared smiling.

Grandmother became shaky and nervous and said: "Every time he gets a few highballs in him, he starts shooting off his gun."

"It's rather touching," said someone, understanding the grandfather's desire to cause a sensation.

Grandmother said: "You should be ashamed, it's dangerous, you're drunk, and you might have killed me."

This threat, combined with that of the fireworks, sent the children running to climb a tree.

"Oh, that tree, that tree is so brittle, you will fall off," cried the grandmother.

"Don't spoil your new dress," shouted the mothers.

The fireworks continued but the little girl felt safer sitting high up on the tree.

As each one flared up, red, or gold, or green, as sprays, or petal-shedding flowers, as comets, as nebulas, as volcanoes, grandfather would say: "There goes sixty-five cents! There goes ninety cents! There goes a buck!"

Perhaps this remark accelerated the fall and the turning to ashes of the fireworks, perhaps it was the implication that so much of his labor was being foolishly exploded and wasted; but in the eyes of the family the sparkle and elation began to peter out, like the fireworks that did not go off.

"In my time they had prettier fireworks," said the grandmother.

"You mean in the time of the dinosaurs?" asked one of the grandchildren.

It is true that there are elevations in art, in music, in writing which sustain us, help us to live. They transmute our sorrows into beauty. But it is also true that there are pitfalls from which art cannot save us, and then it becomes necessary to find an understanding of our human life, of our illness. I have found this understanding, this quest for healing and wholeness, necessary to me and to others. The poets, as I observed from my studies of the classical and modern romantics (whom we call neurotics), always end in catastrophe, in tragedy, illness, death. They were the victims of life rather than its conquerors. See the tragic life of Baudelaire, of Rimbaud, Verlaine, of Dylan Thomas. Only recently Virginia Woolf drowned herself. Rimbaud walked out of his poet's life and into oblivion.

Part of our reality is that we invest others with mystical qualities; we force them to play the role we need. We do not take into account the strength of these myths and thus deny one of the most powerful motivations in our character. We invent situations, we live out, independently of others, a private dream relationship, and a private drama, and the frustration of this relationship is acted in a void, taking the greater part of our energies.

I have chosen to write about artists first because I know them best, then because the expression of fantasy and imagination is more clearly manifested in them than in other lives. In other men most of their life is repressed by the bourgeois structure, their professional, social, and community mores. The artist retains his sensibility; it is the element he needs for his profession. The artist matches his life to his needs and lives by his own design and does not conform to patterns made by others. The artist lives more in harmony with his own character and is closer to freedom and individuality, and therefore integrity.

We say the realist describes what he sees, but what we see is formed, shaped, altered, and colored by what we feel. The same city would change its face a hundred times according to our mood. It may appear desolate, menacing, lovely, or hospitable. The change of mood is like the change of lighting.

The role of the writer is not to say what we can all say but what we are unable to say. Most of the writing today which is called fiction contains such a poverty of language, such triteness, that it is a shrunken, diminished world we enter, poorer and more formless than the poorest cripple deprived of ears and eyes and tongue. The writer's responsibility is to increase, develop our senses, expand our vision, heighten our awareness and enrich our articulateness. "Ersatz" in literature. Gangsterism in literature. And in John Hawkes' *The Cannibal* I am not sure yet, but it seems like an artificial unconscious. Writing should develop our senses, not atrophy them.

Gertrude Stein wrote: "Something is always happening, anybody knows a quantity of stories of people's lives that are always happening, there are plenty for the newspapers and there are always plenty in private life. Everybody knows so many stories and what is the use of telling another story? There is always a story going on. So naturally what I wanted to do in my play is what everybody did not know or always tell."

The secret of writing. The experience resembles the knot one brings to therapy, where one learns to unravel it. Analysis begins with the cryptic phrase out of a dream, usually. The phrase is the key to a condensed tangle. Then there is the process of untangling by a method of associations, chain-reaction sequences, analogies.

In the novels I begin and end with a poetic phrase. I was always haunted by the poetic phrase. Now I find the story begins and ends there, with the unraveling of its meaning. The poetic phrase contains the mystery, leads one to investigation and also sums up the meaning, crystallizes it. What takes place during the unraveling is the revelation of character. In between is the dilution of the crystal. When I suffered in the process it was because I was achieving this by a series of crises, as one does in analysis. But I see now the poetic phrase is the key phrase of the theme to be developed, and it is also a summation.

From Jim Herlihy's diary:

Anaïs swims in the waters she was made for, twenty thousand leagues under the heart, as naturally as a cobbler mends shoes.

I have not yet found my own waters, but I think I know those who have and have not.

I like to write, but half the time the typewriter keys are nothing but sticks and I use them like a man on stilts. I think B.N. and I will be coming later into our purities.

Anaïs functions even in her melancholy, Bill drowns in his, I strangle in mine. Anaïs wins over her demons by recording in the journal, in a language that is her own, pure. I don't have mine yet. I fight for it. I've heard familiar echoes, watched a certain ghost grin, experienced moments in which there were wings on the keys. Not comfortable yet. Pepe is one of us, I think, searching for his own voice.

Work: work doesn't solve everything but when a person is practicing the work that he loves, you can always tell; there is a rhythm in their absorption which shows in the eyes; their eyes glitter with sights brought back from private places: when the right words come together the world becomes at that moment mathematically perfect: so with each stitch of the cobbler's machine, the tailor's needle. They are seeing unity, peace, in some tiny fragment of the world and they know that this fragment is themselves. Pepe sews hats and dreams of Madonnas in galleries and of the books he may write: but before he will have reached the kind of purity I'm trying to talk about, he will have to sew the hat and know that it is his, paint the Madonna and likewise, or write his book. Then he can withstand, as Anaïs has, the hurts that come into us and at us from other levels of our living.

I hear the cries in Jim's diary. I understand them. The agonies, the rebellions, the angers, the compassions. Waiting for a letter which never comes.

Letter to Jim Herlihy:

First let me say that the story of "Black William" is one of your best stories. It needs very little tidying up. What you did was to take an incident which written in an ordinary way might have been ordinary and cliché but written as you did becomes more than a fine piece of realism. It is far more than that. It is a study of the curious relationship between compassion, identification, and choice of object, of the agony lying behind the writing itself, the struggle to depict, to enter the man's feelings. The ending was a surprise, because you built up the man's pride and honesty. You went behind the stage and exposed the relation between Black William and you, the man and the writer. Wonderful your wish to have a place to long for, to return to, and your preparations to rescue him. I think it's very very good.

I am also glad you sent me that section of your diary. I enjoyed reading it even though it depicted one of your infernos, because the dramatization of our personal infernos is our only way of salvation, of separating ourselves from them.

[August, 1954]

Every time I went to visit my mother at Oakland, I felt it might be for the last time. She was over eighty and although not ill, she had one light stroke some years ago. I was always preparing myself for the separation. I would have liked to be able to sense when I should be there. I would have liked to know, but then it might have been more terrible. I would have liked to know so that I could express my love, which something in her prevented me from expressing fully. I would have liked her to die when we felt the closest (during her last illness).

But it did not happen like this. I had no premonition. It was an ordinary visit. I arrived when Joaquin had just finished his summer job. I arrived at night. Mother was already in bed, at midnight. She got up to kiss me and to drink a glass of milk. The next morning Joaquin made breakfast. The maid had not come for a week and they were looking for a new one. Mother read her newspaper sitting in her favorite chair by the window. On the sofa was her bobbin lace, on which she had been working. I worked on my rug and we talked. I teased her about the rug, saying: "Would you like to finish it? I don't work on it enough." Mother answered: "I don't like rug making."

"But you like the rug, I hope, as I am making it for you."

Then I asked her if she would tell me her life story and that I would write it in the diary. She laughed at that, made fun of the idea, and I gave it up while Joaquin said to her: *"Tu n'est pas gentille."* But this did not change our good-humored mood. Joaquin worked at his music copying, a page, and then asked me to play canasta. Mother did not like canasta. She preferred solitaire. She quietly played solitaire while Joaquin and I played canasta, clowning to amuse her. At times she closed her eyes as if tired.

After dinner Joaquin and I went to a movie. I wish I had stayed with her, but as she always went to bed at eight or nine, I did not feel it mattered. But before dinner, to please me, Joaquin made martinis. We became very gay and clowned for mother. I always tell *Marius and Olive* stories with a real southern French accent. Mother would smile but she disapproved of the cocktail. Mother's expression of anger, like my father's expression of severity, was reserved for our actions. The laughter, exuberance, was given to strangers. I missed the in-between moods: tenderness and gentleness.

Before we took the cocktail, Joaquin took us for a ride, the "long drive," as they call it, over the mountains of Oakland. Why did I not notice mother was more subdued than usual? Why can't we know those we love are about to die, so as to give them the words of love they need, the last praise or reassurance? We could not bear to know, but that is not true, for it is in the not knowing that is prepared all the sources of our suffering later. We are still like animals; we do not tell our thoughts or our feelings. Mother must have had a million thoughts that day. She may not have sensed death approaching. She did not sense it because her last words to me were: "When you come next time will you stay more than two days?"

That afternoon passed quickly. When we returned from the movie, mother was asleep. The next morning we rose early to go to Mass together. Mother wore the fur coat Joaquin gave her and her black mantilla. She and Joaquin received communion. On the way out of church we were stopped by Arthur Schnitzler's widow, a converted Jewess. Joaquin stayed to talk with her while mother sat in the car. Mother complained that Joaquin had squeezed her arm too tightly when he was leading her up to the altar. Joaquin explained he could not find her arm in the big sleeve of her coat.

We had lunch. We ate a sponge cake mother had baked. Joaquin scolded her for not eating. We should have been alarmed, but we weren't. We took another drive together, the "short drive." I saw my mother's small eyes looking at the hills and fields, which were sepia colored. I should have known she was looking at them for the last time. And I could have been tender and said: "Mother, I love you." After death, that is what you weep over, but after death the one you love is not there to place an obstacle before your tenderness. Mother inhibited my tenderness. She had a generous, valiant, rough-hewn, cheerful, combative, aggressive temperament.

After our drive Joaquin and I played cards. My mother had refused to get a hearing aid. She could hear concerts but not the voices at the movies. She did not like the detective story she was reading. I left her the one I was reading. I apologized for having leaned over her bobbin-lace cushion and bent the pins (the piece of lace she was never to finish) .

Then at seven thirty I left.

At the airport I did not let Joaquin stay until I left. Noise, crowds make intimate talk impossible and the separation begins really as soon as one arrives at the airport, so it is better not to delay it, to hang on, to talk like the deaf and mute in the deafening roar of the propellers. "Go home," I said, and Joaquin agreed. Stations and airports are rehearsals for separations by death.

In the plane I took a martini and a sleeping pill. Anxiety awakened me at midnight. I did not know that when Joaquin returned home Mother was ill with what she thought was stomach trouble. She had vomited and felt pain. She had a heart attack.

Joaquin called me. Mother was rallying under oxygen and drugs, and had talked with Joaquin. In the afternoon she talked with a young priest she asked for. But the next day she was semiconscious, and did not recognize Joaquin, answered feebly when she was called. That evening she died, unconscious, painlessly. Joaquin called me at midnight.

The pain of irrevocable loss. A greater and deeper pain because there was no sense of unity, of fusion, of closeness and I had hoped to achieve this. The loss is greater and more terrible when closeness is not attained. All my life I had struggled to come closer to her, and now she was lost to me. It eluded me. Pain of remembrance. The lace unfinished. Her game of solitaire unfinished. That ordinary family last day, nothing to lift it from an ordinary family day, with family disharmonies stemming from childhood. Pain, her shrunken body in part dying, withering, but when she was very ill and I rubbed her body with alcohol her back was white, smooth, unwrinkled, shockingly smooth and not ready to die. Pain. I could not look at my bathing suit she sewed a few stitches on, without a pain as great as the stab of a knife. Pain not to have been there, to see her, to help her and Joaquin. Joaquin having to live alone through all the horrors, the loss itself, and all the details attending death. Once I called him. He had been fixing her room. I heard him weep.

"Joaquin, remember, you made Mother's life very happy for many years. She had a happy life. You were the best of sons."

But I tormented myself with regrets and guilts. Why did it happen the night I left? Why did Joaquin and I drink a martini? It displeased her. Not only my mother had died, but my hope of fulfillment, of union with her, of an understanding, penetrating love.

I rebelled against death. I wept quietly. Every now and then the sorrow pierced me again, in the street, in a movie, at dawn, any time. The guilt came from my rebellions against her. The anguishing compassion for her life.

She started at fifteen to be a mother to her six brothers and sisters (because her own mother ran away with a lover, to a life with many lovers), and to give them the same fierce protectiveness, fierce courage she gave us. Her brothers and sisters speak of her as children do: "A tyrant with a heart of gold." Perhaps, then, marrying my father when he was only twenty-two years old and she thirty, another motherhood, and sacrificing her life to her three children may have been what gave her so much anger. She loved to sing. She had a very beautiful voice, she was sociable, natural, very cheerful.

But for the last ten years I had no discord with my mother. Her buoyancy and gaiety made her beloved. Her frankness was total, her honesty absolute, as was her generosity and her spontaneity.

I am now awaiting Joaquin, who took her body to Cuba where she wanted to be buried beside her father.

Why do people carry away with them so great a part of our knowledge of them, of their thoughts and feelings which would make us love them better.

We are still like animals. We think we understand intuitively. We do not. My mother closed the door on me the day I sought an independent life from her, and after that I spent endless effort and time returning to her, being a good daughter.

What a burden of guilt when a mother serves you, does all the menial tasks, feeds you, works for you, but then does not approve what you become. Do we all withhold our feelings and our thoughts because of this fear of condemnation?

A confession Mother made to me once, but she made it with pride. Her father, whom she adored, was dying of cancer of the liver. He was suffering agony. His death was long, drawn out. The doctor consulted the family. Grandfather was asking for an end to his misery. Mother, as head of the family, had to decide if the doctor should continue with injections of morphine in an increased dose because the present dose no longer relieved him. In increasing the dose there was danger of hastening the death. It was my mother who had to take the responsibility of consenting to the increased dose.

Caring for their children physically but not approving their final development, is this an epitaph for all mothers?

Her courage and her generosity were immense.

It hurt me to remember that even when we gave her new dresses, she still wore her rich sister's castoff clothes. Until the end she hated perfume and gave me whatever perfume or cologne was given to her. Whenever anyone admired an object in her home she would say: "Do you want it?"

Once she stayed with me in New York. An Irish carpenter was building bookcases and singing Irish songs. My mother sang with him, laughed and talked with him. I want to remember always the image of her at that moment, carefree, happy that her voice at seventy was clear and beautiful, happy to be singing. I asked myself then whether she would always have been happy and carefree if she had followed her first passion, singing. Music brought her and father together. She had dreams of concert life. At the beginning he tutored her to sing the most difficult songs, and she was praised by Gabriele d'Annunzio for her rendering of old Italian songs. When she sang *O Cessate di Piagarmi* I wept. I do not remember her singing very often until she went to Spain and there Enrique Granados made her a singing teacher at the Granados Academy. She was happy then.

In New York she tried to make a career again. She gave a concert at Aeolian Hall. She sang old Italian songs, Catalan folk songs, and Granados' *tonadillas*. But nothing came of it.

Was this a secret wound? When I was a girl of sixteen, she sang for the young men who came courting me and I was wistful to be so thoroughly outshone.

Her singing moved me. What would her life have been without children, concertizing, traveling, as pampered by the public as my father was?

This is the image I want to preserve, of my mother at seventy with the crystal-clear voice of a young girl, singing for and with the Irish carpenter.

On the way to New York I stopped at San Francisco to see Joaquin. He had been at the opera and stood far away at the end of the gleaming airport terminal. Small, in black and white, with, even at that distance, a tragic way of standing. It is the way of standing of those pierced by an arrow. I felt I was right to have come. The basic, fundamental Nin sadness, or is it the Spanish tragic sense of life? We are doomed. But gallant. Gallantly creative, active, even gay.

He talked more than usual on the drive to his home, about his plans, his desire to go to Europe for a year, his musical projects, his practical problems at the University, his tiredness after fifteen years of teaching. It is strange, when my mother died, the contact between Joaquin and me was re-established. It had been interrupted. When? I do not remember. Perhaps in Paris, when my mother felt I might be a bad influence on Joaquin. As children we were very close. Now this contact was open again. He talked. This new intimacy began when he came to New York after Mother's death.

When we arrived at the house, I was silent. I missed my mother's face at the window, or her standing at the door, or, what was more often true lately, she would be asleep when I arrived and would turn on her light to greet me. Perhaps even rise to have a glass of milk with us. Her bedspread was of crochet, made by her own hands. The room was bare and simple. There was a crucifix over her bed.

When I entered the bedroom I broke down. I slipped to the floor and sobbed. Joaquin wept. I kept saying: "I am sorry, I am sorry" to Joaquin, because I had come to cheer him, not to heighten his sorrow.

I was to sleep in my mother's bed. It was utterly painful. But my concern over Joaquin was so strong I forgot what I felt. He was in bed and weeping. I sat on the edge of his bed and said: "Mother is resting. She would not want you to hurt yourself. Don't hurt yourself." He went to sleep, and I too.

I awakened resigned to the ordeal of helping Joaquin dispose of her belongings. She owned so little! A box of holy medals, rosaries, and a prayer book for the Society of Saint Vincent de Paul. A box of lace remnants, those we carried all through our lives and travels, from Europe to America, my mother always saying: "Someday we will make a whole tablecloth out of all those pieces of real lace." Some came from the dresses she wore as a debutante in Cuba. A box of sewing threads and needles which I wanted, as well as her gold thimble, in hope of inheriting my mother's ability to sew. I accepted mending and sewing now, and asked for the sewing machine, the knitting needles.

My mother's jewelry were gifts from me, gold earrings from Mexico, trinkets from Italy, pins and a few rings from her sisters. I wanted her unfinished bobbin lace, the pale-blue pillow with a pattern pinned to it, and the white thread on bobbins which her hands wove in and out, changing the pins. There was an unfinished piece of lace on it, and Joaquin preferred to give it to a nun who makes bobbin lace and would finish it. The unfinished bit of lace would have caused me sadness.

Her bookbinding press and bookbinding material Joaquin sent to a pupil of hers in Williamstown. The pain was deeper which came from the handling of small objects, her bobby pins, her comb, her face powder. I never saw anyone who possessed so little. A few dresses her sisters gave her, a fur coat from my brother, a half-empty closet. The stark simplicity of her taste, her stripping away of possessions. She took nothing, possessed nothing but what was given to her by her children. But she kept all mementos, our childhood teeth, our first locks of hair, my first piece of embroidery, our first notes to her, all our letters. Three enormous boxes of my letters to her. *I had expressed my devotion.*

It was a comfort to give her clothes to the sisters of Saint Vincent de Paul for the poor, because that is what she would have wanted; it seemed a more sacred way of dispersing them.

Then came the sharing of photographs in three piles: two for the sons and one for me. Still we felt like criminals dispersing parts of her, the coat which had warmed her, her modest handbag. I can now understand those who lock the door upon everything and never enter again. And yet, was it not better that those objects should continue to live. The final casting off of objects which belong to the dead is full of taboos and full of the pains of the ritual of separation.

The final dispersion. Separating from my mother, separating from my mother. As you disperse these objects which hold a terrifying life, you feel the separation is now final.

But each one has his way of remembering. Mine is to enclose her in the diary. And for days after her death I felt possessed by the spirit of my mother. I wanted to express love by cooking, sewing, mending, lacemaking, bookbinding.

We worked all afternoon. Some of our decisions were dictated by an austere mourning. We cast off Christmas-tree ornaments as if Christmas were no longer possible to celebrate without her, we cast off the playing cards with which she played solitaire, as if we would never play cards again. We cast off the detective stories she liked to read in those days when I had the feeling that she was waiting for death. But we kept the black lace fan, the one she waved with a Latin rhythm in church, which seemed irreverent to the American priest.

Joaquin looks mortally wounded. When he cooked he talked about his discovery of the monotony of woman's work and the endless rounds and repetition.

I hide myself to throw away my mother's toothbrush because I know the sight of it will hurt him, yet he won't be able to throw it away. I did it for him, and hurt myself.

The black lace mantilla I brought her from Spain she was buried in.

I knew that Joaquin wanted me to go to church with him, and that he was embarrassed to ask me, knowing my estrangement from formal religion. He was happy when I suggested it. I waited for him, but refused to pray as I had as a child. I watched the little blue lights wavering in their glasses, some freshly lit by penitents, some already burned out, and I could not bear it, my mother's life burning out, so I went and lit a new one, and Joaquin thought I was offering a renewal of my faith.

Every Saturday evening Joaquin and my mother went to church. When he left me to go to confession, he said with one of his half smiles: "It won't take long," alluding to the brevity of the list of his sins.

Joaquin's sadness, the austerity of his life, which I spent a lifetime running away from, rebelling against austerity, and my mother's humble, sacrificed life.

But some bonds are never broken. I inherited from my mother not only her gold thimble, a sewing machine, but the maternal passion and care for others.

The pain deeper than at my father's death.

I didn't love her well enough.

Except from the age of eleven until twenty, when I was completely and utterly devoted to her, thinking only of helping her.

But later when I began to grow in a different direction, when I left her house, became independent, then conceding my love and admiration of her would have meant an acceptance of beliefs and attitudes which I considered a threat to my existence. Her belief in motherhood, so strong that in Paris when my life was in danger, she felt the child should have been saved even at the cost of my life, and would not listen to medical explanations that a child would always be strangled by old adhesions. My mother wanted me to be someone other than the woman I was. She was shocked when I defended D. H. Lawrence. She disliked my artist friends. She wanted me to be as she had been, essentially maternal. While she was alive, she threatened my aspiration to escape the servitudes of women. Very early I was determined not to be like her but like the women who had enchanted and seduced my father, the mistresses who lured him away from us.

When did I first feel this? When did I repudiate the model of my mother and decide not to be a wife or a mother but a mistress? In spite of this I did inherit from her a strong protective instinct toward human beings. But I also cultivated what would give men not only their down-to-earth needs, but euphoria, ecstasy, pleasure, delight.

When she died I remembered only her courage. Her beautiful voice which was a balm, her care.

During her life she condemned my freedom. She often harked back to the lovely, submissive child I once was, and frowned upon what I had become.

It was not the loss of my mother which reawakened my love for her, it was because my mother's disappearance removed the stigma of her judgments, the dangers and guilt brought about by her influence, and left me a simple human being no longer concerned with my own survival, but able to recognize her qualities.

During her life I fought her influence, and she fought in me the kind of women who had displaced her.

When she died I could recognize our similarities. She did not recognize a form of maternity in my protection of the weak and helpless.

As soon as she died my rebellion collapsed. She left me a sewing machine, a gold thimble, the diaries she had bound by hand in France. I became "possessed" by the spirit of my mother. It was my only way to maintain her alive within myself.

How wise the primitives were who retained their ritual of possession so they would know when it took place and also know how to exorcise it.

My aunt Antolina telephoned me today. She censured the entire family for not being present at the burial of my mother; but during her life they caused her much unhappiness by interfering with her, censured one aunt for being a Christian Scientist, censured all of us for going to live in other countries and not keeping the family together, praised Joaquin only for his goodness, not his music, me for my devotion to my mother, not for my work, upholding the family as a sacred unity which should never be broken, and ending with the reproach I have suffered since childhood, when I rebelled against the succession of family rituals, feast days, birthdays, arrivals and departures, weddings and baptisms, funerals and hospital visits, this huge Cuban clan, proliferating children and endless duties; as soon as I could I freed myself of all of them and became the "indifferent" one in the family.

Joaquin so pale, and this reawakened in me my past role as a substitute mother while my mother was working. I had to control my impulse to enclose, hold, and protect him, had to control acting as my mother. Had to remind myself he is forty-five years old, mature, and fully able to make his own decisions. Do parents never change their vision of us as helpless and inadequate? When I took care of my mother during her illness, and found so many ways to make her comfortable, when I massaged her, she turned to me naïvely and said: "I did not know you knew so much about caring for others."

Joaquin successfully reversed the roles as my mother grew older and dependent. He imposed his will on the household and assumed great responsibilities as Chairman of the Music Department at Berkeley. He handled her death, the problems of her funeral, his relationship to the whole family, his trip to Cuba, exceedingly well. He respected the taboos, the family customs, the religious rituals with perfect grace.

Joaquin has no anger. He has become a saint, a human and tolerant saint. He is returning to the house two weeks after mother's death. I would have delayed that. Death of a loved one is like a mutilation, a part of your body is torn from you, you die a little. And then following that, the spirit of the dead one enters into you, as if in this way you sustain his life, assure his continuity. I who had refused to iron and wash clothes long ago, washed and ironed Joaquin's shirts and felt myself becoming my mother. I took on her maternal virtues. But I also carry within me her defect, anger, and all my life I had to struggle against this anger.

Better than the cult of objects, better than the keeping of physical reminders is this moment when we cease to struggle against the parent's own image of us and accept our resemblances as part of our being.

In ancient mystic beliefs, the spirit of the dead entered a newborn child. Surely our parents give birth to us twice, the second time when they die, and as they die, in rebellion against death, we accept the legacy of their character traits.

Joaquin inherited my mother's wholeness, I my father's dualities. But Joaquin also proved that the only way to remain close to the parent is to become this ideal figure they desire: the respectful and devoted son, religious, who never loved anyone more than his mother. I tried this when I was eleven, twelve, thirteen, fourteen, fifteen, and almost up to my eighteenth year. I was the perfect daughter; I submerged my personality into the personality of my mother. She chose my dresses, and kept me at home when other young women were out working. I was lost in my submission to her. But my first rebellion came when I decided I could not bear the passive suffering of poverty and I insisted on going to work. My mother opposed that. A friend helped me to find work I could do (being untrained in any profession). I became an artist's model, joined the Model's Club, and began to earn money to help the family. I may have lost her love before that, when at sixteen I rebelled against Catholicism.

I am at work on Lillian's return to her home and children, and in musical terms, Lillian is struggling with the *muted* tones she had not been able to hear.

I was no longer inhabiting Sierra Madre. I was in Paris with Moricand. Henry Miller had sent me a newspaper clipping of his death. And I remembered all that was not included in the story of the Mohican. I had first read his *Miroir Astrologique* in which he had, in a beautiful style, drawn astrologic portraits of Picasso, Max Jacob, Louis Jouvet. We were giving a party. I wanted to meet Moricand but was shy of inviting him. I took up the telephone and introduced myself. Later he said he had accepted immediately because the voice inviting him came from another world. He came. We barely talked. He was exceedingly formal, a *grand seigneur*. And he sent me a horoscope which read like *House of Incest*. We saw him often after that. I persuaded all my friends to have their horoscopes done. We took them to the hotel where he had a small room.

The room, an attic room, with the roof slanting over his bed, though shabby, was immaculate. He had a new white blotter on his work table and had covered the bedside lamp (probably a whorehouse pink) with white paper. He talked about Max Jacob, Picasso, Jouvet. He was wealthy then and could entertain them. This moment must have been the peak of his life, because he talked of nothing else. We all felt he was not interested in us, but finally both Henry's gaiety and my protectiveness penetrated his isolation and we made a deeper friendship.

One day at the houseboat he brought me a revolver. He thought I would need it. He thought I lived on the houseboat because I took opium and wanted isolation. He inferred this, he said, from reading *House of Incest*. He expressed desire: "I am so utterly dispossessed of everything." He asked for my love as one begs for life. I was gentle but gave him no hope.

I remember the many farewell dinners we gave him when the war came and he joined the Foreign Legion. He showed us the tin cup and tin set of spoon and knife given him. We sat with [Jean] Carteret and sometimes with other friends. What we all forgot when we looked upon the tragedy of his life was his determination to destroy himself. This impulse was so strong that I marveled he had not succeeded much earlier. His destructiveness was apparent in all he did.

He once found a wealthy patroness who lived in a castle near Paris. She wanted to help him, and all he had to do in return was to "grace" her salon. He enjoyed her world, he enjoyed her company. She helped him discreetly and without damage to his pride. Finally, she offered him a guesthouse on her property (he was literally starving before he met her).

There was a prostitute he saw once or twice a week, a little streetwalker with bangs on her forehead, a cheap fur piece, and a poodle the color of the streets themselves from so much walking and sitting on them. They did not live together. He talked about her unromantically. "She is like a cat to me, a companionable presence." If she had been his beloved mistress it would have been understandable. If she had lived with him, and she were indispensable to him, he could have refused the invitation of his patroness, or he could have visited the little prostitute once a week. Instead he asked the patroness to let him bring the girl to live with him on her estate and to be given an allowance directly.

After his failure to live with Henry Miller at Big Sur he began to look for me, but by this time my own self-destructiveness was ended. I could see his suicidal trend, and wondered why I had taken on such desperately hopeless burdens in Paris. Did I really believe I could reverse the negative process? Rescue them? I knew, at the time, Moricand's perversity, and his weights pulling him downward. I knew the origin of them. Because of his homosexuality, his family disinherited him. He lived for years by producing erotic drawings. He and Max Jacob decided the erotic drawings were bringing upon them the punishment of God. Max Jacob destroyed his, and Moricand did not. Max Jacob became a Catholic convert and found other ways of atonement. Moricand did not. Yet I fought desperately to keep him alive in Paris.

To cover up my help I let him translate *House of Incest,* which he did mostly by intuition with very little knowledge of English, just as Artaud translated Lewis's *The Monk.*

I knew what vast amounts of secret lore and occult knowledge died with Moricand. His love of playing the mysterious and enigmatic personage, his reticence, his inability to share his knowledge, made it all like the gold of the miser. It sank with him into oblivion. I do not know who inherited his papers. There was silence around his death. He died in the houseboat his rich family had endowed for the hobos of Paris, on the Seine, very near to where mine was anchored. Henry wrote about him in *A Devil in Paradise.* And what I had skimmed of beauty and poetics I kept in my story "The Mohican."

Felix Morrow says over the telephone: "I have the statements on the sale of *Spy in the House of Love.* Only 2400 copies were sold in three months. I am disappointed."

René de Chochor says: "I did not expect more. All I expected was to enlarge your circle of readers. I do not delude myself, you are a tough case, but your recognition will come."

"In view of this, in view of the possibility that Morrow may not want my next book, why do you make me work, why do you make me write? After all, I could spend my days at the beach, and save you from a poor financial venture!"

I said this playfully. We always talk playfully. He is good-looking, neat and charming. He answered me quite seriously: "Anaïs, you are one of the great writers of the world. We have plenty of writers who sell, and that is very nice, but I would not be happy just to be handling them. They cover my living expenses. You are my pleasure. I am proud of you. I think we have accomplished what I wanted to accomplish. More readers. You are alive. People have seen you. Now the question is your next book must sell better. It may be wiser to give up trying to finish your Proustian work which requires the reading of four books which are out of print, and to write an independent novel. You may have to do that."

He speaks so gently and reasonably that I always listen. I wrote him a humorous letter. I always think I am reaching a dead end in my communication with the world.

Herbert Alexander did not fulfill any of his promises about a paperback edition, but it is not his fault. He does not have power over the system, and the system obeys orders only from the god of commerce.

This should have been the era of deep probings in the novel, the era of Freud, and instead it is the era of Marxism and Mobocracy. It is the era of persecution of individual development that is not of immediate or obvious use to the community.

People think that today the most useful member of the community is the one who sits through the McCarthy hearings, little knowing that the fascination they feel is not that of participating in or altering the course of history but witnessing projections of their own *personal* dramas. They are watching the drama of their own prejudices, aggressions, hostilities, fears; they feel virtuous because it is clothed in a political form and seems to be part of history.

Letter to Ruth Witt Diamant:

I forgot to write you about the Poetry Center. . . . I wish you would extend your support to that in-between bastard, son of poetry and prose, the poetic novel, which is much in need of legitimization. The novels of Djuna Barnes, Anna Kavan, Isabel Bolton, Giraudoux, because someday they will inherit the kingdom of Freud.

It is quite possible that each one of us may have a different way of expressing love, that my mother's may have been physical care, and my father's his aesthetic delight in photographing us. Once when I told Dr. Bogner my father did not love us, was not interested in us, she pointed out that his obsession with photographing us was an expression of interest but on another level—aesthetic.

What blocks compassion often is an overestimation of the other's power. Power does not inspire sympathy. But often this power is imagined, such as the power we imagine held by the parents. True, at one time they had power over us, power of life or death, but this did not mean that they themselves did not have fears, doubts, pains, troubles, tragedies, and that at any moment they might need us desperately. Their strength was relative to our childish helplessness, but later they had a claim to our acceptance of their human fallibilities. In fact, I would say that compassion for our parents is the true sign of maturity.

Irwin Edman: "A study of fine arts is of equal importance with social studies and perhaps more decisive morally."

Adlai Stevenson: "I am most deeply concerned over a trend toward conformity, a growth of anti-intellectualism, which manifests itself in a sneering attitude toward education, science, and the arts. The tendency is to stifle mental freedom, which is the very basis of a democracy's life and growth."

[Fall, 1954]

On one of my trips to New York, I went to visit Dr. Jacobson, now very famous and very much in demand. Powerful patients would send for him on chartered planes. This time I was told "Dr. Jacobson went to Egypt."

He had been called to take care of Cecil B. De Mille, who was filming *The Ten Commandments*. The set was so large, covered so much ground, that Dr. Jacobson never went outside. His trip to Egypt was on a film lot, with artificial pyramids and streets. People used cars to go from one point of the set to another.

Starting as a refugee from Germany, as a doctor practicing in a modest French apartment, Dr. Jacobson's life had soared. He is still dark-haired, dark-eyed, red-cheeked, vital, running through Central Park on his way to his office. He does not have a doctor's mannerisms, the attentive ear, the habit of elaborate tests, the patient diagnosis, the watching for signs. He seems to proceed from some intuition which functions suddenly, beyond symptoms, reports, tales, descriptions. It is as if he does not want to be enmeshed in the details which the sick conjure. It is as though they interrupt the trend of his perception at work. He is clairvoyant. At times he makes a diagnosis as a person enters the room. When he became famous, he concocted a way to remain in flight. He has several rooms. Each patient is allowed to enter a room and lie down. He arrives brusquely, gives an injection, exchanges a few words and rushes away as to an emergency. When a person pursues him with elaborate details he is already in another room, and thus he maintains a balance in flight, a perpetual motion. But the secret of his power is his very genuine and open duel with death. His face shows such joy at the effect of his injection, that it is part of the cure. He acts as if the patients have brought contagion and he must be like a Japanese sword fighter, constantly on the alert. His dynamic war against illness and his joy when he wins is keen. Whether he hates death and illness or is proud of his skill, I cannot tell. But every celebrity in New York is in his waiting room, performers whose livelihoods depend on being fit for a first night, to sing at an opera, or at a jazz concert, to speak at political meetings. It is always someone playing a major role in the life of New York. He also invites doormen, messengers, postmen, policemen, as well as poor artists and refugees from concentration camps. At one time he kept all his patients busy finding homes for camp refugees. A guest room here or there until they could get on their feet, and his labor consisted of repairing the physical ravages. He was generous when needed, harsh with the spoiled, demanding with rich patients. Death was his enemy, and every triumph over it was his personal triumph.

To a wealthy woman who was weeping over the telephone and who was saying "I cannot stop crying," he answered: "Go ahead, you won't need to urinate as much."

Whatever he uses for medicines, or injections, his attitude has much to do with the efficacy of his treatment. It is his absolute faith in what he is doing, his confidence, his love of life which he transmits. He mocks self-indulgence, is impatient with depression. He holds up his wealthy clients for contributions to his research on hepatitis and cancer.

Once his apartment was broken into, and his radio and cameras stolen. The police came to investigate. Half an hour later the huge burly men lay on his couch and accepted injections.

He comes to parties with his injection needle sticking out of his pocket.

During a period of regular visits when I fought against anemia, I met Maya Deren there, Frederick Kiesler, Eleanor Carrington, singers, actors, producers.

He enjoys playing the magician: "You *will* sing tonight. You *will* act tonight." He only resents the investigators, who want to know what the medicine is.

His own young wife had fallen from a horse in Germany, and lay wrecked and paralyzed in a wheelchair when he met her. A year later she was walking and he had married her. Young, and vulnerable, she suffered from jealousy of his patients. She felt anguish at closed doors, and she knew that Max often completed the cure with a kiss or a compliment.

Behind closed doors did he give life to women in another form? He believed in the transmission of life!

Notes on writing.

Language of common man is not to be literally transcribed because it is his own prison and he wants to be helped out of its restrictions. Language which matches not his ignorant vocabulary but his feelings, which are always more subtle than his words. The common man neither feels nor thinks as he talks. He has not learned to talk. And that is our role, to talk for him, exactly as the virtuoso violinist plays for him a violin he cannot play.

Artists who seem to be of no value to any movement immediately (not concerned with sociological themes) nevertheless become valuable to those who understand that individual dramas are reflections of the universal ones (Kafka, Proust) just as the universal ones are projections of individual dramas (Hitler). A person who joins a political movement for private reasons, personal or neurotic, is less useful to the political movement than the one who abstains because he is not qualified for such activity.

Many romantic rebels against bourgeois society were of very poor caliber for social usefulness when they might have accomplished other tasks more efficiently.

In movies not all directors are gifted in the handling of large collective scenes. A largeness of theme is not necessarily a universal one. The giants are those who by their self-development become the main source of nourishment for the tributaries. America is erroneously fighting such individual development. Hart Crane, the poet and a distorted personality, is just as much a part of the history of American literature as Dreiser. There is a misinterpretation of escapism.

The only nonhuman existence is what we call our human life. If we live our human life and none other, directly, then we subject ourselves to the most inhuman of all conditions: slavery to family and national taboos, wars, illness, poverty, death. Even the phrase, "earning our living" is inhuman. Without religion or art or analysis to transpose the stark horror, we fall into the malady of our age with its great devotion to naturalism. A painting in a house is there to represent a color, a form, a realm we may not have been able to possess. A book opens a realm which our need to earn a living may have made unattainable. Everything that helps us to transpose the unbearable into a myth also helps the creation of distance from our inhuman life, to allow us to mix a little objectivity with the harsh, violent torments of our human bondage.

Art is our only proof of continuity in a life of the spirit. When we deny it (as we have en masse and massively), we lose all that gives us a noble concept of human beings. Otherwise we would know only humanity's repellent aspects in war and commerce.

What people really fight in the artist is his freedom, his attempts at freeing himself from human bondage. He forfeits and repudiates his human family if they seek to enslave him to a profession or a religion he does not believe in. He pays the price with solitude. He may repudiate his country if his country acts inhumanly, as many artists repudiated Hitler's Germany.

In all my books there is a return to the dream, the source of the mystery, where the character seeks the key to its own meaning. In *Winter of Artifice,* there is a return to the dream at the end.

Sierra Madre.
When I cannot bear outer pressures any more, I begin to put order in my belongings. I get satisfaction from perfect order in my papers, in my clothes, in the house. I carry this to excess. As if unable to organize and control my life, I seek to exert this on the world of objects. There is a mania for discarding the useless, uncluttering the house, beautifying, tidying, a mania for superefficiency. I spend hours on this. It gives me peace. I remember being told that the symmetry of the gardens of Versailles was intended to give serenity, that symmetry was the symbol of classicism.
I do have moments of peace. Yesterday in the garden. The sun was gentle. The dog was lying nearby, content.
Turnley Walker had just left. He is big and powerful, physically. He has a big round face, green eyes, an earthy, humorous face. His legs are crippled by polio, he walks with crutches of steel. He avoids stairs, has difficulty getting up and sitting down. He is intuitive, intelligent, warm. He wrote a book about his polio experience. It was a best seller. He is writing other novels. After our interview on television *(Book Review)* , we made friends. Once in a while, when he is working nearby at the Ford Foundation, he drops in.
Moments of peace.
I read Wassermann's *Doctor Kerkhoven* for the second time. The first time I had an emotional response. The second time I realized that from a psychological point of view the book is full of massive errors. Dr. Kerkhoven's way of analyzing his patients, his own lack of awareness about his feelings. After creating characters one does feel for and believe in, he draws the wrong conclusion, and the very "insights" of Dr. Kerkhoven are constant errors of diagnosis. It would show the terrible blindness which existed before Freud.

Both psychological blindness and the incapacity to help others by illumination of the path. In the past I was not able to see this. Now I have greater lucidity. But I cannot make in my life, as yet, a synthesis, achieve wholeness and unity. I am still living by my dualities.

Within the last two weeks archaeologists unearthed two more magnificent "Ships of Death" in a secret chamber within the shadow of the Great Pyramid at Giza.

The ships were made to carry the soul of Pharaoh Cheops to the afterlife. They are curious constructions but quite comprehensible to the modern archaeologists who no longer believe that the pyramids and tombs were built in some metaphysical or little-understood relationship with the sun and the stars. Many kinds of Ships of Death are known from the tombs. But Cheops, the greatest Pharaoh of a great dynasty, was taking no chances. After building the greatest pyramid in the world, he built great boats for his posthumous peregrinations. He believed he could sail in them through the light of Heaven and the dark night of the Hell-river.

Two Ships of Death had been built for the day of his death. The ships were called *Manzet* and *Mesketet,* one for the day voyage, and the other for the perilous course through the night realms.

The image of these ships began to haunt me. I wove them into the pattern of my book on Lillian in Mexico. They inspired the title *Solar Barque.* The images connected in some way with my recurrent dream of the ship which I pushed through a waterless city. It connected with the boat sliding through lagoons in Mexico, with my obsession with boats, houseboats. It all formed a pattern.

When a couple dropped in, while Renate visited me in Sierra Madre, they bored us so much that Renate confessed afterward that she wanted to bark: "Because if these are human beings then I would prefer to be a dog."

Renate may have the key to the end of *Nightwood.*

Paul is a Caspar Hauser who did not die, who navigated out of danger, and managed to remain in a world of fantasy.

He has a great knowledge of the old myths. I became aware that they do not interest me because I feel we have to create our own myths. The old myths do not satisfy us.

Some of the artists I know are so young and yet they use outworn symbols. The fixation upon the past seems to be a homosexual trait and may be connected with the fixation on the mother. In their films they love the twenties, their mother's period, their mother as they saw her in her youth. In Kenneth Anger, in James Broughton, in Truman Capote, in Tennessee Williams, in Proust, the time which counts is the time of the mother's youth. They like antiques, objects from the past.

In this I am their very opposite. I seek to escape from the past, I prefer unfamiliar landscapes, unfamiliar atmospheres. I love change of setting, futuristic designs, changes of fashion, frequent metamorphosis, shedding of the past in all its forms. After a while I discard a dress not because it is worn (I cannot wear out my dresses, I hardly fray them) but because the self which enjoyed that particular dress has changed, has outworn it, needs to assume another color, another shape.

A day of lively pleasure with Renate and Paul.

Renate told me a story: "Paul's car broke down and I had to go to Los Angeles, so I accepted a ride with an old man. He told me that a long time ago he was a lifeguard on the beach. And today at sixty he sleeps out on the rocks in a hollow, and the seals sleep on the other side of this rock. He got arthritis and his family insisted he come back and live in a house, but his first night in bed he fell and broke his arm (he was driving to a doctor to check on the healing of this arm) and he returned to sleep on the rock. One night he felt lonely, and so he tried to slip over on the side of the seals, but they nudged him gently away."

"What does he look like?" asked Paul.

"Like a seal," I said.

From Renate's talk about the old man I went home and wrote about the old man and the seals [later included in *Collages*].

Paul talks. But one does not remember his words. One remembers an elfin, mysterious smile. Pan's smile. He does not open his mouth to smile.

Renate said: "Let me tell you my dream. I was listening to music. My body became compressed into a column. At the top of this column grew antennae of science-fiction design with three lassos of blue electric lights revolving in circles. In their centrifugal motion, they captured other waves. The waves of the brain. Seeking to contact other vibrations? The radiations of my brain not only designed fever charts but they were neon-lighted and threw off sparks like electric short circuits."

Behind Renate's house, on top of the mountain, a red-tailed missile was planted in its steel cradle, pointing skyward, all set to soar.

The sea had been there once and left imprints of sea shells and fish skeletons on stone. It had carved deep Venusian caves in the sandstone. The setting sun deposited antique gold on their walls. People on horseback wandered up the mountain. Rabbits, deer, bobcats, and snakes wandered down the mountain and came quite near the house.

Jim Herlihy writes me: "Altitude fairly good this month."

Working on *Solar Barque*. The ancient city of Guatemala, volcanoes, fireworks.

A moment of peace.

The children next door are playing. The birds are singing, the squirrels are looking for food.

Dream of the Blue Mobile:

A whole ceiling hung with icicle blue mobiles in all shapes, utterly beautiful, and tinkling against each other, swaying and spreading diamond-shaped darts of light.

Renate and Paul discuss the conflict between humanity and creation. It is their drama. Hers is a warm, unstable, vulnerable, emotional nature, in pain. Paul says severely: "You insisted on entering a world which was locked to you. You crashed through. And now what you found hurts you. And it's only your insecurity which hurts you. *I have never given anyone else what belongs to you.*"

Renate does not see this. She only feels blindly and wholly the "agonia" of Paul's body given to another. In her faulty Viennese English she uses "agonia" instead of "agony," and it sounds so much more terrible. It brings images of torture, of Christ's crucifixion. In English "agony" is not used except as a prelude to death. Emotion does not reach such proportions. In Spanish it implies all the slow torture of jealousy.

I feel for both.

You have to protect human beings from the terrors of mythology, of what happens when you live with all the parts of yourself, all your dreams, all your desires, all your infatuations.

The room Renate forced open is that of Paul's multiple lives. She could no longer avert her eyes.

We are sad to see them struggle, for together they create a world of fantasy and magic. When they are creating together, whether with paint or parties, they are joyful and spirited and filled with inventions.

It may be that what a lover most hates in the other's promiscuities is the very revelation of minor selves, selves which do not resemble one's dream, one's passionately designed great love. Paul may diminish himself in Renate's eyes. In jealousy there may be this struggle to maintain a fervent integrity between the idealized lover, container of all loves, and one's idolatry, to exclude the proof that there exist other Pauls, unrelated to Renate, who can admire mediocrity or lesser loves.

Just as when I resented Alfred Perlès I should have known that he was revealing to me, against my will, a diminished Henry, by his shrunken imitation of him, a Henry I did not want to see, who could be related to Fred.

Thus jealousy is not only an effort to keep a love all for one's self, but to keep the unity of a lover's image, caught in the dream, and prevent reality from corroding this image. It is the minor Paul and his minor loves which threaten Renate's love of him.

Jealousy can only be annihilated by the recognitions of all the Pauls which are foreign to Renate, and allowing these Pauls to exist, because warring with the unknown aspects of Paul or those not related to Renate will only bring separation and loss.

Maturity is first the shedding of what you are not, and then the balancing of what you are in relation to the human being you love, and allowing the selves of that person which are not related to you to exist independently, outside of the relationship.

New York.

Met Arthur Miller in his country home. We were talking about how Hollywood will never change its image of the Indians galloping in circles around the pioneers and being shot one by one.

I said: "The most they will do is place the Indians in the center and have them shoot arrows at the galloping pioneers."

Met Montgomery Clift's brother, who suffers at being Montgomery Clift's brother. He made a film of Puerto Vallarta in Mexico which reminded me of Acapulco. He is full of tenderness and gentleness, and in love with Kim Stanley.

Saw *Gate of Hell,* a Japanese film of such beauty that you hold your breath. At last, beauty, the art of the film, poetry mixed with realism, the unique eloquence of shadows, mystery, suggestion, the perfect blend of naturalism and dream.

I telephoned the Geismars. "Are you angry with me?" "No," he answered. "We had a dull and wholesome summer and are waiting for you to bring life."

I called Jim: "What's the altitude today?"

Felix Morrow tells me not enough copies of *Spy in the House of Love* are selling, but it does not hurt any more. A culture which cannot create a *Gate of Hell* cannot read *Spy in the House of Love.* Not yet.

Over the telephone a voice:

"Are you a Protestant?"

"No."

"What are you?"

"I am not interested."

"Wait a moment. You don't know what I am going to say. We are approaching families about a marvelous place called 'Beautiful.' It is a burial place. . . . Wouldn't you like to select a burial site?"

I hung up.

At the United Nations I breathe the air of internationalism, my favorite country.

Lunch with Jim at a café where we ask for a Polish drink not knowing what it will be. It is a warm sweet wine with cinnamon. We talk about tragic things with our particular invention; it is a celestial bicycle pump, it pumps air into all suffocating human traps, recommended for all tragic situations.

Jim going through a difficult period. His novelette unpublished, his novel unpublished, and his job at "Paper Plates" brings him just enough for rent and food (and a paper-plate regime for all his friends).

A Haitian evening. A wealthy couple who own many Haitian paintings. An American Episcopalian bishop, an earthy, humorous, generous, and lucid man who lived in Haiti eleven years and was responsible for starting the Haitians painting, encouraging them, and developing a rich and impressive folklore painting, primitive, colorful, and enchanting.

He came to find someone to make a film on Haiti.

He told about the hurricane. The water was five feet deep on the peninsula. Helicopters came to pick up the victims, flew them to Port-au-Prince, where they were clothed and fed. After a while they noticed the number of victims multiplying instead of lessening. Thousands of poor Haitians were throwing themselves into the water to be rescued for the sake of a meal and clothes.

He also talked about Albert Mangones. He was typical of the privileged class who received the best education in France and in the United States and dreamt of returning to his people and helping them.

But the black Haitians did not want to be helped by a nearly white, educated, bourgeois architect. His projects were frustrated by the lethargy, passivity, and indifference of the Haitians themselves.

Josephine Premice arrives from Paris. Her hair is cut boyishly, with bangs over her forehead. Her black eyes look bigger and more brilliant, as she is now very thin. Her laughter is still continuous like a breeze and the beautiful husky voice entrancing. She wears a long clinging jersey sweater with a turtle neck which enhances her long neck, and over that a black-jersey loose square coat.

She is now rehearsing for *House of Flowers*. She likes Truman Capote.

At one A.M. we are leaning over a bar, Jim and I, and I am stressing the primary importance of the *wish*. Not knowing what we want, not wishing for it, keeps us navigating along peripheries and tributaries formed and shaped by external influences. I said: "Forget about the probable and improbable. There is no improbable. Just a few hours ago I met Shirley Clark. She had no money at all but wanted to go to India. She is a film maker. The *wish* was the orientation. When an offer came to make a film about French children for UNESCO, she accepted, and it led to her being asked to make a film on an Indian dancer. Her wish, for years, was the beacon. The probable and improbable are only negative concepts we have to transcend, not accept."

How we love people after their death. In the same way we love certain artists after their death.

The traits which were in opposition to our own, which threatened to alter us, to infringe upon our ordered universe, are forgotten. It was not that the dead disappeared, which created in us the capacity to love their qualities; it was that their disappearance caused the death of our ego, our ego died, and in the absence of danger to its needs, wishes, left in its place a human being not concerned with his own survival but with the recognition of other's values. Conceding with love and admiration to my mother meant an acceptance of traits inherent in me which I considered a threat to my existence, as, for example, my maternal qualities, and I had to fight them in her. She sought to make of me the woman I did not want to be, who capitulated to wifehood and motherhood, and while she lived she threatened all my aspirations to escape the servitude of woman. When she died I was forced to take into myself this conflict, and I realized I had long ago lost the battle. I am a woman who takes care of others on the same level my mother did. As soon as she died this rebellion collapsed. I loved my mother, who had visited upon us her own angers and rebellions, who had not known how to escape from feminine servanthood and had not achieved her first wish to be a loved and pampered concert singer, a wish which her marriage to my father had seemed to make possible (he trained her as a singer) but which ultimately was destroyed by the burden of motherhood and an egocentric husband. Mother's singing did not survive. She had to surrender all hope of a career in order to raise and later support her three children.

The loveliest, the most carefree aspects of those we love we are rarely given, because of the conflict we engage in, each one, in each family, to assert our individual existence against the clan's rules and taboos.

"The Paris you loved is dead!"

It was René de Chochor who said this to me while we were having lunch in a luxurious restaurant in New York, and I wept right then and there. He had just come back from Paris, where he had been a student. I had not been there since 1940.

"I want to prepare you for the changes. I don't want you to have a shock. I am sure that people engrave an image of others in their memory and keep seeing them unchanged, and they do the same with cities. I knew the Paris you loved. And it is not there any more. My friends have changed, those I went to college with. America has changed them, and I know the Paris you remember and wrote about."

His words shocked me so much that as I was preparing to leave for Paris I also tried to prepare my mind. The first image his words brought to me was that of a cemetery. I tried to turn my face away, but all I could see at that moment were tombs. In Paris I had once lived overlooking the tombs of the Montparnasse Cemetery. Now I saw tombs. The tomb of my father, once the pampered concert pianist of Paris, the tomb of Antonin Artaud, of René Allendy, of Otto Rank, of Conrad Moricand, of Hans Reichel, Pierre Chareau, and then I saw a list of those who had disappeared during the war, emigrated, moved, died in concentration camps or in Spain. And I felt like dressing in black, and wearing widow's veils, and postponed the packing of my valises.

Then I reread the stories in *Under a Glass Bell* and wondered what had become of the characters I had described, what had become of the houseboat, of the family who gave *Under a Glass Bell* its title, of Villa Seurat.

Then I conquered my depression, and dressed my mind and my body for the present. I wore warm colors, and thought about a new Paris, an unknown Paris.

I left Europe in a hydroplane in 1939 and returned in a jet. I drove along a speedway and not through overcrowded poor quarters. But as I passed I saw a café, a café on the street, with an open door, and one small round table outside, just big enough for two persons, two glasses of wine, two small iron chairs, a diminutive café like the cafés in Utrillo streets, shabby, with a faded sign, a dull window, lopsided walls, uneven roof. The smallness of it, the intimacy of it, the humanity of its proportion, the absence of American arrogance, the absence of gloss and glitter touched me and once again opened me to tenderness as Paris had always done. A human being feels one can sit in such a café even if one's hair is not perfectly in place and one's shoes are not shined, and even with a run in one's stocking. One could sit there and feel unique, feel in tune with the world, or out of tune, feel human and open to human emotion and wanting to weep. One could sit there if one felt the world too big and too barbaric, and feel once more in a human setting, a proper setting for a human being who does not feel arrogant, glossy, powerful. The small café and tenderness were not gone, the patina of much living, the worn and the tired and the wistful, my café, my Paris, where a soul can be a little worn and does not have to be shop-new, shop-glossy, hard and brittle.

So the small café was there as I sped to the Hotel Crillon. The Square was planted with United Nations flags waving for famous visitors.

The room was again, like the café, not new. It was softly, gently, touchingly imperfect. It was not new, the bedspreads were not new, the rug was not new, the chandelier was not new, the paint was not new. But mysteriously, this room which would not have seemed beautiful to an American, had a glow. I could not find its origin.

I lay on the bed for a few moments and looked at the crystal chandelier. I felt distinctly that this room was not empty, as most rooms in American hotels seem empty and new, as if never inhabited by anyone, spotless, new, and virginal. There are no traces of other visitors in American hotel rooms. Whereas here the soft mild-yellow wallpaper, the slightly faded rug, the heavy velvet portières, the telephone and the bells all exuded a presence, many presences. I had the feeling that I had taken a drug. That the room was full of erotic brilliance, and of past visitors. Names came to my lips, Nijinsky, Diaghilev, Madame Du Barry, Ninon de Lenclos, Marcel Proust, Jean Giraudoux, Colette. Lovers, aristocrats, generals, men of the world, whoever they were, had been alive. Words had been said, expressive, articulate, eloquent, emotions had been displayed, gestures had been made, talented and inspired love made, wine had been drunk, dreams cradled, and the warmth came from the bodies, and from delicate suppers. All the life of Paris like an exquisite intoxication crowded in this room without need of steam heat, of electric gadgets, of anything but people who had lived richly, that the past could not erase. They remained like a perfume in the air, in rooms that had been lived in, enjoyed, loved, leaving psychic, voluptuous secretions.

First the diminutive café, one which could be carried in the heart, and then the softly lighted rooms, the window open on the gray slate roof and a softly lighted city, the mist and the fogs serving as deflectors, diffusers of light. Diffusion. When one laughs or weeps too hard, the world is thus diffused, the hard boundaries are melted, and a hundred other persons lean with you to look out on the square.

Why did I feel warmed by imperfections, discomfort, and patina?

Because intense living leaves scars, and I could not find such scars anywhere in America. Inner scars, softened, human wear and tear.

I felt a human relaxation, a slipping into a more human city, a place where, everyone being so busy living, there were no voyeurs, no journalists, bystanders, groomed, unruffled judges standing on the edge.

As I walked I found the hobos by the Seine I once knew so well when I lived on the houseboat. They were not angry, they were not dour or frightening, as on the Bowery. They were comical, humorous, and their delirious speeches at the corners were ironic and witty.

And there by the Seine was the bookshop, not the same, but similar to others I had known. An Utrillo house, not too steady on its foundations, small windows, wrinkled shutters. And there was George Whitman, undernourished, bearded, a saint among his books, lending them, housing penniless friends upstairs, not eager to sell, in the back of the store, in a small overcrowded room, with a desk, a small gas stove. All those who come for books remain to talk, while George tries to write letters, to open his mail, order books. A tiny, unbelievable staircase, circular, leads to his bedroom, or the communal bedroom, where he expected Henry Miller and other visitors to stay. There is a toilet three floors below, in the cellar. There is another room, full of books, and in the hall, a small stove on which he cooks for everyone.

How did George come to have this small bookshop by the Seine? He had read the "Houseboat" story years ago. He had come to Paris to search for a houseboat. He started his bookshop there, and was happy, but the books mildewed, and he had to move. He moved as near to the river as possible, and often from his window, watching the river, he had the illusion he was living on a houseboat.

On Sundays he made ice cream, which he felt homesick Americans needed. He had fixed the guest room, the front room, expecting all of us would stay there, books and authors offered communally to those passing by, printed words and their voices in unison. He forgot that these writers from old Paris now had wives, children, mistresses, homes in America, fame, and hotel reservations. He forgot they could not always give themselves as freely or there would be no books to give, no books written.

George could not understand why they did not stay there, by a fireplace often without wood to burn, in a room without a door. In the hallway there is a hole in the floor with an iron grille through which one could see what was happening in the bookshop below. A spy window on the floor, and those from below, if they had looked up, could have seen George as he stood by his dusty stove baking American pies for his expatriates, who were looking for a drink.

So it is no longer Sylvia Beach's Shakespeare and Company visited by André Gide, François Mauriac, Pierre Jean Jouve, Léon-Paul Fargue, Caresse Crosby, James Joyce, and Henry Miller. It is The Mistral, visited by James Jones, Styron, Ginsberg, and Burroughs, the beatniks and the new bohemians. The difference is that where there was a warm, hospitable, friendly, demonstrative, affectionate fraternity between writers and artists now there was often a sullen silence, a disinterested attitude, and the young bohemian lying on the couch reading a book would not stop reading when another writer came in. I marveled at their insulation. Unlike Miller, when they had cadged a meal, they did not rush to their room to write twenty pages in exultation. They sought drugs to help them dream, they had no appetite for life, no lust for women. They read like people waiting for a train. They are spectators. Xerox artists, perhaps obsolete in a world of science. To Paris they brought expectations, but they contributed no fervor, no curiosity, no excitement of the blood. The visitors were different.

From The Mistral I went on a quest of the houseboat, *La Belle Aurore,* which I knew would not be in Paris, but it was not in Neuilly where I left it. I was told there was a cemetery of houseboats in Bougival.

The taxi took me up the Seine, close to the banks. In Bougival I found a place with hundreds of discarded houseboats. Some were being repaired and repainted. Some were lived in as they were, by hobos, or by families with numerous children. They had been dragged to shore and dumped on the mire. Even then, the occupants had flowerpots on the window sills, and made gardens of sea shells or oyster shells. There were all kinds of barges. Most of them were the very long, flat barges used for the transportation of coal, bricks, and wood up and down the Seine. A few were corroded yachts which had once been white and glossy.

But there was no *La Belle Aurore* among them. Had she disintegrated from old age? When I lived in her she was already unsafe, taking in water and having to be pumped. I felt melancholy not to be able to catch a glimpse of what had been a deep and rich adventure.

I returned to Paris. I walked the streets as I always did, for hours. Looking at art shops, bookshops, antique shops, all of them unchanged. The bookstalls still there. With their erotic books wrapped in cellophane. With pornographic postcards, and rare books for the connoisseurs.

Around Saint-Germain I noticed a bookshop where they were having a gathering for book-signing. Through the window I saw Louise de Vilmorin, the heroine of *Under a Glass Bell*. I entered and bought her new book. I took my place in the line waiting for autographs. She was sharing honors with a motorcyclist who had written about his life. He was all in black leather and kept his jacket on. When I faced Louise she recognized me, and I recognized the eyes sparkling with irony, the smile of superiority, shaped for wit, the face which reminded one of all the paintings of French history when they depicted aristocracy and pride. And to see her standing beside the motorcyclist was the most incongruous, comical, modern fable. She signed my book, said she wanted to see me, always fresh and cool as a flower, the quick intelligence speeding up time, while the big-handed motorcyclist signed his books laboriously.

I went to see Zadkine in his old home again, the two small houses with a garden in between on the Rue d'Assas, one his home and one his studio full of sculptures. His face is still ruddy and his eyes sharp, but his limbs tremble a little.

On the doorstep of his studio stand two wooden sculptures of women.

The Germans did not take any sculptures away.

The two women, full-bellied, undulating, long-necked, had, during the war, and during the time he spent in New York, sprouted a vine and flowers, which half covered them, and grew at the top of their heads. Zadkine looking at them wistfully said: "You see, even in death there is beauty."

The next day he was at a vast exhibit of modern art. Some of his own sculptures and murals were on exhibit. But as he walked into the vast building, once a palace, at the very entrance, where the winter cold rushed in, he saw an abstract birdcage built like an intricate and convoluted spiral, in which two bewildered parakeets had been placed and could not find their way to food and water, and remained in one corner baffled by the maze. Zadkine thundered in his loudest voice: "What are these birds doing here in this draft? They will die of cold, and if they do not die of cold they will die insane locked in such an abstract cage. One should not experiment with live birds in a dead cage; let the designers try this on their own children, and then they'll know if a human being can live in an abstraction." Moricand was part of the cemetery. But Jean Carteret was alive, and his apartment which I described minutely in "The All-Seeing" in *Under a Glass Bell* was absolutely unchanged. It seemed darker and dustier, that was all. I could not tell whether it was time which had layered dust on the objects from Lapland, from Africa, from South America, from all the places he visited, or whether my own vision of them had lost the sparkle of poetry I once saw. He still seemed like an astrologer, a fortuneteller, a mysterious character whose constant activity did not manifest itself in a body of work. He had found writing difficult, laborious. Now he was enthusiastic about the idea that writing was disappearing, and that he could talk into a tape recorder. He wanted a tape recorder. Then all this profuse, imagistic talk he spent so lavishly in cafés would become a work, there would be a record of his endless dissertations on esoteric subjects. At the café he talked abstractions. He made drawings. He seemed more than ever removed from the present and from humanity. He was dealing in abstractions so esoteric and obscure that we could only listen. When you know someone well, and have once followed the traceries of his fantasies, been familiar with them, you do not recognize as easily the signs of schizophrenia, but this time I felt it. He had gone too far into space. He spoke a language which could not be shared. It was far beyond astrology. It was like a vast web in which he entangled himself. His eyes were unseeing. I once described them as all-seeing because he was then a visionary, and he guided his course by psychology and astrology. But now he was spinning, spinning words, concepts, so far removed from our reach that I wanted to grasp him physically and rescue him. It was an evening which dissolved in a long monologue, unanswerable, unreachable.

I felt chilled, desolate. What had kept him bound to earth and human beings, and permitted him to lose gravity, and be pulled into a void?

———

I visited Richard Wright. We spoke of our first meeting at Canada Lee's apartment, at the time *Native Son* was being produced on Broadway with Canada Lee in the star role. This was in the 1940's. We both lived in the Village. He came several times to the studio on Thirteenth Street for dinner. Then George Davis, hearing of his difficulties, invited him to stay in his house in Brooklyn. An amazing house, we remembered. Filled with old American furniture, oil lamps, brass beds, little coffee tables, grandfather's clocks. He liked antiques. Many famous people stayed there. Auden, Carson McCullers, Gypsy Rose Lee. George Davis was born in February and so were Auden and Carson McCullers so I called it the "February house." My Haitian friends, Josephine Premice, and a Russian poet friend all went to serenade Richard Wright with drums and songs and dances. He did not respond fully, and I did not know then that he was mistrustful of our friendship. He did not believe in it. He admitted this later and told me so on one of his trips back to the States. And asked forgiveness. Living in France, he had learned that such friendships were possible. He had recovered his faith.

He is a handsome man, quiet, simple, direct, his speech is soft and modulated, his ideas clear.

He was happier in France. He could go anywhere, to the theater, restaurants, his children were going to good schools.

He described again the void in which the American writer works, with nothing to support or enrich him, and how this void, for the Negro writer, became a real danger, an aggressive threat. How the response to *Native Son* had been mostly cheers like those given to a baseball player. He objected to such phrases by a critic as: "Richard Wright hit the jackpot."

"What kind of a response is that?" he had said bitterly.

He also talked against the New York hostesses who were willing to invite him because he was a best-selling author but who objected when he arrived with a Negro friend.

When George Davis invited him to stay in his house in Brooklyn there were difficulties. The Negro who tended the furnace resigned because he would not tend the furnace for another Negro. To mark their disapproval of his marriage to a white woman, Helen, people threw stones at the windows.

His first impression of France was going to buy bread and having the baker woman say to him: "Mr. Wright, we read about you in the paper, you are a writer, is there anything we can do for you?"

He felt that he was becoming obsessed with the racial problem in America to the point where he could not develop as a writer. He was possessed by destructive antagonisms. He felt that if the constant humiliations of daily living could be removed he would be able to grow, expand, and fulfill his role as a writer.

He seems happier, more relaxed. We sit in a café and talk about his new works. He feels that a writer cannot forever write about the same theme, that the irritants of American life would have destroyed him.

At George Whitman's bookshop, when you stand on the upper stairway, there is an opening which enables you to see into the bookshop. I saw a gypsy woman stealing books. When I came down she insisted on reading my hand. She predicted I would have many children and never knew why I laughed.

In spite of being considered thieves, of being humiliated, of resorting to begging, gypsies' pride is not broken or corroded. It remains smoldering and strong. It is as though our morals were not acceptable to them, as if they lived by other values, and did not feel ashamed of their activities.

The Paris I loved is not dead. The lovers still love each other. The Seine still glitters with barges and boats. The fountains still play. The shopwindows are still dazzling displays of imagination and style. The galleries are crowded. The bookshops are crowded. The parks are filled with flowers, gardeners, and children. The shops are small and intimate and the shopkeepers attentive. The cafés are crowded. There are people who have time to stroll, time to sit out of doors, time to look at each other with curiosity. Conversation is still sprightly and entertaining. The taxi drivers are witty, and the hobos are clowns and beg with charm. The skies are opaline, and the buildings engraving colors. Each stone has a history, and each house bulges with lives well-lived, deeply loved. There is a festive air, as with all people in love with pleasure. There is a patina of shared lives, through high literary articulateness. It is still the capital of intelligence and creativity, enriched by the passage of all the artists of the world.

[Winter, 1954-1955]

The homemaking skill of Stanley Haggart in such a transient, ephemeral, rootless city as New York was beautiful to see, because it was a physical replica of his gift for protection, care, and he was as sensitive to the emotional well-being of his friends as he was to creating an atmosphere of warmth and shelter anywhere and with little means. The grayest of cold-water flats was transformed. The simplest Long Island house rented for the summer would immediately become a place where you might want to stay. Disappointments or frustrations never changed the mood of hospitality and delight he created. One never knew of the difficulties; he was, according to the Varda philosophy, creating paradise for others. His personal sorrows or losses did not intrude. He acted as the fate for the mariners of New York City, predicting hopeful journeys by way of handwriting, offering faith and loyalties. It is no wonder he came to believe that his decorating of an apartment could repair disintegrating marriages, could reconcile estranged lovers, could heal children of discords. In his case it was true. The hearth. The home was the symbolic hearth. He lived with courage and style. He retained a youthful enthusiasm, curiosity, experimental openness toward experience and relationships. People gathered around him. He was himself the hearth which the city so often denied.

Once in Paris in the late thirties, encouraged by Maxwell Perkins' interest, I prepared according to his suggestion six hundred pages of excerpts from the diary. He had read one or two complete volumes, and thought selections could be published. But when he saw the excerpts he was disturbed; he felt it was a pity to do that, that it should be published in its entirety or not a all. Today I burnt these pages in the fireplace. If the novels are symbolic and composites, the diary at least must be intact. I must find a different way of editing.

Dream:
A vast church in a state of dilapidation as if it had been bombed. A small temporary building of wood had been erected like those wooden houses built by the workmen during construction of big

apartment houses. It is subdivided into many rooms. In one room there is a play going on, but in such a limited space and completely hidden by low walls, beams, doors, narrow hallways et cetera. I am watching the play. There is a person seated on each side of me. Then I realized that from where I sat in the center I was the only one who could see the play clearly. I got up restlessly to see what could be done. I felt the player's work was wasted.

I awakened thinking I must remember this dream.

I feel the play only I could see, the work that is wasted, may be the diaries.

At New York City College yesterday, talking with the students. One of the professors commented on Henry's immaturity. I said: "It depends in what realm. He may not be academically mature according to your standards or ideologies, but in life, in the flow and vigor of his actual living force and experience, he is far more mature than any of your other pusillanimous writers who merely dip the end of their toes in life experience."

I had arrived incensed by Malcolm Cowley's fanatical narrow-mindedness on the obligation of the novel to treat only of political or historical BIG themes of the day, not themes unrelated to the essential function of American life! In other words, only power and war are of importance, not life, not human relationship, not psychology, not neurosis, not personal history. The Age of Mediocrity. Age of the Functional Novel.

In the New Jersey library there were two signs: "Useful Arts" and "Fine Arts."

Malcolm Cowley also urged novelists to "give up the inner world that has been enfeebled as a result of its isolation."

This is almost as obtuse as Cyril Connolly's remark on Miller: "He is the man of the street. It is too bad that his streets are in Paris and that they are lined with bordellos."

I told Dr. Bogner that after the lecture I was depressed. She finally uncovered that I am distressed because the tension I feel at facing the world (because of my fear of being hurt, mocked, rejected) blocked my natural human contact with the students. I kept the contact on an intellectual level. All the time, as in life, I am fully aware of the human sympathy which is imprisoned by my greater fear of vulnerability to derision, irony, or hostility.

Some of the sympathy must come through on other occasions or else people would not, as they invariably do, confess their intimate life to me. But in public I am tense. It is an ordeal, a tournament, not a pleasure. I fear attack.

Now after saying that America has a lack of contact, I find that in some cases it is I who do not make contact with the harsh aspect of American character.

The simplistic American concept that everyone concerned with politics is altruistic, and everyone concerned with development of the individual is egocentric, is an error which will have dire consequences. The quality of human beings diminishes each day because of this taboo.

If my work were merely egocentric would *everyone* feel they can confide in me, from the rough, uncouth woman hairdresser in Sierra Madre, to the old hobo who lived in a cabin in the mountains, to the taxi drivers, always and immediately; would everyone call me when in trouble, would I know every detail of Millicent's life, her feelings, her children's lives? Who would want to see an egocentric person alone (as everyone asks to see me) so they can talk intimately about themselves?

Dr. Bogner: She has patience and skill in teaching one how to expose one's projection of the personal drama onto an external situation. Today, for example, I finally understood why the social criticism constantly accusing the artist of egoism made me suffer, because as a child my mother constantly spoke of my father's selfishness, and we grew to dread any resemblance to my father. The idea of being selfish seemed the most horrendous of crimes. I was happiest when I acted unselfishly. Later I realized how many of the acts I considered altruistic were not truly so, and I became more sincere. But I have remained vulnerable to this particular accusation, so prevalent in criticism today.

Dr. Bogner said what I said to the students: there is no objective novel. In fact there is no objectivity at all. Even a reportage on the waterfront is probably biased. As for example Schulberg's film *On the Waterfront*.

I am confused about selfishness and individuality because my father, who was selfish, deserted us and my mother, who was unselfish, was possessive. Consequently my father did not love us. My mother did. On such a primitive basis do we create our image of the universe.

An evening at the Brooklyn Public Library dedicated to Henry Miller's exhibit of watercolors. I was asked to be one of the speakers. The Ghouls and the Spectators. I don't know which are the more contemptible. The first feed on the artist only when he is dead (or at least very old) while refusing to feed the artist while he is alive.

The second stand passive, watching. The voyeurs of the Western world. Watching the artist's life, his loves, his struggles. Watching the critics and reviewers plunge their puritan and personal beaks into the artist while he is alive. They sit. They do not live, laugh, or love.

They are the dissectors, the taxidermists, the mummifiers, the embalmers.

Miller's watercolors sparkled with delight, delicacy, fantasy, a child's work, innocent and gay. They hung unframed. People talked. James Laughlin. Kay Boyle. The painter Abe Rattner. But no one entered the playfulness, the lightness, the aerial spirit of the watercolors. No one showed humor or osmosis, empathy or shared delirium. It was like a wake. I tried. I read Henry Miller's own statement on his watercolors where he juggled words as colorfully as he juggled colors. Later, because the discussion was going on as to whether the government should subsidize the artist or not, and it was all so serious and mournful, I tried again to stress the essential theme of Miller's contribution to the flow of life by reading my preface to *Tropic of Cancer*.

Instead of a celebration, I felt this was a premonition of gatherings to come when Miller would no longer be alive. It saddened me. I asked James Laughlin why he had not fought the battle against censorship (he had a fortune to do it with). He answered coldly: "I consulted my lawyers and they decided I had no chance of winning."

The librarian had wanted to avoid this theme. There was a policeman at the door. But people persisted in discussing this and nothing else.

One man insisted: "I get no insight into life from reading Henry Miller." I answered: "Perhaps insight is not what you need, what you need perhaps is to be immersed in living itself, in the living flow. Most of our writing today is dead."

I came away depressed and disturbed.

To see all that I knew as wild living and abundant creating, wild faith and wild desire and wild aliveness, to see it all exhibited on museum walls, and people immune to the messages of the watercolors, to see it as a wake.

The original intent of the evening had been to help Miller because he needs money.

Marino Ruffier, the librarian, said: "I must confess that I have not continued to read Miller. I was discussing this with my colleagues the other day. One of them suggested that there is a time when we read everything of vital importance to us, a formative period when we are seeking our way of life, our orientation. Then when your life has taken a certain form, the books which caused great changes one leaves alone. It is an experience already lived, done with." Fear of change?

Dear Henry:

You will hear about the exhibit at the Brooklyn Library from different people, but I want to tell you what a marvelous sensation I had seeing the new watercolors, many I had never seen, and all there, with the fantasy and delicacy and sensibility, the richness and airiness of tone, the fluid, melting transparencies. They were a joy to behold. Also they broke the sense of eclipse I have had all these years which made me unable to enjoy or read anything of yours, and I am glad of that. Ignited by the joyousness of the paintings I was able to navigate through the kind of evening I find utterly depressing, like a wake to me, the way people come to listen and look at what was done in moments of great beauty, fervor, and pleasure. Later I kept repeating, the ghouls and the spectators, the ghouls and the spectators, who do nothing courageous and tremendous for the living artist but who can only enjoy what the museum keepers and curators place in glass cases. This, of course, was not altogether fair. The truth is you had good friends there (it's the passivity I caricature, the inertia) and they may help you.

James Laughlin was seated at the back and I attacked him openly and firmly on why he had not fought a case for your work. He answered lamely about having abided by the advice of his lawyers. . . . It was also a disgrace, which I am sure he was insensitive to, that everyone there was concerned with your need of selling watercolors, which reflected on his lack of generosity toward his writers. The atmosphere was so somber that I decided to remind them of the pleasure you manifested in the watercolors and read them passages from *The Angel Is My Watermark*.

I don't know what the practical results may be as the sales have to be handled by others than the library, but Kay Boyle and her husband were there, and the Baradinskis, and several librarians, and a Spanish woman friend of Buñuel, and a Swedish woman who was told to read you because you were a pacifist. I said and did all I could in the discussion which followed. Kay Boyle was asked to speak but withdrew shyly. Ruffier was really courageous because he knew all the time that if there had been a scandal he might lose his job. And people did persist in discussing not the watercolors but censorship. But the evening passed without explosion. The watercolors on the walls shed a light of joyousness and lightness which I hope they will buy; but they cannot truly possess this as you did.

Exchange with James Laughlin: "You made me very happy writing a letter to a friend of mine in which you said my writing was deteriorating, because for years I have felt that your taste was deteriorating."

His hostility began way back in Paris, when he felt that I was the "poetic" or "mystical" influence which might turn Henry Miller away from the sort of writing Laughlin was interested in. He told people I was a dangerous influence. It showed how little he knew Henry, who could never be influenced by anyone, and how little he knew me in spite of the contents of my preface to *Tropic of Cancer*.

He came to see me at the houseboat and I had friends there from Peru who did not speak English, so I stepped out on the bridge and told him to come another time, that I could not see him that evening.

Back in America, everyone felt he was the logical one to publish me, but he persistently refused. He did not include me in *New Directions,* and only once admitted I was an avant-garde writer and he said he would let someone else, of my own choice, write about me. My choice was not fortunate: I chose William Carlos Williams, who did not understand my work.

Laughlin is not known for his generosity to writers. When Henry needed money to sail from Greece, he did not send any because he said Henry would drink it all away, something Henry never did, for he was never a heavy drinker at any time.

Letter from Henry Miller:

Dear Anaïs:
Was indeed moved by your letter about the exhibit. As a result I sat down and made several new ones, last few days—the best I ever made. I still give away most all I make. Now I am invited by my Japanese pub-

lishers to give a show in Tokyo—they guarantee to sell at least one-third of what I send. Rather unusual, what!

I also forgot to tell you that when in Paris, Eve and I visited the moving man in Louveciennes—and together we went to your house and took a photo outside. It didn't look the same. I went up and down the place three times before I recognized the place. But Louveciennes itself is pretty much as it was. And that man, Marius Battedou, is adorable. We had a good talk.

And now a word about Lotus di Paini, an author Moricand recommended to me long ago. See, if possible, her *Les Trois Totemisations*. (I'll send you a long clipping about her work—she died recently—if you like.) Moricand is dead, I hear. Have no details. But this Paini woman will certainly excite you, I think.

If you are coming back to Sierra Madre soon, try to stop by and see us. Eve wants very much to meet you.

June, by the way, was taken to a mental institution some months ago. Must stop—mailman due any minute. Henry.

I wonder why *Spy in the House of Love* arouses such antagonism. Why can't people laugh at the characterizations of Cold Cuts, of Jay. I see Sabina as a portrait of modern woman, seeking to break taboos but still a prey to guilt. Why can't they read the poetry and hear the music and feel with her?

Larry Maxwell, commenting on my reading the preface to *Tropic of Cancer* at the Brooklyn library: "It was good that you read that, to remind people of what they seem not to have nowadays, capacity to live, to desire, to flow."

So much takes place within me each day that by comparison I find a paucity, a stinginess, a silence in people which drives me to excess. I would at times be less of a rebel if people did not seem so inert, cautious.

Am I creating my own isolation? It seems to me that most of my acts are acts of integrity. It is true I do not share with the many the cult of Dylan Thomas and T. S. Eliot. It is true I broke with The Living Theatre after seeing a play by Kenneth Rexroth, and another short piece by Gertrude Stein. I wrote a letter and asked that my name be removed from the list of sponsors.

But for these differences, do I deserve this solitary-cell treatment?

Those I call my relatives, Giraudoux, Djuna Barnes, Proust, Isak Dinesen, Anna Kavan, Pierre Jean Jouve, were they treated as I am treated now?

Dr. Bogner's concept is that if you are already angry you tune in on what feeds your anger and on the experience of other angry people. The anger is increased and multiplied. If you examine it at its source, the origin of it, you can deal with it alone, but not with a magnified anger out of one's control.

I spend a great deal of time trying to find the culprit, the origin of my angers. Dr. Bogner said it was because I cannot bear to see myself as a person capable of anger. I always tried to divert it, by understanding, by compassion, by justifying others' behavior. But repression of anger causes intensification of it.

"You pick up the waves you want to pick up. There is always hostility and cause for anger in the air. But like radio waves, you pick up what confirms you in your anger, what harmonizes with the image you wish to make. In your family everyone was preoccupied with shifting the blame. Your mother blamed your father for everything that went wrong, and your father, in his own way, built up a case against her in his letters, as you told me, a perfect logical and rational brief."

This is probably the major occupation of most people, this fixing of the blame on others, a projection of a personal drama onto others, onto countries, art, science, philosophy.

I am trying to find the cause of hostility to my work, so I will not be angry at America.

My talks with Jim are like jam sessions. Last night in a drizzle, we walked to the White Horse, my favorite café, all in wood, with old-fashioned mirrors, huge mugs, imported May wine. The barman, an old Scotch miner who had been in a mine explosion. Photographs of Munich. Dylan Thomas liked it, and many other artists. A workman in workmen's clothes with a giant poodle, who looked sad and innocent watching his master drinking. Artists in house painters' uniforms. Beards, mustaches, corduroy trousers, soldiers, Negro jazz players, a Chinese girl out of a Chinese print. And the rapid machine-gun talk. Directness like a thousand arrows and utter freedom. We can say anything. There are no pauses, no examinations of what we are going to say, and no effort at sequence. It is elating and invigorating. Euphoria comes from the freedom of improvisation and the fact that we never judge each other. We have set no moral, social, or realistic limits. All we ask is the electric charge of vital life dynamics, and the next day, as after listening to jazz, no hangover, no backtracking, no censorship, no malaise.

Whereas with Max Geismar, whose friendship I valued, this is what happens. He is a spiritual crab. He is writing about American writers backward in time, starting with the dead ones. He comes to see me for a few minutes when he has business in New York. He is hurt that we all label him a "social critic." But when I invite him to come to New York to meet someone who admires him, or to hear jazz, or to see a Japanese film, or even to read Wallace Fowlie on surrealism so that, as I explained, he may move into the future when he gets tired and bored with [William Dean] Howells (as he tells me he is), he can't come because he is working, and does not want to be sidetracked, so he negates living (he always says I am the only one whose company he enjoys). When, to attenuate the sting of my having accused him of being a social critic, I say: "Let's make an anthology of surrealist elements in American writers such as Nathanael West." He says: "No, you do it, I don't know anything about it."

"But you say you are bored with Howells" (so bored he wrote a long letter to Edmund Wilson, who answered with a lecture, a sermon, a paternal castration, infuriating Max, who revered him when he was young and was always being disparaged by Wilson). Now Max knows that Wilson is no longer reading exploratively. He is preparing himself for death by studying religions (a map for the next world) and genealogies and ancestor worship to assure his own portrait for posterity. When I remind Max that he is lonely in the past, in the historian's solitary cell, he says (with the coquetry of a woman playing hard to get), "But I am comfortable in the past." He knows I will not follow him there. As I once said to him, "I was born modern, I was born contemporary."

Reading a few fragments of the diary disturbed him. Conflict? The diary is a blueprint for living, a Baedeker to freedom. So I took it away and gave it to Jim, who nourishes himself on it.

Dear Max:

I know you are genuinely concerned about the diary and want me not to feel blocked. And I am grateful for your advice. But I will try to explain something now that will make you happy and improve our friendship on the ideological side (nothing needs improving on the human side). This year I finally achieved objectivity, very difficult for a romantic. The divorce from America, as I call it, was painful, but has proved very creative and liberating. It was like breaking with a crabby, puritanical, restrictive, and punitive parent. As soon as I overcame the hurt, I began to write better than ever. America, for me personally, has been oppressive and destructive. But today I am completely free of it. I don't need to go to France, or anywhere. I don't need to be published. I only need to continue my personal life, so beautiful and in full bloom, and to do my major work, which is the diary. I merely forgot for a few years what I had set out to do. To prove that problems are primarily psychological, and that no Marxism, no economic security, and no social obsession will solve them. American history has proved the fallacy of this. You have to begin with the self, the personal and the human being, and *then* proceed to the community. Psychoanalysis was right. And in that sense it is altruistic. We live in a country which tried to destroy the growth and the development of the self in the name of social growth, and look at the monstrous human beings it has produced, the crime, the tyranny, the corruption, the political horrors. Having settled this in my own mind, I have settled down to fill out, round out the diary. I am at work now on what I call the volume of superimpositions, which means that while I copy out volume 60, I write about the developments and conclusions which took place twenty years later. It all falls into place. It is a valuable contribution to the faith in the Freudian system. It can wait for publication. I feel now that all America's attempts to batter this self into submission have failed, and I am the stronger for having withstood it. So I am doing my life work quietly now. I feel free of the prying eyes, of irrational criticism. I am in a cool, serene laboratory. The self, in the narrow sense, as you know in all creations, in all experiments, in all research, in all exploration and invention, is not important. I have proved something that I believe will be of value to humanity when they get weary of trying to solve everything from the outside. This has to wait far beyond my own existence because the world is in its material phase. It has to see that dialectical materialism is leading it to destruction far more effectively than romanticism or neurosis. It is an interesting stage. And now I understand why I hurt you, but will never do so again. Because this is no longer a hurtful, emotional thing, but history, psychology, philosophy. I also can explain to you why I felt so compelled to take the diaries away from you. It happened after I read your review of Hemingway in which you took him to task for living outside of the United States and for not keeping his nose to the political grindstone. At this moment you were no longer my well-loved friend but a symbol of what I do not believe. How dare anyone go so far in tampering with another's life? How dare anyone pass such judgments of how and where one should live? But now the ideas you have, or the beliefs you have, no longer threaten me. *I don't live here any more. I live in the future.* And it is anywhere, and it is a lighter and freer and more humorous place. This is quite different from escape (which you would also look down upon as a Marxist). In escape you abandon your life's work. This is more like the scientist going into his laboratory and keeping the uninitiate out merely so they won't break the bottles and shatter the formulas, and spill the precious liquid.

It is altitude, and a preparation for a task which may take years. It is good for work.

Edmund Wilson disturbed and hurt you. I was able, when he telephoned me to meet him for dinner, to say: "I have no desire to see you."

I feel so strongly about this, that I would add that if the whole world went through the same quest I went through in search of reality and truth, that would be the end of war. Remove the power of what makes you angry; then you are ready to live for bigger aims and better friendships.

So Max withdraws into the sterile world of Howells (because he is a museum piece) and Max feels the necessity of making a literary history or catalogue (a taste I consider necrophilic when it relates to the truly dead but a resuscitation when it relates to Léon-Paul Fargue, who will always be alive because he was alive when he was living). Actually, one should only trouble to resuscitate those who were alive, not those who were stillborn.

So I go to the White Horse with Jim and we have a word jam session, and people ask me why I frequent the young rather than my mature friends.

I gave Max all of Rank to read. No comment. Possibly he gets overstirred, overstimulated, and feels fear. Anyway he returned to Mr. Howells. As Anne puts it (her wit is magnificent always): "At this moment Max is Mr. Howells, and I am Mrs. Tolstoy and we are getting on well."

The contact with the young is contact with the future. But some of the young I have known were amazingly traditional and far from modern; they stratified early.

With Jim I share a disrespect for Dylan Thomas, for Eliot.

Last night he gave me an interpretation of the end of *Nightwood* I had failed to see: the woman, after considering the girl as a human being and being blinded, baffled, destroyed by the non-human behavior of the girl, finally sees the girl as a dog, as an animal and not a human being.

So very well, Dr. Bogner, you awaken angry and you tune your radio to the anger of the world. You pick up on your wavelengths the crimes, the wars, the polemics, the floating insults, the passing curses, the flying bullets. You select your world's composition for the day. It is your choice. There are other events taking place. It is all a private symbolic drama. The anger must be dissolved, it is toxic, and it corrodes the joy of being alive. I am laboring at this. At the antitoxics.

The diary is like life itself—*une oeuvre inachevée,* ever incomplete. Sometimes I would like to live long enough to terminate it in every detail, make of it a Proustian work. But to follow the life line is always of greater concern to me than the perfection of detail. I put enough perfection in the novels.

Dream: Dr. Bogner has a pain in her stomach. She has just finished analyzing me. Then she ceases to be an analyst, expresses her own pain and confesses that she really wants a husband. I respond warmly, feeling happy that she should confide in me. I offer to give a party for her, and to invite every charming man I know. I keep saying: "He must be sensitive and brilliant."

Dr. Bogner: "Do you think that in your dream you are saying you need no more analysis?"

"Oh, no, I do know I will not be finished with analysis until I have reached a resolution of my life and work, economic independence, and a better relation with the world. I am fully aware of that. Analysis is one of the powerful elements I have complete faith in to attain harmony and wholeness."

Dr. Bogner: "There is an identification with me in the dream, for you are the one who has had stomach pains, not I. And even though you are going to take care of finding me a husband, the particular qualities of intelligence and sensitivity are, as you tell me, both those you believe I display in the analysis, and those you personally prize the most."

On the plane, Flight 5 nonstop New York to Los Angeles, I summed up the month's analysis with Dr. Bogner. I feel so much better, so much less angry, so much lighter and full of energy and buoyancy. I have had anger but no depressions. More humor, more confidence. I am more aware of my fear of the world's cruelty (dreams before facing the public about bats, snakes, leeches, tarantulas) and I understand how the fear has made me hostile. I accomplished a lot this month. Tracked down the French translation of *Ladders to Fire* lost by my French publisher, repaired my friendship with Geismar, who definitely does not understand my work, was able to speak for Henry, enjoyed my buoyant friendship with Jim. Less guilt and less oppression. Less fear. As I discover the personal drama behind all I did, I also discover the personal reason why people attack me, such as the woman who wrote me angrily: "I lived with a Sabina . . ."

Kimon Friar included Djuna Barnes in an anthology of poetry, but not me, when it was he who invited me to Amherst College as a writer of poetic prose.

I am working well on Lillian's return home. René de Chochor and Felix Morrow keep saying I must abandon the *roman fleuve* and write a BIG BOOK if I am to continue publishing. My temptation is to give them five hundred pages of fragments from the diary.

But Jim writes me:

The important thing is this: nothing you or anyone else has ever written has remained with me so substantially as the first portion of your work in progress—*Solar Barque.* This is something I wanted to mention all during your stay here but we had much to talk about and this seemed too important to do in conversation that I can't formulate again, as clearly, so I'm trying to do that now. But here is what has transpired: I find that at important moments now, and each night before I go to sleep, my mind brings out for viewing images from this work. In some important ways, I think this experience in reading has possessed me more entirely than anything I've read before, anywhere. The ancient city and the fantasy flight of the solar barque, the girl sunning herself, awakening in horror from death which has lighted on her shoulder, and then the flight of the boat again.

I think I have a private image that has grown from these; a personal view of the composite that is nearly impossible to describe, except imperfectly, clumsily (perhaps because if it were sayable in direct language, easily translatable, there would be no need for the artist to evoke it as you have done) something that has to do with the soul being the body; mysticism become a physical thing, as if the high moments (art religion love) can, for people, only coexist with real, physical life. By being purely what one is, a living animal with five senses. And the five of these, operating at their top efficiency, create a sixth; and the sixth sense the artist reaches and functions from in his moments of flight. Now perhaps you see why I have been unwilling to launch into this. It comes out flat. I can only hope that these platitudes suggest to you what I'm trying to convey. It is the most difficult writing job for me; this effort to describe the best thing that can happen to one. We have spoken before of the difficulty of describing experiences that are the opposite of painful. Most artists can describe pain exquisitely without much effort; the chore, an almost impossible one for most of us, is to convey the essence of something that has been beautiful. For this reason, I have suspected that your final book in the long tapestry would be a dull one. Health does not make very good reading usually. People who are winning their battles and who remain readable, vital writers are few. Frankly, I did not believe you could do it, not because I think you are less than a great artist, but because so few have done it that I felt it would be too much to expect. But as it has developed, you have done this better than any example I can think of; and the book is more readable, exciting on more levels, than any you have done in the past. I think there is a word better than maturity to name what you have reached. It is what you have lived for. It's the reason for all the human risk, the pain, everything you have endured, experienced, enjoyed. The ability to transmute it purely, perfectly. The volumes and volumes of rehearsal. I wish there were some way to shock you, if necessary, into realizing that this is exactly the moment (I refer to the book itself, not to the clock or the day of the week) at which you must demand of life the conditions under which you are able to finish this work. And to tell you the truth, I am disgusted with you as an artist for having permitted De Chochor's words to enter this sacred part of your consciousness—or the publisher's words about bookkeeping, etc. As a human being I am sympathetic to this, because I fall prey to even pettier discouragement myself—but I expect more of your artistry—having seen more distinguished examples of it (the diary, writing under fire, not when the mood strikes, or when the room is warm, or when the coffee is boiling, or when the money is in the pot, or when everyone is crying for more, but writing under fire, personal fire, peril, risk—*under fire;* this is why I expect more of you than I have reason to expect of myself—at the moment anyway). And I don't mean to shock you when I use the word disgust. The difference between this human reaction and the work itself is almost grotesque. They have nothing to do with one another. I don't mean that you should be at this moment writing in the book. I only mean that there should be a different reason for not doing so . . . more absorption. Or pure repose, like the earth in the winter, the roots and juices working deeply warm under the cold and motionless crust; call it the winter of the heart, the time between. But Jesus, agents may die in the wintertime, publishers may go bankrupt, perish, cities may fall, but the artist, in this winter, has nothing to do with these events; he bears real relationship only to ancient cities, the flights of the solar barque, the memory in the senses, the anticipation of his own springtime. As we know, there are moments at which the artist must victimize the human being he inhabits, and assume his higher life, tell the world to go to hell. And this is not difficult for an artist to do, or, I should say, not nearly as difficult as preserving himself from pressures during gestation periods. The world thinks that when the writer is not at his typewriter, he is ready to talk business, talk anything, because he is not working. So I don't blame the publishers, De Chochor, and I don't blame the part of you that the world sneaks into. And I'm not talking to you now, Anaïs, but to the woman who writes the books.

And now about the man who writes my books: I haven't a beginning point in my head, and I don't even use the diary (my own) as well as I could. But I have a feeling that something is going on, so I continue pleasantly content on the surface and trust that something is going on in there. During these periods of nothing I usually suspect of myself that I am dry; but now I have a sense that some inner activity is in progress and that pretty soon I'll sit down and begin to make something on this machine. There is a terrible kind of comfort connected with this apartment, and walking to work every day, and having dinner and company, and seeing shows, and I would probably be mortally frightened except that there is always that one inside who screams at me, and reminds me that I am not dead. I've stopped being intimidated by the possibility that I am not an artist. I know that I am. I'm not sure how this came about, but I don't question this fact any more. I am, as they say, cocksure. The only trouble is the discomfort of not being actively working on something, but this will end very soon, I think. Your work with me on my diary is more important than any other thing. Of course there are combinations of infinitely varied forces that bring this confidence about; but the most important is probably you. I know damn well I can fool De Chochor, and the *Paris Review,* and the American theater, but I know perfectly well that I can't fool you. My own private fraud detector. And the way I know is that I have tried now and then (unconsciously in my work) and have always been found out.

I would like to have the portrait of myself in your diary. It is the best I have. Not only because it is beautiful, but because it is also the way I want to be, and feel that at my best I am. And I would like to have the part which has to do with the evening at the White Horse, a wonderful evening for me.

At the risk of repeating, I must say again that *Solar Barque* is inside of me as no other book has been. I know that I have personalized this experience, but I have not exalted it. It exalts itself. It *is* that power. And I talk about it, and think about it. Not the power itself but a sense of what you did. There are sentences I am able to quote, and would like to, even now, but I won't because they are not a total but a partial view; and the book's great virtue is its perfect balance of life and death, the barque and the sunning. The sensual beauty of the earth combined with the beauty of flight. Death as it is used in this book (and in reality, I believe) charges life with meaning and significance and force. The senses of man, the most beautiful animal of them all, require such urgency; it stalks him into life. I think that if you said nothing else in your life, this alone qualifies you as a great woman and a great artist. And it has a stunning effect on a reader, an awakening, empowering effect.

"Now get with it, honey, get with it."

Kay Dart, looking like a Hawaiian queen, and John dressed in a dark suit like a missionary (his father was a missionary in Africa) were sitting at Zardi's while Shorty Rogers played on his horn a poliphony never to be imitated in life and which I would give my life to equal in writing. John was saying: "We need roots. We want a home, a garden, a job, all of which our American culture has developed in us, and neither Kay nor I have had it."

I flipped my eyelids and my billowy Italian dress and said: "My roots are portable."

Sierra Madre.

Dream: Atmosphere of gloom and sorrow. I have learned that my mother did not die a natural death but took her own life. Joaquin and I are desperate. She left a valise like a salesman's valise, in which are neatly placed all the parts of a lunch box, Thermos bottles, plastic spoons, sandwiches, et cetera. My mother had written under each one: "More picnic boxes to fill. Another lunch box to fill. Everyday more lunch boxes. Lunch boxes again. Nothing but lunch boxes."

The implication to me was that my mother had filled too many lunch boxes and had finally gone mad and committed suicide.

I have always felt the role of woman as half-servant or total servant with keen rebellion. Yesterday Christie gave all her clothes to her mother to carry from the pool, saying: "You make a good servant."

I have taken up first aid because I was called upon three times to give first aid and felt helpless. Monday I went from eight A.M. to twelve. I faced one of my greatest fears, the fear of looking upon physical wounds. I never feared psychological horrors. But I dreaded to witness an automobile accident. I was always impressed with Thurema Sokol's courage. She rescued a man in an automobile accident who had been cut by glass. His head was open. Thurema closed the wound with her hand and stopped the blood.

I love to take care of Chris, Kitty, and Mollie Campion to relieve their parents. They are fairy-tale children, sensitive, delicate, and poetic. I genuinely love them.

But the children on the other side of my house seem made of badly cooked oatmeal. But when the mother went to the hospital to await the third oatmeal baby, I took care of the other two and cooked dinner for the whole family. Awaiting news of the baby I felt excited, even without a personal love. For a moment I was reintegrated into the fraternity of a community life, *la vie de famille,* which I spent my life evading. Acceptance of the human in place of the marvelous.

Lecture at Pomona College.

The *Paris Review,* I introduced Jim to, accepted his story "A Summer for the Dead." Jim celebrates. He was the center of attention.

In Caresse Crosby's copy of an old *Transition,* in which a fragment of *House of Incest* appeared, there was mention of me as included in the "heroic period of surrealism."

Caresse, author of *The Passionate Years* in a passionless era, appears. Her dress is airy, winged. It is of black but transparent material, it is inflated and crisp by new chemistries, as organdy once was by starch and ironing. It gives her the silhouette of a young woman. Her hair, though gray, is glossy, and brushed and also starched and the opposite of limp, because the spirit in Caresse is airy and alive, serving the Citizens of the World, traveling to her land in Delphi, which will become the center of her project, its symbol. Age can wrinkle her face, freckle her hands, ruthlessly drop the eyelids over opened eyes, can tire her, but it cannot kill her laughter, her enthusiasm, her mobility.

Her second husband, Harry Crosby, committed suicide at the side of another woman (but Caresse had been invited first to share the suicide pact). Her adored son Bill died asphyxiated by a faulty gas heater in Paris. She lost two fortunes, but she wears at her neck a huge bow because dress and body and hair reflect the alertness and the discipline of her spirit.

"I went to a cocktail party in Washington at Huntington Cairns', and I was appalled at how little interest people had in each other."

Perhaps she did not live on the deepest levels, but the level on which she situated herself, that of an elegant grain of pollen, a smiling international serpentine, a *chargée d'affaires* of the heart, a public-relations expert among lovers and artists, a personal representative of the artists, a publisher who played the writers as others of her set played the horses, the purest example of the *mouvement perpetuel* of the fervors. Certainly a woman like this is worth more than those who are deaf, dumb, and blind to other human beings.

At another party there was a lady who, unlike Caresse, aged without illusory fiesta dress, without the blessings of cosmetics, and without skillful reconstructions. It may have been that she decided from the beginning that no art and no charm could reduce the prominence of her nose. At this moment, with her memory almost gone, with her hair like an accidental pile of hay, her skin dry and coarse, she seemed partly animal and partly mummy. But she told a story:

"When I went to Nairobi, and went out lion hunting in a jeep, one African was driving, and the other carried my gun. The rule in this kind of hunting is to remain in the jeep and to keep driving. Well, when we reached a particularly deep gully, the jeep got stuck and while they were working to get it going, I left them and went for a walk along the gully. I was walking back peacefully when I saw, across the gully, an enormous lion walking parallel to me. I was calm. I continued to walk toward the jeep. So did the lion. Then where the gully turned to the left, the lion went in the opposite direction to mine but before the parting of the ways he looked back at me as if to say goodbye."

I felt that the lion had determined Mrs. X did not belong to the human race. That furthermore, there was an affinity between her hair, skin, bones, and some aged animal. Or that perhaps there was nothing there to stimulate his appetite. The friendship, in any case, the peaceful walk, was understandable. If I had been walking along the gully, and I spotted Mrs. X, I would also have walked in the other direction.

American writing poses as realism. John Goodwin writes about Haiti. He mentions politics, economics, prices, costs, size, aspect, and establishes the realism so dear to America. To all appearances it is an objective novel (in contrast to mine), but soon the characters appear and they are thoroughly distorted and absolutely impervious to Haiti, never having grown any closer to it than to each other. However, the realism has been established. Their madness is never perceived. The book, they say, is a documentary. It deals with the white and black problem. With magic on the black side, and alcoholism on the white side. It never revealed either Haiti or its parasitic inhabitants.

At Millicent's birthday party, her granddaughter, now six years old, asked the Reverend: "When you baptized me, was God there?"

What I see around me is that the disillusioned Communist is more bitter than a disillusioned lover. Because politics are so narrow and demand such single-mindedness, the rest of the personality is atrophied. When disillusion comes, there is nothing left to renew faith. In the disillusions of love, there is still the habit of love left, and faith in love itself. It is a personal failure, not the total ideology.

Talk with Dr. Bogner. Discussing the three things I failed in: to make money, to drive a car, to run a camera. The three were symbols of man's prerogatives: leadership and excellence. I was afraid to take over masculine activities. The man was in the driver's seat. As soon as this was clear (which means actually to separate the pure from the impure motive), I felt free. Dr. Bogner added: "When you took a job to help your mother, it was seemingly a pure motivation, but you felt guilt not because you stepped in to help in a crisis, but because originally you had wanted to take your mother's place in your father's affection, because originally (original sin!) you were angry with her for driving away your father, angry with her for bringing you to America, so far away from him, when you were happy in Spain, nearer to him. So these hidden angers, covered as they were by good reasons for taking a job, became in the dream your moving into your mother's place when she drove badly."

This may even explain why I repudiated music (my father's prerogative), why I never entered politics (Gonzalo's attribute). But writing? Why did I not fear to write, when that was Henry's profession and vocation? Perhaps because I felt he was so strong a writer, I could never surpass him.

The pure and the impure motives mix. The conscience is aware of its deeper intentions, and becomes uneasy.

My earliest memory is of sociability. In Neuilly when I was four or five years old, I went out and invited everyone who lived on our street for tea.

From my childhood diary, age eleven: "I have decided it is better not to love anybody. As soon as you begin to love, it is time to leave. Look at my grandmother. I love her, and I love Barcelona, and now we have to leave. The best thing is not to love and then going away will not hurt any more."

Advice that fortunately I did not follow.

Note from Geismar:

Just a line in haste to say that your Xmas card was sweet and touching and nice to get; yes you showed your fangs or claws or the tips of your anxiety when your last book appeared and I was hurt; but all authors go through this period when their progeny are born, and fight with all the critics, even when the critic is trying to do his best for the author, whom he sincerely admires and respects, and even loves in a sociological way; but the critic knows this mood, being himself an author more than a critic, God knows, and he felt the artist would get over this mood, as she did, but it was just as well she was a lady artist, because that is a great thing, and he can always blame it on being a woman at heart, which is a great thing, and there is no reason that both of them now cannot look forward to such years of amity, of mutual admiration, and, I think, a rather touching affection for each other. You are nice.

[Spring, 1955]

Yesterday I asked myself whether I had lost my power to create because of the many humiliations America had inflicted upon me and the commercial failure of *Spy in the House of Love*. Am I defeated by the coldness of the critics?

The answer came this morning. The inner music started again. I reread what I had done on *Solar Barque,* and liked it. Tonight I hear the music and all my feelings are awake.

My greatest problem is one inherent in the experiment itself. Because I follow the pattern of free association the design is sometimes chaotic, even to me.

The attempt to construct a novel in this way is difficult.

I wanted to show how the adventurer does not forget his past or escape it when he goes to the paradises. The doctor gave the drug of remembrance and refused the drug of forgetfulness. He is killed for that, because people want to forget. Lillian does not escape. She returns to remember and liquidate the past.

Lecture at Evanston. Felix Pollak was at the station, after driving through flooded roads in a taxi, poor Felix, an extravagance for his modest budget. He looked like his handwriting, small, delicate, with big, sad Spanish eyes, a gentle smile, the hands of a violinist. In the taxi he kissed my hand like a true Viennese, and during the drive we had a long talk. He had been nervous, he was not nervous any more. As I found out later he was being metamorphosed from a man of forty to a man of eighteen. A metamorphosis not without inconvenience, for with it were reawakened his adolescent romantic longings for other lives.

All of Chicago's sky rained angrily upon such lyrical states. They tried to drown the Curator of Special Collections as he rushed to meet a "famous writer," a character who confirmed his inner world. It made him dissatisfied with the present, with Evanston, the library, the small daily routine of an eight-hour office day, the unfulfilled potentials of life, *la vie triviale.*

His violin is there, his beautiful chess pieces, the piano, Sara's cello, many books, and once more Europe and America trying to live together.

His great love is Hermann Hesse. He has written about him. He wants me to write him a letter. He has not received his due. Felix wrote to me:

Hesse's writings are vivid and vital and immediate enough to be understood by themselves, but to be really appreciated he should be seen against the background of Jakob Boehme and Novalis, of E. T. A. Hoffmann, and Jean Paul. . . . None of his novels have what is called "social significance," they are concerned with the individual.

Felix Pollak had quietly and gently manipulated the whole situation. The library's purchase of forty-three manuscripts, the exhibit in glass cases, originals of books, engravings, records, publicity on the campus. But so quietly, so subtly nobody knows it, has noticed it. So he is overlooked, not invited to lunch and dinner, invisible. He was, however, asked to introduce me, which he did.

When you give someone a flavor of other worlds, you also give the poison of discontent. Life is dull at Evanston. I took a walk. The lake was bilious. The wind cold. The houses big and without charm. An atmosphere of a hospital, school, factory. I know what Felix feels. People live here as if disconnected from each other. There are no relationships because they have denied the self. The students stand about, glued to each other, saying good night, but, I am sure, like puppies in a warm nest, still blind, not seeing each other. Felix struggles to make them read Hesse.

The hall for reading was a cold, wind-swept place. Always the massive podium I try to avoid, to face the public with all of myself. There was noise from other rooms, and the light was bare and violent, as in a cafeteria. I was frozen physically and emotionally. Afterward Professor Douglas had a gathering at his apartment. People talk but it is in a void. It could be me. I felt a stranger. No one said anything I could remember, though I listened with all my attention. They talked about their little daily business. The rain. Examinations. The effect of spring upon the students.

Dream of a revolution. Men, many men, in a place like Mexico. They have just finished a revolution and are surreptitiously returning to work. The leader does not want me to hear about the details, but I say with exaggerated detachment: "Oh, don't be concerned over me. I understand revolutions require violence and terrible acts. But the end justifies the means." Then I am drafted too. My job is dangerous. I have to push some earth into a pit and I'm in danger of sliding down into the pit with the moving earth.

The dream of the lake that cures everything. I am swimming in it. But other people take boats and these boats endanger the swimmers. The boats are like carnival floats. They ride over the swimmers and I get angry and I bang on them.

This month came the great discovery that I could never learn to make money because of my father's disdain for money. He always proclaimed contempt for it, and, toward the end of his life in Cuba, it is said that when the gasman came to collect his bill my father handed him his wallet and said: "Take what I owe you. I refuse to handle such dirt."

The paradox was that while he disdained money he was protected from disaster first by my mother's inheritance, and then by his wealthy second wife.

In analysis one studies the constant displacements. The habits you cannot bear in others are those you fight against in yourself. I made superhuman efforts to discipline a dreamy and chaotic childhood. I succeeded. And so I hate absent-mindedness above all things. My father's absent-mindedness. Thinking of other things. Not paying any attention to us. He did not know we were there. Absent. And I developed its opposite. I try to be ever alert and rarely absent for anyone.

Did AA discover that people could more easily fight alcoholism in others than in themselves, fighting on two levels?

Coincidence, or effect of analysis? I have handled my life so well this month.

"Get a load of this," says Jim over the telephone when he has a story to tell: "Get a load of this," I said to Jim. "I met a man who has a publishing house downtown. He is a poet. His whole family works for him. He gave me one hundred dollars for the right to reprint six short stories. He makes his money on pornography, a nude magazine, and an anthology for subscribers only, where classical and trash mix under the sign of the Planet Sex. The same formula as Girodias and the Olympia Press. He is in and out of jail constantly. Should I give him the diaries to publish anonymously, in a limited edition?"

Jim was excited. "Because Anaïs, I have just read volume 46 and

I almost called you up at two A.M. That volume 46. It contains the most beautiful writing ever done in the English language. I was ready to explore."

To balance the indifference of the big critics, I have this personal, intimate fervor.

From Jim's diary:

Anaïs' journal is having a powerful effect; her power to breathe life through writing, into even the most difficult periods of her neurosis. I cannot help but be inspired by this, and strengthened: the spectacle of beauty from ashes, the phoenix rising from flames; something sur-really fundamental, the great indefatigable life. Life drawing one through the thickness and the mud, giving one survival power against the death rays everywhere. Anaïs, who is at this very moment in bed with bronchitis, suffering from low energy, is the strongest woman alive. If at times there are manifestations of weakness it is only because her sensibilities are greater. She needs desperately all the staying power and resilience which she definitely possesses because she enjoys the curse and the privilege of a kind of sainthood, sainthood being the name for high sensitivity and awareness and an inhuman or rather superhuman sort of vision. Laugh loud, weep deep.

A telephone talk with Anaïs: blues chaser. I can't write any more tonight but yet I would like to capture the quality that is constant in her: her way of raising, without effort, one's view of life; and without dissemblance, making it more exciting.

Yesterday Anaïs between the sun and me in the room. The hair illuminated, the cigarette smoke rising all around, gray and then blue like a dream. I wanted to get up and walk through the smoke and investigate, touch her hand. I see from her journal that I am not the only one who has found her illusive: everyone has seen her that way, as if one dare not blink one's eye for fear that . . . poof! It is part of her beauty, this quality of being not quite there, dreamlike. I see it less often now because our friendship is a human one, stronger, and has a fiber in reality, but at moments like these I see the essentially spiritual appearance.

Anaïs will never be a mistress of artistic forms. This flaw is the price her novels pay for the perfect integration of art and life achieved in the diary. Where is the form in the diary? The life. The life is the great work. Its consistency is in the person, not the artist. The unity of the diary is created by the person, not the artist. There is a brilliant, super-electronic light, the person, born blind, and working at only one thing, to remove the walls and veils and films and layers that stand between the light and her vision of it.

The art of Anaïs Nin is the art of improvisation, its glow and beauty the result of jazz moments in the world of perfect vision.

Jim is the twin in writing I had wished for. Copying this from his diary and reading about his moods, struggles with writing, dreams, refurnished the loneliness and barrenness of my writing world. Working blindly on *Solar Barque,* with Jim's faith.

Made my peace with Max Geismar. He had said: "I hurt easy."
I explained that I did an unrealistic thing. I set him up as a symbol of *the critic.* He was going to make an absolute statement, the voice of America, to say what no other American critic would say, total allegiance. But I see now that I was wrong. He could not do that, because he had his own integrity.
"I could show allegiance to the diary," he said.
"I believe that."
"But I do admit I let you down about *Spy.* I did not write what I felt but what I thought would sell the book."
"Yes, that was wrong. I didn't want that. I wanted you to write what you said over the telephone: 'the book is alive.' But I am sorry I hurt you. I felt you were my only link with America. After you failed me, I broke away. I accepted America's rejection. Then when I resign myself, and give a lecture, I discover a small and fervent following."

The need to clarify one's projections. What we project onto others, and they onto us is bound to be destructive because it is a fantasy. Whether they are ideal or critical images, they are not an understanding of each other as individuals (like my placing the critic role onto Max Geismar), and they make for bitter disappointments.

The dream of the Godmother. She invited me to stay with her at the beach. But the weather was dark and we had to stay in the house. I was unable to swim and felt disappointed. The clothes she loaned me did not fit me. We took a plane to leave the place, but a helicopter flew near us, so close that it frightened me. I felt they would collide. I even felt it must be attached to us, the way it followed us about.
This led me to talk to Dr. Bogner about my real godmother, who never gave me presents I liked. Once a dark-haired doll when I

had wanted a blond one, and other times real jewelry which I did not like because it was accompanied by long instructions as to its value and the care it required. She and my mother quarreled often. I turned against her. I showed no feeling at her death, which hurt my mother. I had been meditating on my sudden and irrevocable breaks (once there is a break, I cannot feel any more).

I saw an automobile accident in Sierra Madre. One car hitting another caused the gas tank to explode. The fire's violence and my fear of *more explosions* paralyzed me with terror. Fear of explosions in coal miners' stories, all sudden explosions. My awakening each time during atom-bomb tests although I could not hear them, and in one instance, did not even know it was to take place.

Dr. Bogner asked me if she was the godmother. I smiled because it seemed absurd.

"You never disappointed me."

"But perhaps you wanted to swim in the joyous waters of Acapulco and instead I asked you to examine your angers and your inner explosions. To examine that you are not free."

My fear of my own explosive nature, so often curbed.

Dr. Bogner focuses on my need for independence. It is true that there is a superimposition of my economic status as a child so filled with anxiety. My mother was overoptimistic. She started a purchasing-agent business, to shop mainly for our wealthy relatives who bought everything in New York. She would come home and tell us she had made so much on commissions, but as these purchases were charged by clients, some clients paid very late, and some did not pay at all, and so we accumulated debts and were hounded by creditors. The secretarial work for my mother which I did was overwhelming. The bills from the shops had to be examined and a separate list of items made for each client, charged to a different person.

The house in Richmond Hill needed repairs. The furnace did not work. My mother started to rent rooms again, but here it was a home, not like the separate floors of the brownstone house, and we lost our privacy. My reaction was to take a job. My mother objected to that. She maintained Latin standards, and I had to be sheltered. I was not equipped for any job.

Fortunately an Irishwoman who rented rooms in our house made a suggestion. She sent me to The Model's Club in New York where

I began my profession as an artist's model, later as a fashion model. But even then my pay was not enough for four people, or to cover old debts. I went without lunch to pose extra hours (and to write in the diary). All I wanted out of the economic factor in life was a modest, quiet, undisturbing income. I did not want moneymaking to have primary importance. But my work does not bring me this.

Dr. Bogner tries to tell me independence is a feeling not always to be taken literally. My life today does not resemble my childhood and adolescence. I should not feel helpless and overwhelmed by destructive forces.

I am baffled when analysis seems to arouse the need of self-sufficiency, but then it questions one's direct efforts to reach this.

In the life of the soul, the emotions, there are these undertows, these treacherous downward forces.

Yet I feel the sun, the spring, and I go out and I enjoy the Easter windows on Fifth Avenue.

Jim is breaking through a surface writing into a subterranean level. His best writing is still in the diary. Why does one's best writing require secrecy, silence, and darkness?

Neurosis is a "possession." You are possessed by the devils of destruction. They drive you. They make you compulsive. They make you destroy. It is not you, your voice, your true self. But it inhabits your body. It is the spirit of the past. It is the past selves superimposing themselves over the present, blurring it, choking it. An Anaïs of fourteen seeing her mother working so hard, work accumulating and debts, baffled by the bookkeeping, feeling helpless. Later clear-minded and judging her mother's errors, then working for immediate needs, a small salary for four people. And then one day, when I returned from modeling all day at Jaeckel's and posing all evening for a painter, I find my mother has signed a contract for a sidewalk for six hundred dollars, when we do not have a proper heating furnace.

The irrationality of the mother, that was the terror. The impossibility to reason. The illusion I believed that my father was logical, because he was always talking about logic, and so I believed that man was logical, I believed in man's logic. And when I met my father, the shock of realizing his fictions, what was later diagnosed by Dr. Bogner as schizophrenia.

I carried from this childhood the conviction of helplessness in the material world and fear of its workings. But a new Anaïs is emerging, proving her capabilities, her practicality, her clear mind.

Talk with Dr. Bogner: she made the subjective metamorphosis very clear. I could see it. I could see also how it all originates in the self and returns to the self. But when she seemed to imply that I use the subjective in my work too, I became very disturbed, because that is used *against* me by the critics. I am willing to admit errors in my life and relationships, but not in my work. I took her implication as a threat to the integrity of my work. She did not mean that. She meant that all truth lies in the relationship between subjective and objective, not in one or the other.

"But subjective has been used as a judgment against my work . . ."

I had misunderstood. Although I defend the validity and value of my subjective art, when she expresses a doubt, I feel she is implying a doubt of the validity of this vision. (Neurosis? Psychological blindness?) But she is not. She said that truth was an interplay between subjectivity and objectivity. Hemingway was not an objective writer. He wrote a case history. It was Hemingway's vision of war and bullfights.

The only other time I misunderstood Dr. Bogner was again in reference to writing. To remain objective she has not read my books. She seemed to disagree when I said I used psychoanalytical ways of approaching the truth about character. She meant that this method would only reveal one aspect of the character, the subconscious or the neurotic. She meant that was not all of the character, only the focus on neurosis or the secret or irrational self. I felt she of all people should understand what I was doing, and that if I chose to stress the neurotic or subconscious aspect, it was because this lay at the source, it was the secret origin of the character. We cleared that up. But she questions all extremes, all separations. Nothing is either or, separate. I have separated them. Everything is interrelated. Outside and inside. Body and psyche. In my work I meant to begin in the subconscious and arrive at objectivity. I intended to unite them.

Her emphasis on interrelation is finally becoming clear to me. I feel now that the warring factions inside of me are slowly integrating, fusing. Every fusion puts an end to some warfare. To some loss of energy.

Twenty-six years ago in Paris a boy was born to whom I paid little attention. He was the son of Gilbert Chase, my American cousin, famous now for his books on music, his work for the State Department in South America, and his teaching. Twenty-six years later I receive a neat, precise letter from Paul about my books. He wrote from the University of North Carolina, Chapel Hill. I sent him the books he did not have, and we corresponded. He announced his marriage. He planned my visit to the college. He was enthusiastically helped by one of my first readers, Kenneth Ness, of the Art Department.

So yesterday I arrived on a small plane, and found waiting a neat, slender young man with a delicate, narrow face and enormous, beautiful eyes. Alert and quick and with finesse. We recognized a genuine bond, not that imposed by families. He drove me to his little house where I met Deirdre, a gentle and beautiful girl. We had barely time to talk together, about Kathleen Chase having wanted all her life to write about my work, when Kenneth Ness appeared. Teacher of painting, dressed negligently, blue eyes distressed. I thought he was nervous at meeting me and I wanted to follow my impulse to ask: "Are you in trouble?" We talked only about the plans for the evening. Later I went to his house for dinner. I met other members of the faculty. I saw a few of Kenneth Ness's paintings, which are bold, alive, and full of charm.

Good attendance. Party. After the party I talked with Paul and Deirdre until one o'clock. To bed exhausted. Awakened aching with fatigue. Stood on my head for five minutes. At ten I saw Kenneth Ness's other paintings, all of them. The paintings are joyous and rich. Yet he did not feel ready for an exhibition. Lunch with Jessie X. Jessie is direct and lusty, and humorous in spite of inner distress. Free from tradition, recovering here, which is her home, from a breakdown. Writing a novel.

The lives of these people touched me, the great distress in such peaceful, relaxed surroundings. The loneliness of college life.

I had a lively discussion with Jessie's class. Jessie told me the following story: Her mother asked her one day: "Jessie, tell me something about this subconscious I've been hearing about."

"But, Mother, I've been talking to you about it for twenty years!"

"Oh, that, but the way you talked I thought it was something you had which I didn't have."

For a neurosis such as mine, to take roots means to be rooted to a situation of pain. To have a fixed home, a fireplace to sit by, a view, seemed dangerous (concealing as they do the bars of a cage). To take roots to me means cutting off avenues of escape, avenues of communication with the rest of the world. So that against the wish for repose, there is an impulse to remain mobile, fluid, to change surroundings.

At times I do feel like a snail who has lost his shell. I have to learn to live without it. But when I stand still, I feel claustrophobia of the soul, and must maintain a vast switchboard with an expanded universe, the international life, Paris, Mexico, New York, the United Nations, the artist world. The African jungle seems far less dangerous than complete trust in one love, than a place where one's housework is more important than one's creativity.

I think what I should do is devote the rest of my time to preparing diaries for publication, no more novels. And earn my living some other way like everybody else.

Lawrence Maxwell without his beard would have looked like a small boy who had been inflated with a bicycle pump. He had roseate cheeks, a constant smile and a highly polished style of speech, indulging in the indirect. When I first met him he had a small bookshop at 45 Christopher Street. He handled my books. He gave me autograph parties. He was very fond of young girls, either the pretty ones or the gamins. Larry had been in politics before he had the bookshop. He had been to college. His knowledge of books was general. Politics were still at the center of his interest. But the shop gave him a bohemian life which he liked. He loved to talk and people dropped in and listened. He sold very few books. He loaned books to the attractive young women. He threw beribboned phrases like serpentines on New Year's Eve. When I left and examined what he had said it tore like tissue paper. But through him I met Lila Rosenblum, Marguerite Young, and many other friends.

He lost his wife, and his bookshop.

All the time he was captivated by the whims, the fantasies of the artists, like a child by the glitter of toys, but he never became one. He remained on the periphery. I had never met anyone before who made me feel from the beginning that I was a celebrity and that whatever I did would become the subject of an anecdote. It was distressing. It was artificial. I tried to break through this to a human relationship, but the self-consciousness was there. Certain of his speeches were similar to official receptions, they were reserved for me when I went to the shop. I tried to break down the barrier. But he never abandoned his formal speech or talking about me as if he were writing my biography. "I will never forget the evening at Thirteenth Street when we arrived and you calmly walked to the porch and said: 'Oh, I must take down the laundry.'" I felt everything was being registered for future use, being lived by me for the future anecdote because of the way he commented on the experience while it was happening as if it were the product of a conscious creation of an anecdote. He had no innocence, and could not imagine innocence.

When I had my autograph party at the British Book Center and Isabel Bolton appeared (whose *Do I Wake or Sleep* I love), I introduced everyone to her, I told everyone who she was, I created a stir around her and Larry immediately commented: "I will remember this, it is your party, we are here to praise you, and you make Isabel Bolton feel it is all for her." Which took all the spontaneity out of the event.

Or: "I shall never forget the time when you were on the eve of going into the hospital for a serious operation and you never dwelt on it, treated it so lightly."

He considered his own life an anecdote and played the roles assigned to him in a manner which indicated they were roles: consoler, shelterer, helper, confidant, ambassador, *entremetteur,* companion.

He gave to everything the air of a performance.

He returned to his deepest love, politics. The political life of Mexico, of the birth trauma, of the bottom of the sea.

And concluded that art was not a useful or beneficial contribution to the life of the masses.

And so Larry passed on into another world.

Reading the diary of Virginia Woolf. It seems so confined, so narrow and dry in the conveying of experience, that it drove me not to suicide but to write in my own.

My last entries were of the kind known as the Stagnant Cycle. I was ruminating old, worn material. But I managed to re-enter the present.

Jim's fascination with the diary warms me. He is my only link with the future. His reading me makes me feel that even if America succeeds in destroying literature (which is what it is doing actively), it cannot afford to destroy life, and it is the life in the diary which Jim is drinking up in contrast to the writing of contemporaries, which he finds dead.

Yesterday he called me exaltedly: "There is no relation between the best of the writing being published today and yours. They simply do not meet on any common ground. I feel I am getting your secret in my diary, there at least I feel I can reach something deep, sincere."

Dream: I am in a carriage, dressed in a fantasy costume, a veil around my head like the veil over the head of the Japanese woman in *Gate of Hell*. The men in the carriage are curious, and want to unveil me. I get angry, get out of the carriage and take another one. I am on the way to a festival at which I am to play a part. On the way I stop at a small village. My mother and Joaquin are there. Joaquin is weeping quietly at being imprisoned in this out-of-the-way place.

The first time I heard the music of Harry Partch was during the film-making of Kenneth Anger's *Pleasure Dome*. It was the music Kenneth wanted, but Harry Partch disliked his music being used as background for a film. But when I heard the recording I had the same sensation as when listening to Balinese music (I had heard so much of it through Colin McFee). I recognized the sensation of fluidity. It was as if this music and his was an entirely novel and modern expression, had the power to dissolve the senses, to multiply their receptivity, to expand the range of receptivity, to involve the senses completely.

It was a delight, it was as if one had drunk the music instead of accepting it through the ears.

Then I heard about him from Kenneth. He was an unusually handsome man, a man preoccupied with metaphysics, born in San Francisco and exposed to its Oriental influences. He had designed his own instruments. He lived a difficult, independent, individualistic life. He had to sell his own records. I saw a photograph of him with his Cloud-Chamber Bowls. "Played on the edges with soft small mallets, also on the flat tops. The bowls give a bell-like tone, and each has at least one inharmonic overtone."

The instruments themselves had wonderful names:

Marimba Eroica
Bass Marimba
Boo
Diamond Marimba
Spoils of War

Kithara 1
Kithara 2
Harmonic Canon One
Harmonic 2 (Castor and Pollux)
Surrogate Kithara
Chromelodeon 1

The recordings came from "Gate Five," Sausalito. In New York I saw a film showing him at work, the instruments being played, and Harry packing and mailing his own records as I had packed and mailed my own books. He explained "Gate Five" in a pamphlet: "Beyond the prosaic fact that Partch lived, wrote music, built instruments, organized and rehearsed ensembles, and manufactured records here, there is the more intriguing circumstance that 'Gate Five' carries an occult meaning in sundry ancient mythology. In ancient pictographs, the city, the center of culture, has four pedestrian gates. These are tangible; they can be seen; physical entrance can be shown. But the city also has a fifth gate, which cannot be shown because it is not tangible, and can be entered only in a metaphysical way. This is the gate to illusion."

Janko Varda, too, lived at "Gate Five." His ferryboat was moored there.

I saw Harry Partch's instruments in San Francisco. I played his records. I loved the color of his music, the fluidity and the new combinations of sounds.

He has extremely blue and candid eyes, a spiritual face, and arouses great devotion in his students.

At the beginning of his career, Harry found that the extremely subtle tones he wished for his music (he devised his own scale with forty-three tones to the octave) could not be reproduced by conventional Western instruments. To solve this, he not only designed his own instruments but constructed them as well, often using exotic materials like glass carboys or Plexiglas. But he said: "I am not an instrument builder but a philosophic musicman seduced into carpentry."

He had to train gifted and devoted students to play each instrument. And again, because conventional music notation could not encompass the tremendous range of notes or the very complex rhythms, he devised his own system of notation.

The affinity of his music with water, with the poetry of space, with fusion appealed to me.

The affinity with nature, the sounds coming out of Sitka spruce, Philippine bamboo, Brazilian rosewood, redwood, Pernambuco reeds, played with picks, fingers, mallets, and felted sticks. The affinity with Oriental music, which has a flowing, enveloping, oceanic rhythm. Rhythm was an essential part of Partch's music, a native, contemporary rhythm. The richness of it gave to contemporary compositions the depth and dimensions which so far existed only in the music of the East.

When I go to the laundry in Sierra Madre I see the man who runs it and who mystifies me. He is tall, dark-skinned, dark-eyed. He wears a red shirt which sets off his foreign handsomeness. But it is not this which makes his presence here so unexpected. It is the pride of his carriage, and his delicate way of handling the laundry. He greets me with colorful modulations of his voice, trained to charm. He bows as he greets me. His hands are long-fingered and deft.

He folds the dry sheets as if he is handling lace tablecloths. He is aloof, polite, as if laundry were a country gentleman's natural occupation. He takes money as if it were a bouquet, and returns the change as if he were offering flowers too.

He never comments on the weather, as if it were a plebeian interest. He piles up the laundry as if he were merely checking the contents of his own closets. He is proud and gracious. He, like a high-born valet who overlooks his master's lapse in manners, pretends not to notice the women who come in with hair curlers looking like Medusas with plastic snakes.

For me he has a full smile. His teeth are strong and even, except for one milk tooth protruding, which gives his smile a touch of humor.

I never mention the weather either, as if we both understand weather is a mere background to more important themes. We agree that if human beings have to attend to soiled laundry, we are given at the same time a faculty for detaching ourselves, for not noticing, and for forgetting certain duties and focusing on how to enhance, heighten, add charm to daily living.

I tell him about my life, friends, the masquerades. As his fine-bred hand rests on my package, I notice for the first time a signet ring on his finger. It is a gold coat of arms.

I bend over it to examine the symbols. The ring is divided into four sections. One is engraved with a lion's head, the second square with a small castle, the third with a four-leaf clover, and the fourth with a Maltese cross.

"I have seen this design somewhere. Could it be on one of the shields of Austrian titles?"

"Yes, it could be. I have ancestors in Austria. My family has a castle forty miles from Vienna. My parents still live there. The coat of arms is that of Count Osterling."

He brought out his wallet. Instead of photographs of round-faced babies I saw a turreted castle. Two dignified old people stood on the terrace. The man wore a beard. The woman carried an umbrella. One could see lace around her throat. Her hand rested on the head of a small boy.

"That is me."

"How did you come here?"

"After the war we were land poor. I felt our whole life growing static and difficult. Tradition prevented me from working at any job. I came to America where any job was honorable. I went to Chicago. I was only seventeen and it was all new and exciting. I felt like a pioneer. I liked forgetting the past and being able to work without feeling I was humiliating a whole set of relatives. I did all kinds of jobs. I liked the freedom of it. Then I met the Rheingold Beauty Queen. She was unbelievably beautiful. I married her. Her father owned a chain of laundromats. He put me to work as an inspector. At first we traveled a lot, but when he died my wife wanted to stay in one place and raise children. So we came to Sierra Madre."

"You never went home again?"

"We did once, but my wife did not like it. She thought the castle was sad. She was cold, and the plumbing was not efficient. She didn't like so much politeness, moth-eaten brocades, yellowed silks, dust on the wine bottles."

I call him Count Laundromat, as I watch the gold signet ring flashing through detergents.

I study the style of Simenon because he is a master in the physical world. But in an interview he claimed to be a poet, the one thing he is not. He is a realist, a recorder, a psychologist, accurate and profound, but not a poet, because a poet transfigures all that he touches and he discards the appearance to penetrate beyond. Simenon has always selected the characters who submitted to destiny, a destiny formed by their character. This character they could not change, it had no power except to sink into destruction. Not one of his characters had passion, heroism, or the power to transform his life, his character, his destiny. Not one of them had the power to break through the isolation, the nonlove. It is one vast novel of failure, of frustration and revenge. The tone is always fatalistic, joyless, and the characters are victims of their own suicidal destructiveness. He has described all possible variations on destruction and self-destruction.

All my recent meditations have been on the aspects of life I leave out of my writing, because I am so intent on the heightened moments, on the living moment. The story of Henry begins with my fiery enthusiasm for his work and his first visit to Louveciennes. It could have begun with Henry spending the night in an empty motion-picture theater, with the detritus, and having to get up and move when the cleaning woman arrived and prodded him with her broom. It could have begun with Henry not believing in himself and I believing, with Henry angry and I not angry. But always I would write a story different from Simenon's, different from the story everyone expects. Now I realize that my physical world is subject to such intense emotional lighting that it becomes for most people *invisible*. It is a world of psychic transcendence. And it is this realm of the material world I want to complete now, as you clothe a revelation.

That is not the world of the poet, Mr. Simenon. The poet lives in the transfigured night, the night of symbols.

Even when he mentions dreams, and interweaves them, Simenon reveals but a part of the blind unconscious patterns and compulsions. And he never mentions the battle against them, only the passive yielding, the submission to them. He does have a knowledge of the inner structure (he refers to the time when Mallard seeks a certain sordid café even though he is now rich and successful, because it smelled the same way as the scene of his early childhood). He knows all the inner fatalities but never conceives of defiance, of mastering, of changing, of altering, of escaping these fatalities. No victories and no rebellions against these invisible tyrants. And none of the flights by way of art, and fantasy and love, only flights to Tahiti, to Africa.

[Fall, 1955]

In New York I received a telephone call. The voice was deep and rich. "I am Father Michael, of the Greek Orthodox Church. I would like a set of your books and a photograph, autographed. I will send a messenger."

The messenger came. He was about twenty years old, pimply and diffident. I gave him a set of books, a photograph, and because he seemed so admiring and worshipful, I gave him one book for himself.

A month later I received a letter from jail.

Here I am in jail. They caught me at the Doubleday office, when I was picking up books for Father Michael of the Greek Orthodox Church. There was no Father Michael. It was my way of earning a living. I don't mind about the big publishers, but I do mind about you because I truly loved your books and hated to sell them. Will you forgive me? As soon as I get out I intend to work and pay you back. It really upset me when you gave me a book for myself. Do please write me.

I had to write to him and deliver him of guilt. Who was the person with the deep rich voice who did the telephoning? I meant to ask him. For the young Michael in prison did not have such a voice, a voice you believed in.

Because I described once the delights of the birds and tropical plants department at Sears Roebuck in Pasadena, Peggy asked to be taken to the Botanical Gardens in the Bronx. We arrived too late. The huge glasshouses with domes were closed. We could see from the outside the giant palm tree pushing against the glass ceiling. We could see the cactus, the flowers, but not smell the pungent earth and feel the odorous heat.

To think we were reduced to looking through glass at what could be touched, felt, and smelled in Acapulco.

The relativity, the shifting quality of character becomes more and more apparent. As people disappear from your life by estrangement or death, you take on the traits they symbolize.

My mother's death caused a shift in my character.

I wonder if she felt the humiliation, the enslavement, the submissive role of woman and expressed the anger not directly at her mother role, but displaced onto other causes. The role was thrust on her when her eight brothers and sisters were left without a mother. It was thrust on her by my father's flightiness and by three children. She never spoke against this role of woman. She was not cast for it. She had qualities of leadership and power. My father needed her courage, yet glamorous mistresses occupied all his attention. Untrained to earn a living, she felt the helplessness of a woman with three young children. Her rebellion could only assume a negative form: anger.

To trust the world with the diaries. Nothing the world has done so far will convince me that it can be trusted with the truth. The world to me has been like a jungle, full of fierceness, meanness, and malice.

America hates the artist. It will not admit: the artist is my soul and I want to kill off my soul.

Jim and I were walking down Fourth Street when a woman (or I should say many women) sprang toward me and said in a chanting tone as if she were singing a theme: "You are Anaïs Nin," giving to Nin all the overtones and musical resonances it contains, and adding with perfect lyrical logic: "I am Nina," as if a woman called Nina must of course address a woman called Nin, and I hesitated because I felt I must know her, yet I did not, and murmured: "I do not remember. . . ." But as I said this I realized it was not exact; no one could ever remember Nina because she was simultaneously a thousand women: a beautiful Medea, without jealousy, long, luxuriant hair that had never known repose, like the black hair of Martha Graham, a patrician carriage of the head, a Balinese expressiveness of the hands, shoulders, and eyes. Ophelia, I thought, too, Ophelia and other Graces. No sadness, no weight. Her words flew fast and winged and Jim and I, alert as we are, could not follow her. We stood there bewildered by her rapidity, by the enchantment of her words, voice, smile, and total incoherence. Her recitation informed us immediately about Manfred, a name she separated into two syllables as she separated all her words to examine the philological roots and to wander off into her own associations. Man Fred. "Who is Manfred?" asked Jim after a few minutes. "The man I am going to love."

Nina Gitana de la Primavera, as she introduced herself, saying Gitana as if she had been born in Spain of Spanish gypsies, and Primavera as if she had been born in Italy, was utterly delirious and threw her head so far back I thought her very slender neck would break. Jim and I wanted to run away. The thread, the fine thread by which we held on to ordinary life, was in danger of being broken by this trapeze artist of words and gestures who made such perilous jumps between images and thoughts. She did have to account to a man who works with stones, the jeweler, when we asked her if she would come with us and have a coffee.

We sat at a bar. Nina never ceased talking except to stare into our faces, or to touch our faces as if she were blind, and seeking to find the contour of our features, or to gesture like a Hindu dancer loosely jointed, or to say: "I talk too much." When Jim asked her: "Do you know Anaïs?" she seemed surprised at this question and answered: "I live with the Becks. I acted in Gertrude Stein's play and Rexroth's." And then I remembered an evening where the whole cast had been overtaken by hysterical laughter and the play was almost ruined. Could it have been she? Of course she never ceased acting, but I wondered how they had succeeded in placing others' words in her mouth when she had her own overflow and profusion, but she did quote Shakespeare and Stein, and mentioned Mozart and sang a tune, mentioned other musicians, and sang a German song.

Jim asked her: "Say something I will always remember." She meditated, was silent, and then gracefully and calmly made five gestures which paralleled but did not imitate the gestures of Balinese dancers. With her small, delicate, fragile hand she touched the center of her throat, her shoulder, her wrist, then placed one hand under her elbow and held it there and said: "Remember this."

Having answered the question whether she knew me, she recapitulated our encounter. She had been standing with a group of people and one of them said to her: "Do you know who that is? That is Anaïs Nin." She answered: "I see only two very beautiful people. What beautiful people you are."

Her invocation to Astarte, her lyrical philology, her musical accompaniments frightened Jim. I saw him grow pale and knew that he wanted to leave. So we deserted her. We said we must leave. And we walked. Jim said: "I'm frightened. That is how I want to live, but I'm frightened."

"I'm frightened too, but I want to go back. I don't want to lose her. She is beautiful. It is like talking to Ophelia." Having reassured him we returned to the bar. She was not where we had left her. And I felt: "We lost her. We lost her through fear." But we found her in the back room. She was talking and singing to other people.

At this moment she looked like Vivien Leigh. Her black hair was in a disarrayed Grecian style. Her body was very thin but supple as a dancer's. Green, large, vague eyes, a perfect profile, finely curved lean cheeks, a tender, not too full mouth, beautiful teeth which she exposed to hiss through, with her index finger upon the center teeth, to emit a hiss, a breath, which she translated with the same finger on the table, pointed index finger forming a large S, the infinite, she explained. "Julian does not want me to go out because he thinks I'm crazy."

"You are dreaming awake," I said.

The associations were too swift and Jim and I were lost but we surrendered to her performance as if it were a Japanese Noh play and we did not know the story, and occasionally a phrase we understood reached our ears, as when she said later, as we separated: "No, I'm not going to the Becks tonight. I love them but that is not my home tonight. I am at home everywhere, anywhere. I'm going to see Daniel and bring him this I had intended to bring him." The key phrase she repeated was "as if to say" or "that is, you might say" . . . I can't remember. It was a phrase which actually denied connections between her phrases. Jim recited the opening of *House of Incest*. We decided after minute examinations which of our eyes we could see best from, and which hand was the strongest. Nina was never angry or sad. She shuffled musicians and writers and people we did not know. "Silver Fox said to me: 'You have something to give to the earth and the earth has nothing to give you.'" Jim wanted to know who Silver Fox was. The answer was: "This took place in a bar in Provincetown." I watched the very carefully modulated words as she gave birth to them, the motion of her mouth. Perpetual movement. She only relinquished her absorbed, rhapsodic intensity focused on us to throw back her head, and it was only when she threw her head back and turned her eyes upward that she evoked insanity, for there is in insanity always a moment which is not human, and at no other time was Nina not human. Even when she did not hear what we said or did not answer, she held our hands or caressed us with her eyes. Even while passing through those changes from dancer to singer to actress and poet to Joycean puns and allegories, she was graceful, ritualistic, beautiful. She designed an abstract web of images and captured us and Jim wished she had seen *Moon in Capricorn,* his play, and he asked her: "Did you see my play *The Moon in Capricorn?*" She answered indulgently, while waving her shoulders as if to dismiss the superfluity of the question. Indulgent toward our limited use of words? Know Anaïs? See Jim? Such slow wits. "Of course I know the *Moon in Capricorn.* I was there. I was born August 24 in Leo. Leo is your middle name. Why do people separate religion, philosophy, art? They are all one." To make the three of us one she maintained a linking of fingers, touch, to maintain the hypnosis. For the same reason that Jim wanted her to have seen his play, hoping she would recognize his dreams as we recognized some of hers, I wanted her to have read *House of Incest,* as if I expected her to tell me: "I was born there."

She wore a shabby short cape of purple velvet, a dress of Indian print with small designs, which she had difficulty in holding up to her shoulders because her breasts were so small. Pinned where her breasts should have begun to protrude was an elaborate Indian silver pin which held a bell-shaped container (a ball of hashish?). She drank wine but when the glass was empty she held it, warmed it, caressed it against her cheek as if it were full, and I could swear she did not taste her drink.

Toward midnight she refused another glass but said she was hungry. Asked us if we had eaten. Paused to remember when she had. "Oh, yes, I ate this morning." So Jim ordered a sandwich. She ate it as if it were a wafer. The fact that it was big, an Italian roll, only amused her. The big mouthfuls she held as if they would not fit into her mouth, would not go down her slender throat. She looked mischievously at Jim as if saying: "You'll not be able to see it, but I will swallow it."

"You are very powerful," I said, "but I feel like protecting you."

We are always afraid when our dreams or our creations come to life. Her answer was: "That is right, that is the way everyone feels," as if for the first time we had said something completely wise. When Jim quoted *House of Incest* she behaved as if this were known to her already.

The radiance of her face was magnetizing.

Again we asked American reporter questions, heavy and clumsy, because we could not enter her dreams, especially the ones she whispered so low and swiftly to herself. "When did you begin to dream awake, Nina?" Her answer confounded us: "October 21, 1952. Today is September 14, 1955. My telephone is ——— and my address ———" Perfect accuracy. When we left she asked for the time although I am sure she did not care. It was a part of her exquisite politeness toward conventions.

It was my first encounter with someone more removed from reality than I am. She was among the dreamers, the one who had broken through the sound barrier.

She was Ophelia, a young and beautiful Madwoman of Chaillot. Jim was tense and quite aware of the vertiginous heights of Nina's tightrope and aware that there was no net to catch her. I believe we only went home because we felt our tightrope walking was not as perfect as hers. I didn't, as Jim often said, look at the ground, but oscillated on a tightrope of written words which I had not learned to say. I was struck mute by her fluency. I was not in her state of speaking grace. I was in a state of a sensitive paper receiving an imprint, and after sleep I opened my eyes to pull out of the chemicals the combined negative and positive:

NINA

She is Breton's Nadja but far more eloquent. She is Nijinsky before he plunged to earth pushed by his earth wife.

She took her bracelet off. She braided her hair. As if the street at midnight were her own chamber and she were preparing to sleep.

Jim could not bear to leave Nina wandering about at two A.M. and took her to his apartment.

Before that, Jim told me, they had seen some giant pipelines resting beside an excavated street. Nina bent over the opening and laughed into the drainpipe and then ran toward the other end of it to see if her laughter would come out of it.

Arriving at Jim's apartment she said: "The room is too small." Then she opened the window and said: "Oh, but there is so much more to this room than I thought. It is enormous."

Then Nina asked for silver foil. "I always glue silver foil paper on the walls to make them beautiful."

She wanted to mop the floor with beer. "The foam will make it shine."

"Do you want to sleep?" asked Jim.

"I never sleep," said Nina. "Just give me a sheet."

She took the sheet and covered herself with it and then slid to the floor saying: "Now I am invisible."

The next day she must have gone back to the Becks for we did not see her again.

Enjoyments. An evening of rock-and-roll at the Brooklyn Paramount, with an audience mainly composed of delinquents, who tear up the seats when displeased. High-voltage atmosphere. An evening at the Palladium, watching Mambo competitions, the women dressed in the new skintight fashion with a ruffle below the knee, revealing every ripple of the body. And Teddy Brown (who spent one New Year's Eve in Harlem at the Savoy dancing with me only), winning all the prizes, surrounded by beautiful girls all wanting to become his partner. When he saw me he said: "I'm sorry I saw you Anaïs, I will start dreaming about you again."

A teacher of dancing sat at our table. He diagnosed the trouble with the rock-and-roll crowd. "All the evil came out of dance halls becoming too expensive for the young. That is where they spent their energy, in a place like the Savoy. When the exploitation of dance halls started they had no place to go. They could listen to jazz but not dance for a dollar as before. To listen to jazz or rock-and-roll and not be able to dance all night as I did when I was twenty is a way to prime human energy for destruction. We wore out our energy dancing."

I wanted to write the following science-fiction story: twelve persons who do not believe in astrology are invited to take a tour of the planets in a special rocket. At first their various characteristics are imperceptible. But as they draw near to each planet, the characteristic trait of that planet affects them, and then it becomes very obvious that one is a Libra, the other Jupiter, the other Mars, the other Neptune, the other Saturn and so on.

Freedom is an inner attitude, a habit easier to acquire than one imagines. Dr. Bogner and I discuss the issue of time. I am always too early. This compulsion adds to general stress and anxiety. She feels it conceals my rebellion against appointments, organization, discipline. I am afraid of my own impulse, which is to disregard time, so I go early to make sure I do not yield to that. So that the feeling of constriction does not come so much from the duties I have to perform as from the clash between these duties and my anarchic self, whom I have to hold in check. The constriction is caused by my own destructive rebellions, which I have to control like a pair of runaway horses.

This small mechanical examination of reflexes was evidently important, because since I returned from New York I have had a feeling of ease. I have had no destructive, negative rebellions. And because I do not fight my duties, I do them more easily. Also because I do not fight them I can be more humorous about them and they do not seem so heavy.

Jim writes me:

Nina Primavera comes here now and then. Last Friday she arrived depressed and very silent, said that few people understood her, that she talked too much and to the wrong people. She was headed for the Phoenix Theatre to watch the French mime, Marcel Marceau, hoping to learn from him the art of silent conversation.

Second letter from Jim:

To bring you up to date on Primavera: took her to *Isle of Goats* (Tani, Uta Hagen, Ruth Ford, Lawrence Harvey). During the first act when Ruth Ford brings on cheese and bread, Nina pulls out a sandwich from a brown paper bag and whispers in my ear: "I think I'll eat with them." With this she began to devour a pickle and a slice of bread.

After the third act she asked me to take her backstage and introduce her to Lawrence Harvey, whom I don't know from Adam. So I took her back and introduced her to Ruth Ford, thinking that would suffice. After a moment she whispered in my ear: "Lawrence Harvey." Resigned, I took her to the star dressing room, where a Negro in uniform asked what I wanted. I announced grandly that Miss Nina de la Primavera was here to see Mr. Harvey. The Negro disappeared, returned in a moment to tell me that Mr. Harvey was undressed at the moment. Nina Primavera gathered her shawl about her, walked forward, brushing the Negro aside with a gesture, and disappeared into the room announcing: "That doesn't make any difference. I'll see him anyway."

The Negro shrugged his shoulders. I returned to Tani's dressing room. Later when I left the theater, Nina had disappeared, and so had Lawrence Harvey. Haven't seen her since!

To sum up the extraordinary change caused by analysis. A month without depressions, anxieties, or nervousness. Only occasional or less severe forms of it. I feel installed in the present. I give myself to it. I no longer feel anger, walls, hostilities with the world. My criticalness has relaxed. I enjoy what comes. I am not nervous beforehand. I drink, I am gay, I am free. The fears have decreased: the fear of being unable to earn a living, of losing those I love. There is less jealousy and less rebellion. Much more smoothness and lightness in living, an ability to throw off anxiety. There is no bitterness, no friction, no hostilities. My feelings have changed about America. I see people who are in trouble, not happy on a deep level. I want to help, to teach. To pass on the wholeness I feel, and the strength. It took me a lifetime to find happiness in quiet things—not only in the peaks of ecstasy or passion. I feel reintegrated into the human family. I have overcome the neurosis at last.

Ian Hugo spent months filming on Forty-second Street and finally produced *Jazz of Lights*. The title was inspired by James Herlihy's *Jazz of Angels*.

When we become too familiar with certain street scenes we no longer see them. We become a blind man walking through the streets. Ian Hugo filmed Moondog walking through Forty-second Street. Moondog is blind. He wears his hair long and has a beard and dresses like a Christ figure in a long flowing robe. He wears sandals. Ian Hugo photographs the rhythms and interplays of billboard lights without the words which prevent us from seeing their abstract beauty. When he photographs the Empire State Building upside down it is not to break the laws of gravity but to emphasize the upward sky-piercing thrust of it. By shooting the lights of Broadway from oblique angles, or upside down or in counterpoint motions, or in superimpositions, he reveals their rhythm and pulsations obscured by references to Kleenex or Planter's Nuts. Divorced from their function of selling, they create intricate patterns of form and color with a beauty of their own.

The basis is imaginative realism, that is, realism transmitted into fugitive impressions, an ephemeral flow of sensations. Ian Hugo manipulates with skill the elements which dislocate or blur objects to reveal new aspects of them as they are revealed in emotional states. He has added to the phantasmagorical qualities of film images special effects which have caused images to fuse together as if they were notes in a musical composition, to flow into one another and become pure image and pure rhythm.

———

I write Geismar in an effort to repair the friendship:

I am so glad you told me by what words I offended Anne, because I did not know and I could never have repaired the offense. So this letter is for Anne, too, and please let her read it. If I said politics are *useless,* I used a clumsy word I did not mean exactly. I may have distorted a belief I do hold, that we cannot cure the evils of politics with politics, and that fifty years ago if we had gone the way of Freud (to study and tackle hostility within ourselves) instead of Marx, we might be closer to peace than we are. That is what I meant. That is why I gave my devotion to psychology and not to politics or economics. I meant to say politics are ineffectual as we can see by the state of the world. And this Anne will understand, I know. And I hope she will forgive me, for I never intended to offend your religious devotion to politics. I truly believe there is no solution to war, tyranny, persecution, while we look for external remedies (systems, economics, social work) but only when man is faced with the personal hostilities he projects into larger issues. And in America the quest for personal growth is taboo . . . so . . . That is what I meant. Dedication to politics has not brought on civilization.

It was sweet of you to ask me to write something for *The Nation.* But I sincerely feel I do not belong there, and none of my readers are there, and at this moment I can't address the very people who did all in their power to sink me. I need my energy and the very little time I have left to finish my work and I need the tenderness of artists, not the harshness of *The Nation's* political obsessions and bias.

The absurd talk of the objectivists. Simenon is not in his books. He is objective. But of course he is in his books. In his choice of characters, in his obsession with the downfall, the crime, the pathology, the destruction. In his somberness. How few moments of joy, euphoria, of love. He truly paints the negative aspect. It is perfectly told, perfectly motivated. But it is always the catastrophe. In *Coup de Lune,* Africa. The injustice of the whites. Man's sexual bondage and no love. Of course Simenon is there. Always there. His disguise is cleverer, that is all.

The objectivists think they have liquidated the self, that it is an encumbrance, but they only disguised it under the cloak of politics, history, social problems.

As a result of this denial of the self, no one stands out. When I traveled three thousand miles I looked at people attentively, I spent hours watching them in buses, in cafés and cafeterias, and they seemed like extras in a film from which the main character is absent. Nothing distinguishes them.

To give the workman three meals a day do we have to destroy every vestige of man's other hungers?

It is difficult to write to an empty hall, to know I will have to struggle to get the book published, struggle to sell it, and struggle against hostility.

Bella Spewack advises me to write like *Bonjour Tristesse,* to tell a story.

Malraux talks about the hero. I wonder if I can be a heroine, pursue my solitary way, fighting and not minding war, not minding being attacked. Keep my aim in sight. I have a very big, impersonal aim: to impart the discoveries I have made about character. I write about uncommon characters so that we may become them. Proust solved this. He wrote in depth about characters who did not have any depth. His characters swim in his own unconscious. They are ordinary people but Proust looked beyond them and at a collective depth and made profound deductions. Because I write about uncommon characters (particularly in America, where the artist is considered among the freaks with the Bearded Lady, the Fat Man, et cetera), I am under suspicion. Nobody understands that the commonness is but a façade and that what makes people uncommon is what is hidden from view.

I had just read Aldous Huxley's *The Doors of Perception* but it did not impress me as much as Gil Henderson's talk about the visionary effects of LSD. He had participated in an experiment with Dr. Oscar Janiger. He painted an American Indian doll before taking LSD and then again after the ingestion of the drug, and the difference between them was astonishing. The first version was rigid and photographic. The second impressionistic, emotional. Gil asked me if I wanted to participate in an experiment because Dr. Janiger was hoping a writer would be more articulate about the experience. There were to be two other subjects there, a biologist from UCLA and another painter. Gil would be my sober pilot, that is, a person who has taken LSD before and now stands by to help one and guide one if necessary.

It seemed strange to be coming to a psychiatrist's office for such an adventure. Dr. Janiger took Gil and me into his private office, which was lined with books and very dark. I had little time to form an impression of him, for he immediately dispensed a number of blue pills, five or eight, I do not remember, with a glass of water. Then he conducted us to the waiting room, where the biologist sat already with a pad on his knee, pen in hand.

At first everything appeared unchanged. But after a while, perhaps twenty minutes, I noticed first of all that the rug was no longer flat and lifeless, but had become a field of stirring and undulating hairs, much like the movement of the sea anemone or a field of wheat in the wind. Then I noticed that doors, walls, and windows were liquefying. All rigidities disappeared. It was as if I had been plunged to the bottom of the sea, and everything had become undulating and wavering. The door knobs were no longer door knobs, they melted and undulated like living serpents. Every object in the room became a living, mobile breathing world. I walked away, into a hallway opening into several small rooms. On the way there was a door leading to the garden. Gil opened it. The dazzle of the sun was blinding, every speck of gold multiplied and magnified. Trees, clouds, lawns heaved and undulated too, the clouds flying at tremendous speed. I ceased looking at the garden because on the plain door now appeared the most delicate Persian designs, flowers, mandalas, patterns in perfect symmetry. As I designed them they produced their matching music. When I drew a long orange line, it emitted its own orange tone. My body was both swimming and flying. I felt gay and at ease and playful. There was perfect connection between my body and everything that was happening. For example, the colors in the designs gave me pleasure, as well as the music. The singing of mocking birds was multiplied, and became a whole forest of singing birds. My senses were multiplied as if I had a hundred eyes, a hundred ears, a hundred fingertips. The murals which appeared were perfect, they were Oriental, fragile, and complete, but then they became actual Oriental cities, with pagodas, temples, rich Chinese gold and red altars, and Balinese music. The music vibrated through my body as if I were one of the instruments and I felt myself becoming a full percussion orchestra, becoming green, blue, orange. The waves of the sounds ran through my hair like a caress. The music ran down my back and came out of my fingertips. I was a cascade of red-blue rainfall, a rainbow. I was small, light, mobile. I could use any method of levitation I wished. I could dissolve, melt, float, soar. Wavelets of light touched the rim of my clothes, phosphorescent radiations. I could see a new world with my middle eye, a world I had missed before. I caught images behind images, the walls behind the sky, the sky behind the infinite. The walls became fountains, the fountains became arches, the domes skies, the sky a flowering carpet, and all dissolved into pure space. I looked at a slender line curving over into space which disappeared into infinity. I saw a million zeros on this line, curving, shrinking in the distance, and I laughed and said: "Excuse me, I am not a mathematician. How can I measure the infinite?" To Dr. Janiger, who was passing by, I said: "Without being a mathematician I understood the infinite." He did not seem impressed. I saw his face as a Picasso, with a slight asymmetry. It seemed to me that one of his eyes was larger, and this eye was prying into my experience, and I turned away. Gil was sometimes there, but now I became aware that he was a child, that he had a big round face with a grin. Now I was standing on the rim of a planet, alone. I could hear the fast rushing sound of the planets rotating in space. Then I was moving among them and I realized a certain skill would be necessary to handle this new means of transportation. The image of myself standing in space and trying to get my "space legs" amused me. I wondered who had been there before me and whether I would return to earth. The solitude distressed me for the first time, the sense of distance, so I asked Gil very vehemently: "Are you sure that I will find my way back?" Gil answered reasonably: "Of course, I found my way back. I'm here." He asked me if there was anything I wanted, a glass of water or a sandwich. I answered: "I want a pagoda." And after a while I added: "I realize this is an unreasonable request." I returned to my starting point. I was standing in front of an ugly door, but as I looked closer it was not plain or green but it was a Buddhist temple, a Hindu column, a Moroccan ceiling, gold spires being formed and re-formed as if I were watching the hand of a designer at work. I was designing red spirals which unfurled until they formed a rose window or a mandala with edges of radium. As each design was born and arranged itself, it dissolved and the next one followed without confusion. Each form, each line emitted its equivalent in music in perfect accord with the design. An undulating line emitted a sustaining undulating melody, a circle had corresponding musical notations, diaphanous colors, diaphanous sounds, a pyramid created a pyramid of ascending notes, and vanishing ones left only an echo. These designs were preparatory sketches for entire Oriental cities. I saw the temples of Java, Kashmir, Nepal, Ceylon, Burma, Cambodia, in all the colors of precious stones illumined from within. Then the outer forms of the temples dissolved to reveal the inner chapels and shrines. The reds and the golds inside the temples created an intricate musical orchestration like Balinese music. Two sensations began to torment me: one that it was happening too quickly and that I would not be able to remember it, another that I would not be able to tell what I saw, it was too elusive and too overwhelming. The temples grew taller, the music wilder, it became a tidal wave of sounds with gongs and bells predominating. Gold spires emitted a long flute chant. Every line and color was constantly breathing and mutating.

It was then I began to experience difficulties in breathing. I felt immensely cold, and very small in my cape, as if I had undergone an Alice in Wonderland metamorphosis. I told Gil I could not breathe, and he took me to the doctor. The doctor calmed me with words. I had asked for oxygen. He suggested I lie down and cover myself well. Gil was seated near me, grinning. I asked him if he had had difficulties breathing. I still had the impression I had been among the planets. I remembered the illustration from Saint-Exupéry's *Little Prince,* the child standing all alone on the edge of the planet. I lay down and covered myself. I was smoking a cigarette. I looked at the curtains of the room and they turned to a gauzy gold. The whole room became filled with gold, as if by a strong sun. The walls turned to gold, the bedcover was gold, my whole body was becoming GOLD, liquid gold, scintillating, warm gold. I WAS GOLD. It was the most pleasurable sensation I had ever known, like an orgasm. It was the secret of life, the alchemist's secret of life. From the feeling of intense cold, as if I were chloroformed, of loss of gravity of the legs, and diminution in size, I passed to the sensation of being gold. Suddenly I was weeping, weeping. I could feel the tears and I saw the handkerchief in my hand. Weeping to the point of dissolution. Why should I be weeping? I could see Gil smiling, and realized the absurdity of weeping when traveling through space. As soon as the concept of absurdity struck me, the comic spirit appeared again. It was another Anaïs, not the one which was lying down weeping, but a small, gay, light Anaïs, very lively, very restless and mobile. The comic spirit of Anaïs was aware of Gil's predicament: "Poor Gil, you are out with an ordinary weepy female! What a ridiculous thing to spoil a voyage through space by weeping. But before we go on, I want to explain to you why women weep. IT IS THE

QUICKEST WAY TO REJOIN THE OCEAN. You liquefy, become fluid, flow back into the ocean where the colors are more beautiful." The comic spirit of Anaïs shook herself jauntily and said: "Let's stop this weeping. Everything is more wonderful under water (than in space?). It is alive and it breathes." Space was lonely, and empty, a vast desert. After the feeling of GOLD I had a feeling of danger. My world is so beautiful, so beautiful, but so fragile. I was pleading for protection of this evanescent beauty. I thought I was the quickest mind alive and the quickest with words, but words cannot catch up with these transformations, metamorphoses. They are beyond words, beyond words. . . . The Oriental cities vanished and the infinite appeared again, but now it was bordered on each side by celestial gardens of precious stones on silver and gold stems. Temptation not to pursue the infinite, but to enjoy the gardens. Space is definitely without sensuous appeal.

The comic spirit of Anaïs stood aside and laughed at so much Russian-opera extravaganza. But the other Anaïs maintained her pose as a Balinese dancer with legs slightly bent, the tips of the fingers meeting in a symbolic gesture of pleading. I could feel the weight of the brocade.

I watched a shoreline of gold waves breaking into solid gold powder and becoming gold foam, and gold hair, shimmering and trembling with gold delights. I felt I could capture the secret of life because the secret of life was metamorphosis and transmutation, but it happened too quickly and was beyond words. Comic spirit of Anaïs mocks words and herself. Ah, I cannot capture the secret of life with WORDS.

Sadness.

The secret of life was BREATH. That was what I always wanted words to do, to BREATHE. Comic spirit of Anaïs rises, shakes herself within her cape, gaily, irresponsibly, surrenders the abstruse difficulties. NOW I KNOW WHY THE FAIRY TALES ARE FULL OF JEWELS.

After my experience with LSD I began to examine whether it was an unfamiliar world, inaccessible except to the chemical alterations of reality.

I found the origin of most of the images either in my work or in literary works by other writers.

In *House of Incest*, written in 1935, objects become liquefied and I describe them as seen through water. There is a reference to

Byzantium and I was brought up on volumes of *Voyages Autour du Monde,* which had images of Cambodia, Thailand, Bali, India, Japan, and which remained forever in my memory. I have listened to countless recordings of Balinese music, tapes made by Colin McFee.

Images of split selves appear in *House of Incest.*

The image of loneliness on another planet is derived from my frequent reading of *The Little Prince* by Antoine de Saint-Exupéry.

In *House of Incest* there is mention of crystals, precious stones: "The muscovite like a bride, the pyrite, the hydrous silica, the cinnabar, the azurite of benefic Jupiter, the malachite, all crushed together, melted jewels, melted planets."

The sensation of becoming gold is one I had many times when sunbathing on the sand; the sun's reflection came through my closed eyelids, and I felt myself becoming gold.

I could find correlations all through my writing, find the sources of the images in past dreams, in reading, in memories of travel, in actual experience, such as the one I had once in Paris when I was so exalted by life that I felt I was not touching the ground, I felt I was sliding a few inches away from the sidewalk.

Therefore, I felt, the chemical did not reveal an unknown world. What it did was to shut out the quotidian world as an interference and leave you alone with your dreams and fantasies and memories. In this way it made it easier to gain access to the subconscious life. But obviously, by way of writing, reveries, waking dreams, and night dreams, I had visited all those landscapes. The drug added a synthesis of color, sound, image, a simultaneous fusion of all the senses which I had constantly aspired to in my writing and often achieved.

I reached the fascinating revelation that this world opened by LSD was accessible to the artist by way of art. The gold sun mobile of Lippold could create a mood if one were receptive enough, if one let the image penetrate the body and turn the body to gold. All the chemical did was to remove resistance, to make one permeable to the image, and to make the body receptive by shutting out the familiar landscape which prevented the dream from invading us.

What has happened that people lose contact with such images, visions, sensations, and have to resort to drugs which ultimately harm them?

They have been immured, the taboo on dream, reverie, visions, and sensual receptivity deprives them of access to the subconscious. I am grateful for my natural access. But when I discuss this with Huxley, he is rather irritable: "You're fortunate enough to have a natural access to your subconscious life, but other people need drugs and should have them."

This does not satisfy me because I feel that if I have a natural access others could have it too. How did I reach this? Difficult to retrace one's steps. Can you say I had a propensity for dreaming, a faculty for abstracting myself from the daily world in order to travel to other places? What I cannot trace the origin of seemed natural tendencies which I allowed to develop, and which I found psychoanalysis encouraged and trained. The technique was accessible to those willing to accept psychoanalysis as a means of connecting with the subconscious. I soon recognized its value. My faith in it is unshaken. But then there is also the appetite for what nourishes such a rich underground life: learning color from the painters, movement from the dancers, music from musicians. They train your senses, they sensitize the senses. It was the banishment of art which brought on a culture devoid of sensual perception, of the participation in the senses, so that experience did not cause the "highs," the exaltations, the ecstasies they caused in me. The puritans killed the senses. English culture killed emotion. And now it was necessary to dynamite the concrete lid, to "blow the mind" as the LSD followers call it. The source of all wonder, aliveness, and joy was feeling and dreaming, and being able to fulfill one's dreams.

Even the art of reading, lost to America, was a constant nourishing source which revealed countries I wanted to see, people I wanted to know, experiences I wanted to have. How cruelly the weight of ordinary life, *la condition humaine,* weighed upon America, with everything forcing you to live in the prosaic, the shabby, the practical, the quotidian, the down-to-earth, the mediocrity of political life, the monstrosities of history via the media, because they believed this was contact with life, and it was the very thing which destroyed the contact with life.

So the drugs, instead of bringing fertile images which in turn can be shared with the world (as the great painters, great poets, great musicians shared their abundance with the unfertile ones, enriched undernourished lives) , have instead become a solitary vice, a passive dreaming which alienates the dreamer from the whole world, isolates him, ultimately destroys him. It is like masturbation. The one who wrestles his images from experience, from his smoky dreams, to create, is able then to build what he has seen and hungered for. It does not vanish with the effects of the chemical. The knowledge gained without the drugs, as, for example, my feeling for color learned from watching the painters when I was posing for them, is a permanent acquisition. It became part of my being, it was applicable to my travels, to my image of people. It was or became a new faculty, part of my sensory perception, available, but the effort I made to learn was also the strengthening of the ability to create with a sense of color, to create houses, clothes, visions of cities, enjoyment of color not only as a passing, ephemeral, vanishing dream, *but as reality*. And that is the conflict. The drug effect does not strengthen the desire to turn the dream, the vision, into reality. It is passive.

I have to go on in my own way, which is a disciplined, arduous, organic way of integrating the dream with creativity in life, a quest for the development of the senses, the vision, the imagination as dynamic elements with which to create a new world, a new kind of human being. Seeking wholeness not by dreaming alone, by a passive dreaming that drugs give, but by an active, dynamic dreaming that is connected with life, interrelated, makes a harmony in which the pleasures of color, texture, vision are a creation in reality, which we can enjoy with the *awakened* senses. What can be more wonderful than the carrying out of our fantasies, the courage to enact them, embody them, live them out instead of depending on the dissolving, dissipating, vanishing quality of the drug dreams.

I will not be just a tourist in the world of images, just watching images passing by which I cannot live in, make love to, possess as permanent sources of joy and ecstasy.

Index

Pfeffer, Max, 53, 88–89; letter from, 73
Phoenix Theater (N.Y.), 252
Picasso, Pablo, 81, 123, 184, 185, 257; painting of two figures by, 97
Pilgrimage Play, The (play), 27
Plexus, 94, 102
Pliny, 141
Pliny the Younger, 141
Poel, William, 26
Pole, Reginald, 26–28, 29, 30, 130
Pole, William, 26
Pollak, Felix, 163, 228, 229; letters from, 161–63, 229
Pollak, Sara, 228
Pomona College, Calif., 224
Port-au-Prince (Haiti), 198
Porte d'Orléans (Paris), 121
Porter, Arabel, 78, 81
Posada, José Guadalupe, 134
Powell, Lawrence Clark, 95
Powys, John Cowper, 26, 27
Premice, Josephine, 54, 198, 206
Proust, Marcel, 48, 80, 91, 92–93, 112, 121, 122, 123, 149, 191, 194, 200, 214, 255
Provincetown, Mass., 248
psychoanalysis: awareness through, 109–10; changes caused by, 252–53; displacements in, 230; like shock treatment, 111; method of, 122–23; pain of, 147; responses in, 167, 217
Psychoanalysis of Artistic Vision and Hearing, 122
Public Library (N.Y.), 149
Puebla (Mexico), 67
Puerto Vallarta (Mexico), 197
Purdy, Theodore, 76; letter from, 76
Putnam's, G. P. (publisher), 76
Pyramid (Giza, Egypt), 193

Quintero, José, 88

Rahon, Alice, 17, 18
Rainer, Luise, 88, 139
Random House (publisher), 76
"Rango" (character in *The Four-Chambered Heart*), 33
Rank, Dr. Otto, vii, 85, 100, 160, 200, 218
Rattner, Abraham, 211
Rau, Santha Rama, 148
realism: in American writing, 225–26
Really the Blues, 115
Rebels and Ancestors, 125
Red Door Bookshop (Chicago), 42
Reed, John, 134
Reichel, Hans, 200
Revolcadero (Mexico), 152
Rexroth, Kenneth, 25, 214, 247
"Rheingold, Miss," 243
Richards, Mary Caroline, 22, 23
Richardson, Tony, 125
Richmond Hill, N.Y., 233; life at, 74–75
Rimbaud, Arthur, 170
Ritchie, Mr., 64
Rivera, Diego, 7, 161
Robbins, Jerome, 69
Rogers, Shorty, 153, 223
Rolland, Romain, 122
Rollo, Charles, 80, 81, 88, 158
Romulus and Remus, 142
Ronde, La (film), 152
Roqueta, La (Mexico), 19
Rose Tattoo, The (play), 64
Rosenblum, Lila, 43, 85–86, 105, 110, 118, 126, 237; letter to, 110–11
Rosset, Barney, 99
Rousseau, Henri, 75, 125
Ruffier, Marino, 212, 213
Ruggles, Ted, 60–61
Runyon, Cornelia, 30, 31–32, 64; party for, 147–48
Russell & Volkening, 88

Winwood, Estelle, 27
Wolfe, Thomas, 22
Woodstock, N.Y., 88
Woolf, Virginia, 26, 32, 170; diary of, 238
Wright, Helen (Mrs. Richard Wright), 206
Wright, Lloyd, 27, 72, 103, 166
Wright, Richard: in Paris, 206 writing, on: 72, 190–92; American, 160; Dr. Bogner on A.N.'s, 235; letter to a young writer, 149–50; role of writer, 171

X, Jessie (pseudonym), 236

Young, Marguerite, 237
Yucatán (Mexico), 66, 73, 98, 106

Zadkine, Ossip, 204, 205
Zaller, Robert, vii
Zardi's (Los Angeles nightclub), 153, 223
Zayas, Pepe, 80, 125, 172
Zev, 46
Zeyer, Café (Paris), 121
Zihuatanejo (Mexico), 13, 67
Zola, Emil, 47, 123
"Zora" (character in Children of the Albatross), 62
Zuma Beach, Calif., 30

Books by Anaïs Nin available in
paperbound editions from
Harcourt Brace Jovanovich, Inc.

The Diary of Anaïs Nin, 1931–1934

The Diary of Anaïs Nin, 1934–1939

The Diary of Anaïs Nin, 1939–1944

The Diary of Anaïs Nin, 1944–1947

The Diary of Anaïs Nin, 1947–1955

The Diary of Anaïs Nin, 1955–1966

A Photographic Supplement to the Diary of Anaïs Nin

In Favor of the Sensitive Man and other Essays